Theologians of
a New World
Order

Recent Titles in the
RELIGION IN AMERICA SERIES
Harry S. Stout, General Editor

Theologians of a New World Order

REINHOLD NIEBUHR AND

THE CHRISTIAN REALISTS

1920–1948

Heather A. Warren

New York   *Oxford*   •   *Oxford University Press*   *1997*

Oxford University Press

Oxford   New York

Athens   Auckland   Bangkok   Bogota   Bombay   Buenos Aires
Calcutta   Cape Town   Dar es Salaam   Delhi   Florence   Hong Kong
Istanbul   Karachi   Kuala Lumpur   Madras   Madrid   Melbourne
Mexico City   Nairobi   Paris   Singapore   Taipei   Tokyo   Toronto   Warsaw

and associated companies in
Berlin   Ibadan

Published by Oxford University Press, Inc.
198 Madison Avenue, New York, New York 10016

Oxford is a registered trademark of Oxford University Press

Library of Congress Cataloging-in-Publication Data
Warren, Heather A., 1959–
Theologians of a new world order : Reinhold Niebuhr and the
Christian realists, 1920–1948 / Heather A. Warren.
p.   cm. (Religion in America series)
Includes bibliographical references and index.
ISBN 0-19-511438-8
1. Theologians—United States—History—20th century.
2. Christianity and international affairs—History—20th century.
3. Liberalism (Religion)—History—20th century.   4. Ecumenical
movement.   I. Title.   II. Series: Religion in America series
(Oxford University Press)
BT30.U6W37   1997
261.8'7'097309042—DC20   96-34717

Parts of chapter 6 appeared in an earlier form in "Intervention and International Organization:
American Reformed Leaders in World War II," *American Presbyterians*, 74, no. 1 (Spring,
1996), 43–56. Reprinted with permission. Some material in this book appeared in an earlier
form in "The Theological Discussion Group and Its Impact on American and
Ecumenical Theology, 1920–1945," *Church History*, 62 (December 1993), 528–543.
Reprinted with permission.

1 3 5 7 9 8 6 4 2

Printed in the United States of America
on acid-free paper

Acknowledgments

WHILE POLITICIANS DEBATED whether it takes a village or a family to raise a child, I found that it takes a community to make a book. For me, it took a community of scholars, friends, and family.

I had the invaluable assistance of organizations and colleagues dedicated to the study of religion in America. Grants from the Scarritt-Bennett Foundation and the Department of History of The Johns Hopkins University enabled me to make research trips. Revision of the manuscript was made possible by a semester appointment to the University of Virginia's Shannon Center for Advanced Study. Seth Kasten, Archivist at The Burke Library of Union Theological Seminary, made available manuscript collections, including the papers of Henry P. Van Dusen. Likewise, Archivist Martha Lund Smalley and her associate Joan Duffy at the Special Collections of the Yale Divinity School Library pointed out crucial interconnections of the several collections in "Mr. Niebuhr's neighborhood."

I am grateful to those who read the manuscript and offered helpful comments: Stephen Longenecker, Stephanie Wilkinson, Robert Wilken, Mark Toulouse, Grant Wacker, and James W. Lewis. Dr. Timothy L. Smith was my guiding inspiration throughout the life of the project.

No one, however, contributed more to the manuscript than my husband, Bill Burgess. Because of him the book is as readable as it is.

Charlottesville, Virginia   H. A. W.
November 1996

Contents

Theologians of
a New World
Order

Introduction

THIS IS THE STORY of how a group of Protestant theologians forged a theology of international engagement for America in the 1930s and '40s. It tells how in doing so they informed the public rationale for the United States' participation in World War II and stimulated American leadership in establishing both secular and religious international organizations for the promotion of world order. Among the members of this group were Henry P. Van Dusen, Reinhold Niebuhr, John Bennett, Francis P. Miller, Georgia Harkness, and Samuel McCrea Cavert. In creating a coherent, theologically derived position and then bringing it to bear on contemporary international issues, this group combined ideas with public action in a way that set the standard for American theologians' social activism in the years to come. They did this by explaining the import of world events in religious terms that the laity understood, providing a moral calculus to apply to the particular issues leading to war, such as racist nationalisms. They established a reputation for themselves as a "prophetic" band by criticizing the then-dominant liberal theological tradition and the existing social order. They also proposed concrete remedies for social and political ills. Through their writing, involvement in organizations, and connections with people in high business and government circles, they worked to implement their solutions by calling for changes in the policies of governments as well as the churches. They got a hearing in the national press and were regularly published in religious journals that reached the active, influential segment of American society. In retrospect, their story sheds

3

light on the related subject of how attention to international issues became a hallmark of the American Protestant establishment in the mid–twentieth century.

Defining what a "religious establishment" is in twentieth-century America is a complicated matter. Originating in the early 1960s, the term became synonymous with "mainline" Protestantism, meaning an alignment of the white, middle and upper-class churches—Congregational, Episcopalian, Presbyterian, Baptist, Methodist, Disciples of Christ, and Lutheran—that dominated in American society. But this definition misses other essential elements: prestigious seminaries, extra- and interdenominational organizations, and, most important, a network of leaders with a shared theology.[1] This book traces the careers of that peer group to show how one of these networks developed a shared theology that had political as well as intellectual relevance for the churches.

The authors of this theology were men and women who came to maturity in the 1920s with a heightened sense of generational kinship. They believed themselves called to lead Christians in overcoming the evils that had caused World War I and were reemerging with even greater fury in its aftermath. Rejecting the optimism of late-nineteenth- and early-twentieth-century liberal theology as excessive, and holding out hope in a supranational yet self-critical Christendom, they formulated a theology they called "Christian realism."[2] Their response to worldwide dissolution of civilization in the 1920s and '30s also took institutional form as they brought the World Council of Churches into being and influenced the drafting of the United Nations Charter. In all these ways, they laid the theological as well as the organizational foundations of Protestant international engagement.

Contrary to the charges of fundamentalists and evangelicals, this group was not monolithically liberal. In fact, none of them were simply liberal, either theologically or politically. While espousing elements of late-nineteenth-century liberalism, especially its methods of inquiry, they rejected some of its chief emphases, particularly God's immanence and a weakened valuation of original sin. Politically they opposed the pacifism of the liberals who advocated isolationism. Yet like the liberals of the preceding generation, they unabashedly presumed leadership for determining America's moral code, defining its national ideals in terms of foreign policy.

These theologians saw themselves not as thinkers ensconced in ivory towers but as intellectual activists whose commitments took them beyond the academy. So their story forces us to rethink old categories. Institution builders such as John R. Mott and political heavyweights such as

John Foster Dulles usually appear in one category, while theologians like Reinhold and H. Richard Niebuhr belong to another. But no one seems to know what to do with the others in that group, such as Henry P. Van Dusen and John Bennett, who were a bit of both.

Theological scholarship about these thinkers has focused on the continuity between pre– and post–World War I American religious life, the impact of European "crisis theology," and the phenomenon of Reinhold Niebuhr.[3] This emphasis on continuity has made their thought a descendant of the social gospel, liberal theology, and liberal politics, and misses the differences between their program and that of their predecessors. Other scholars' focus on the influence of European "neo-orthodoxy" has obscured the personal and indigenous American sources of the change. The preoccupation with Niebuhr also distorts the picture. This is not to diminish Niebuhr's stature but to balance it with the role his less-famous peers played in the religious scene and in stimulating his thought.

Histories of the ecumenical movement only cursorily note that these individuals had a hand in the World Council's formation. These institutional studies often lack a sense of proportion about the American involvement and do not plumb the depth of theological ferment and engagement over international evils that moved them to be among the founders of the World Council.[4] These Americans had a profound sense that they were living in a time of unprecedented worldwide crisis, and this stimulated them to think and act. The men and women who formed this group drove the Christian unity movement to consummate itself organizationally not because they wanted to avoid divisive issues, such as the fundamentalist-modernist controversy, but because they genuinely feared the perversion of Christianity and humane values that took place in civilized, "Christian" countries under fascist regimes.

Another defect of scholarly studies is that they have downplayed the Americans' role as the organizers of the World Council, evidently trying not to favor one national contribution over another, and perhaps also reacting to a long-standing European tendency to caricature the Americans as activists. But it was precisely their genius for organization that made them unique, a standing association of like-minded intellectuals with the managerial acumen and drive to develop the ecumenical idea into a reality.

Biographies of the "ecumenist" leaders and prominent European theologians in this period also cover some of the same ground.[5] The biographies of the ecumenists tend to mention the Americans' involvement but assume, incorrectly, that the organizers of the first ecumenical conferences in the 1910s and '20s were still the moving force in the '30s and '40s. Though some of the founding generation continued to be highly influential, in particular J. H. Oldham of the International Missionary Council and William Adams Brown of the Life and Work Movement, others had died by 1935, or, as in the case of John R. Mott, were eclipsed by this younger cadre. Their biographers have missed important changes in the ecumenical movement during the interwar decades and the wartime years, a trend the younger theologians seized upon in their climb to leadership positions. They have also overlooked the collective ambition and presumptuousness of their Union Theological/New York–New Haven–Princeton conclave. Most biographies of such European notables as Karl Barth and Dietrich Bonhoeffer, while more accurate about the course of the ecumenical movement, neglect the Americans' significance.

A new narrative is needed, neither exclusively theological, institutional, nor biographical, but one that draws upon these approaches, setting this complex story in the context of American culture and the wider world. This complexity makes for a narrative analogous to musical counterpoint. "Counterpoint," from the Latin *punctus contra punctum* (literally "note against note"), is composition in which two or more lines sound simultaneously. In this narrative several historical strands "sound" at once: the changes in theology, ecumenism, and politics. In counterpoint the simultaneous sounds generally produce mellifluous harmonies but sometimes also create dissonances, parts that sound out of place but press the piece toward its resolution. At times the disparate strands of this story create dissonance, with each variously sounding more loudly than the others. However, they press the story forward to its resolution, providing the narrative structure and gradually harmonizing the strains.

What I have presented here is in large part a history of these theologians' informal association.[6] Seeing them as a group emerging together from the student organizations that shaped their religious life and inclined them to ecumenical projects makes it fully understandable why they acted together for almost thirty years despite their strong-mindedness and the range within their theological and political views. Moreover, scholarly treatment of these theologians' early work rarely extends beyond the outbreak of World War II, with very little written about their ideas for the postwar world and how the war provided the opportunity for putting their beliefs into action.

Fundamentally, what had always distinguished these theologians' outlook from the liberal reformers of the progressive era was their sense of sin—personal and corporate—as the profound root of social ills. Unlike those liberals, they held that it was not enough to create opportunities for progress; sin made it necessary for Christians also to take political action to prevent regression into moral barbarism, whether fascism or communism. Yet they would use the democratic state and the supranational United Nations to prevent it. Therefore, despite awakening to the communist threat, they kept their distance from the contemporary conservatives. Instead they articulated what became the "mainstream" internationalist ideology for American Protestantism in the 1950s and '60s, an amalgam of liberal transnationalism with a sobering emphasis on sin, God's transcendence, and revealed religion.

High Tide of American Protestantism
1880–1920

BORN BETWEEN 1888 AND 1902, Protestant America's future theologians grew up in an era of pell-mell industrial expansion and urban reform. In 1869 the railways connected the coasts, extending capital and goods nationwide, creating a boom economy, and giving rise to large corporations. Inspired by the "captains of industry," typified by Andrew Carnegie and John D. Rockefeller, Americans embraced a new model of personal success. Thrift and diligence no longer sufficed as virtues; the ability to mobilize scattered or untapped resources, natural and human, into great wealth became the ideal. While popular utopian novels and Horatio Alger's "rags to riches" stories equated happiness with leisure and consumption, many individuals cultivated the values of rationality, efficiency, cosmopolitanism, specialization, and, above all, belief in Darwinian progress. These "progressive" Americans shared a sense of being alive in an exceptionally promising time.[1]

Liberal Theology and the Movement for Reform

As industries grew, so did urban poverty. Masses of workers, many of them immigrants, flowed into the cities, attracted by the promise of higher wages. Their numbers were overwhelming, and a host of social ills were manifest on an unprecedented scale. Apartment buildings deteriorated into crowded tenements. Diseases stemming from poor diet and inadequate sanitation became endemic.

Moved by the horrors of urbanization, the Protestant denominations expanded their home missions efforts. They trained thousands of social workers to teach people how to improve their condition through prudent household economy, literacy, and, for the immigrants, learning English. They opened settlement houses where social workers lived among the poor they sought to reach, offering them opportunities for education and rec-reation. Some followed the example of the Episcopal priest William S. Rainsford in establishing "institutional" churches that opened their build-ings for kindergartens, employment services, sewing classes, meetings of mutual-benefit societies, and other programs designed to meet the im-mediate needs of working people.[2]

This missionary work fueled an urban reform movement that swept the country. Home missionaries were joined by businessmen and old-line conservative Protestants in a crusade to improve local neighborhoods. Stirred by newspaper exposés of hazardous factory conditions and frus-trated by the failure of political patronage machines to address such prob-lems, businessmen and ministers worked through their chambers of com-merce and trade associations to make incremental improvements at the workplace and in city government. At the same time, proponents of a religious view known as "the higher life theology" advocated the evan-gelical and social rescue of the urban poor. They believed that a second transforming religious experience would move converts to witness for Christ, inevitably improving society as well as the individual.[3]

These efforts breathed the spirit of progressivism, a middle-class out-look combining a practical reform attitude with an elevated, visionary hope for democracy. A cluster of ideas informed this view: that monopo-lies and corrupt government were to be fought, that human existence is social in nature, and that life would be changed for the better with the new pop science of social efficiency.[4] Progressivism engendered involve-ment in an array of reform causes, which in turn informed middle-class attitudes: trust-busting, regulation of the railroads, civil service reform, women's suffrage, and public ownership of unexploited forests. Under-lying it all was an optimistic assessment of human nature—belief in people's inherent desire and ability to improve themselves and society when given the opportunity.

The progressives' values had two sources in Protestantism: liberal the-ology and its offspring, the social gospel. Liberal theology, bred by the historical-critical method of biblical scholarship, Darwinism, and German idealism, amounted to a cluster of ideas—like the progressivism it inspired. Popularized by Washington Gladden and Lyman Abbott in the 1890s as the "new theology," it sought a comprehensive, conscious adaptation of religious ideas to modern culture, emphasizing God's self-revelatory immanence in cultural development and humankind's movement toward realization of the Kingdom of God.[5] Faculty at the Andover-Newton Seminary editorialized in their respected *Andover Review*: "The church is rapidly learning that many of the social and secular conditions of the present time are providential arrangements in the use of which the kingdom of God can be advanced."[6] Influenced by the progressivism in German philosophy and committed to the social application of theology, the liberal theologians proclaimed the solidarity of the human race against what they saw as excessive individualism.[7] Following the German theologian Friedrich Schleiermacher, they placed greater confidence in knowledge gained from daily experience than from formal logic. As William Adams Brown, a professor at Union Theological Seminary in New York, put it: "What the theoretical reason cannot afford, the conscience and the religious experience provide."[8] This theology put a high premium on a central tenet of progressivism, the call for moral improvement in individuals and society. These "new theologians" believed in a moral God, a moral theory of atonement, and the moral life of believers.

Related to liberal theology was the social gospel.[9] It held that sin afflicted society as a whole as well as individuals, and that just as individuals could be redeemed, so could the social order. The concrete form that social sin took was the socioeconomic injustice of industrial capitalism. Rather than advance a general reform program, the social gospel leaders focused on labor relations and aimed to make middle-class Protestants aware of both the desperate plight of workers and the sources of industrial conflict. Social gospel leaders, like the muckraking journalists, thought that once churchgoers were exposed to these problems, they would strive mightily to solve them to make the Kingdom of God a reality.

To this end, Washington Gladden, Richard T. Ely, and Walter Rauschenbusch (to name the most prominent) gave lectures, formed study groups, and published books that critically analyzed industrialism in light of the Sermon on the Mount. They condemned the individualistic and materialistic ethic pervading American economics and Protestantism, and argued instead for an organic view of society. They advocated the law of love as the ethical standard for individuals and society alike, and emphasized God's immanence in gradually bringing the Kingdom to its consummation on earth. Social gospel advocates believed in the progressive project and had confidence in America's ability to achieve it. Many Americans had faith in these beliefs, too, as evidenced by the best-selling popularity of Charles Sheldon's social gospel novel, *In His Steps*.

As a result, the social gospel combined with progressivism to feed an optimism that disposed the leadership of the Protestant denominations to set aside their differences and work together for social improvement. Their attitude resembled (and may have drawn inspiration from) Andrew Carnegie's "gospel of wealth," which argued the financially strong were suited to dominate for the good of society. Such church leaders took for granted that they were the ones best suited to give America its moral bearings on the landmark issues of the day, to articulate national goals and prescribe practical measures for implementing them. Their cooperation took institutional form when their denominations established the Federal Council of Churches in 1908.

Foreign Missions and the Student Christian Movement

At the same time, a consensus was developing that the United States should take a more responsible role in the world as well as attending to its own social problems.[10] Industrial expansion presented Americans with new opportunities in Asia and elsewhere. Immediately a distinctly American moral internationalism emerged to cope with the challenge to the insular psyche of the country. From the 1880s onward the United States increasingly projected itself as a world power, benefiting from a favorable balance of trade. By the early 1890s the domestic opportunities for capital investment were no longer enough; large firms started to look overseas for new markets. Their need for stable business conditions naturally combined with the progressives' and philanthropists' benevolent yet imperialist intention to promote their Christian way of life throughout the world, reviving the faded belief in America's "manifest destiny" to possess and civilize the continent. Such belief in America's divinely sanctioned, international mission found its most vocal assertion in these people's support for the Spanish-American War. Religious leaders sanctioned these views by endorsing the war. Lyman Abbott, the well-known pastor of Plymouth Congregational Church in Brooklyn, typified the acceptance of the paternalism and nationalism embedded in the progressive view. Favoring the war, he expressed his belief in America's unique role in building a worldwide Kingdom of God and his enthusiastic confidence in America's growing role as an international force. But no one expressed it more blatantly than President William McKinley himself when he explained to his Methodist friends the reason he changed his mind regarding acquisition of the Philippines:

> I went down on my knees and prayed God Almighty for light and guidance more than one night. And one night late it came to me. . . . There

was nothing left for us to do but to take them all and educate the Filipinos and uplift and civilize and Christianize them, and by God's grace do the very best we could by them, as our fellow men for whom Christ also died.[11]

This spirit also found expression in a wave of Protestant enthusiasm for overseas missions, giving rise to a new strain in American religious life.[12] The rapid growth of foreign missions in turn produced changes in American Protestant attitudes. Many missionaries themselves acted with unself-critical altruism, sublimating their imperialist motives. Their reports drew churchgoers' attention to life outside the United States and prepared them to accept a greater role for America in world affairs. Contact with Buddhists, Confucians, and Hindus raised the question of the uniqueness of Christianity. For the missionary the original issue turned on whether these religiously observant but unconverted natives would suffer eternal punishment. At home, consideration of this question attracted the attention of liberal theologians who recast the notion of Christianity's finality in almost completely ethical terms. This view shaped Protestant missionary attitudes well into the twentieth century.[13]

One place where the effects of the nation's economic boom and enthusiasm for overseas missions came together was on college campuses. An unprecedented growth of higher education establishments was a byproduct of industrial expansion.[14] Wealthy businessmen founded such institutions as Johns Hopkins (1876) and the University of Chicago (1892); land-grant universities dotted the nation; technical and professional education evolved standard courses of study; and women's colleges and coeducation brought a growing number of women into such milieux. Campus life changed dramatically. Athletics, fraternities, and a host of clubs proliferated—debating, literary, and drama societies. All this activity invigorated a nationwide community of student YMCAs, "Christian Associations" as they were known on campus.

The leading spirit of the student movement over the last quarter of the century was Luther Wishard, the YMCA's first college secretary.[15] Assisted by Charles Kellogg Ober, Wishard implemented a program that emphasized active personal evangelism and overseas missions. As he saw it, other agencies provided students' social, physical, and intellectual development; the Christian Associations should be responsible for their spiritual welfare. Owing to his inspiration, Associations typically held weekly meetings for prayer and consideration of Christ's claims on their lives. He stirred student deputations to undertake revivalistic activity, which brought hundreds of men to make a Christian commitment and swell the ranks of the campus YMCAs.

Out of the mushrooming growth of Christian Associations during the 1880s came the Student Volunteer Movement for Foreign Missions (SVM). Seeking to boost the collegiate evangelistic crusade, Wishard went about enlisting Dwight L. Moody, the world-famous evangelist and former president of the Chicago YMCA, who hosted Association student staff retreats at his Mount Hermon School in Northfield, Massachusetts. Awaiting an opportune moment, Wishard followed Moody from one evangelistic campaign to another. Late in the spring of 1886, he met with him and persuaded him to sponsor a monthlong, summer Bible study for students. Moody held his first student conference in August 1886 at Mount Hermon. Among those attending were two future leaders of the international missions movement: John R. Mott, then vice president of the Cornell YMCA, and Robert P. Wilder, a student missions advocate and organizer of the Princeton Foreign Missionary Society. Wilder had brought several student missions volunteers associated with the Princeton Society to the Mount Hermon conference where they discretely advocated their cause. The first sparks of interest in missions grew into a firestorm when Dr. A. T. Pierson, a widely known missions promoter, and Dr. William Ashmore, a missionary who had served in China, addressed the assembly. At the final prayer meeting one hundred volunteered, taking the pledge: "It is my purpose, if God permit, to become a foreign missionary." Henceforth they were known as the "Mount Hermon Hundred."[16]

As committed as their elders were to spreading Christianity worldwide along with American civilization, these young people also had a way to yoke the two diametrically opposed rationales that gave the call to missions its urgency: postmillennialism and premillennialism. Postmillennialists, believing Christ's Second Coming would occur at the close of a thousand years of prosperity and harmony, encouraged Christians to spread the gospel in order to improve life so that the millennium would begin. They sought to hasten Christ's return. Filled with the optimism of progressivism, they discerned the signs of the times heralding that event at that very moment. In contrast, premillennialists believed a natural and spiritual deterioration would indicate the world was hastening toward the end of time, and only the Second Coming of Christ would end the horrors, an eschatological event establishing God's Kingdom on earth. Their reading of contemporary trends led them to think the demise had begun: masses of people embraced various apostasies, such as Darwinism and socialism; urban society spread decay worldwide; corruption permeated public life. Premillennialists aimed to spread the gospel to the four corners of the world so that when Jesus returned he would recognize his followers and save them from damnation in that final hour. Uniting post-

and premillennialists, however, was a sense of urgency and the belief that God had put America in the vanguard: Europe was too marred by its legacy of tyranny; Africa and Asia were heathen lands.

By the following year, the number of students wanting to enter missions had so multiplied that they dominated a second Northfield conference. Taking stock, the student leaders decided that a movement had begun, and they committed themselves to building a stable financial base and a permanent organization for it.[17] In December they officially named it the Student Volunteer Movement for Foreign Missions (SVM), and adopted the watchword "the evangelization of the world in this generation." John R. Mott was appointed their chairman. To avoid conflict with the YMCA and YWCA the leaders determined that the SVM would function as the missionary arm of the student Y. In relation to the churches, they meant to serve as a recruiting organization, not as a competing "sending agency." Stirred by the volunteered assistance of missionaries home on furlough, and promoted extensively by Luther Wishard, the student missions movement grew rapidly in the United States and in European countries colonizing Africa and Asia. By 1910 the SVM had 4,338 of its members serving in foreign lands. Over half the American missionaries who went abroad in the previous five years came from the student ranks.[18]

It was at this time that John R. Mott had the vision of a united international student movement.[19] He believed such an organization would both boost the growth of student movements around the world and help the Christian Associations in each nation to lead more students to embrace the Christian faith. Rather than amalgamate the national YMCAs in a single body, he had in mind a federation, which would enable the Associations to retain their distinct identities and autonomy while acting in concert. By 1895 it was decided that the student Christian movements in five countries had matured sufficiently to unite. In August of that year, at a meeting in a castle at Vadstena, Sweden, four European delegates and Mott formed the World's Student Christian Federation (WSCF). They aimed primarily to move students to believe in Christ and commit themselves to missions. In the preamble to the WSCF's constitution they made their evangelical purpose explicit: to "lead students to become disciples of Jesus Christ as only Saviour and God."[20] Mott and his peers also had an ecumenical goal, reasoning that if Christians were united they would bear a more potent witness to the salvation available in Christ. Soon after the WSCF was formed, Mott predicted it would fuse Christian students worldwide "in spirit" and speed the fulfillment of Jesus' prayer that his disciples might be one so the world would believe in him.[21] To the founders of the WSCF, ecumenism was mainly a pragmatic means for achieving evangelical, missional ends. They adopted as their motto *ut omnes unum sint*—"that they all may be one" (John 17:21).

The first WSCF international conference was held two years later in 1897. Delegates from twenty-six countries took precedent-setting steps to highlight the movement's universality. A delegate from China was chosen to chair the general sessions, the first time a non-European was selected for such a role in an international assembly. To enlist women, the delegates decided to make the organization officially coeducational.[22] Through the evangelical fellowship and inquiry that went on at such conferences, at regional meetings, and in WSCF publications, key members made lasting friendships and commitments to evangelism that led them to convene a succession of international conferences launching the ecumenical movement.[23]

The Ecumenical Movement

Between the turn of the century and the outbreak of World War I, very few Americans criticized their country's actions. While their nation's growing influence in international affairs fed young people's zeal for evangelism, it also encouraged personal involvement in international cooperation between the Protestant churches in the United States and Europe. Concerned that competition among Protestant missionaries was working against them in non-Western lands, John R. Mott and J. H. Oldham, a Scottish missions leader, arranged for the 1910 decennial meeting of the International Missionary Conference (IMC) at Edinburgh to address this problem.[24] To lessen dissension they restricted invitations to missionaries working among non-Western peoples, which excluded those who proselytized Orthodox and Roman Catholic Christians in the Levant and elsewhere. To prepare delegates to discuss cooperative work, Mott and his associates circulated preliminary studies on the challenges facing missionaries overseas. Unlike the large missionary gatherings of 1878, 1888, and 1900, which featured inspirational speakers and trumpeted the number of converts gained, Edinburgh was a working assembly. To avoid sectarian disputes, Mott, presiding, prohibited any discussion of doctrinal differences. The result was a conference procedure that modeled the muting of competition in the mission field. The participants also experienced a fellowship that transcended their ecclesial and national differences. They wanted to keep this spirit alive, so a "continuation committee" was established to pursue cooperative work in missions. They made Mott its chairman and Oldham, secretary.

Mott then traveled extensively throughout Asia to set up "national councils of churches." In contrast to the Federal Council of Churches in the United States, which was preoccupied with socioeconomic issues, these councils were devoted to coordinating missionary efforts and promoting evangelism among their people. Meanwhile, Oldham and his associate Georgina Gollock started the quarterly *International Review of Missions* to serve as an international forum for thoughtful discussion about missions. Thus in a matter of a few years an international ecumenical organization was born, claiming the attention of the major Protestant denominations in America.

The call for global evangelism and ecumenism at Edinburgh moved several American churchmen to make preliminary arrangements for an international body dedicated to ongoing discussion and eventual resolution of the doctrinal and ecclesial differences separating Christians.[25] One of the Americans it stirred to action was Charles Brent, the Episcopal bishop of the Philippines. Inspired by Edinburgh's spirit of cooperative expansion yet frustrated by the stifling of doctrinal debate, Brent returned to the United States and addressed a large meeting on the eve of his church's 1910 General Convention. He urged participants to initiate preparations for a world conference on issues of "faith and order." The Episcopal convention endorsed his idea unanimously, appointed a commission to implement it, and chose an influential layman, Robert Gardiner, as secretary. Impressed, the banker J. P. Morgan donated one hundred thousand dollars to underwrite the conference. Like the WSCF and the IMC (called the International Missionary Council after 1921), the Faith and Order Commission expressed its intent to fulfill Jesus' prayer that his disciples be united so the world would believe in him.[26] Within a year eighteen Protestant churches, the Church of England, and several Eastern Orthodox communions were prepared to join.

Between 1910 and the outbreak of World War I, American Protestants waxed enthusiastic for overseas missions and funded ecumenical ventures that promised to promote them. The Laymen's Missionary Movement organized massive financial crusades that raised unprecedentedly large funds; the numbers of students signing the SVM pledge reached new heights; church missions societies sent ever larger numbers of recruits abroad. To the leaders, all this bordered on evidence of divine sanction, reinforcing their enthusiasm over the burgeoning reform movement at home, giving them the heady feeling that evangelization of the world would indeed be accomplished in their lifetime. To middle-class Christian America it seemed the centripetal forces of civic reform and religion were triumphing over the centrifugal ones of urban decay and sin. Hopes ran high.

Then the Great War broke out in Europe. At first the momentum Protestant ecumenism had gained in the preceding decades carried it for-

ward. From 1914 to 1917 the YMCA and church agencies jointly provided relief services for Europeans displaced and impoverished by the war.
When the United States entered the war, the national passion for solidarity brought forth a stream of interdenominational projects, in many
ways paralleling the mobilization programs in the federal government.[27]
The Federal Council of Churches led the way, coordinating the work of
the denominations and such extraecclesiastical bodies as the YMCA and
YWCA, spawning the General Committee on Army and Navy Chaplains
and the General War-Time Commission of the Churches. This success
pushed the Federal Council to shift its primary social focus from labor rights
to international affairs and disarmament, thereby broadening its base of
public support.[28] All this gave the people involved an experience of interdenominational Christianity in practice and demonstrated the potential
for making a better world through united Christian action. While they
shared the patriotic fervor, Protestants hoped the sacrifices of the war
would indeed lead to a warless world.[29]

This whetted church members appetites for postwar international interdenominational work. Immediately after the November 1918 armistice
the Episcopalians resumed promotion of their conference on faith and
order. On 6 March 1919, a deputation sailed for Europe and the Levant
to enlist the Reformed and Orthodox churches. Assisted by sympathetic
local clergy and American consulates, they visited church leaders in Athens, Constantinople, Belgrade, Paris, and Uppsala. The journey bore fruit:
a year later a preliminary meeting in Geneva set up a "continuation committee" to prepare for an international conference. Organizers hoped to
convene it in Washington in 1923. The date slipped, however, owing to
a succession of world events and logistical complications. The conference
would not be held until 1927, and then at Lausanne.

The same wartime experience of interchurch service inspired the formation of a third ecumenical organization, the Life and Work Movement.
Drawing energy and principles from the American social gospel, it arose
from the belief that cooperation rather than competition should govern
efforts to testify to the gospel and improve human conditions worldwide.[30]
The organizational impetus came from the European side at the first
postwar international meeting of Protestant leaders in September 1919,
when Archbishop Nathan Söderblom of Uppsala proposed creating an international Christian council like the League of Nations to coordinate the
churches' work. In contrast, the IMC and the nascent Faith and Order
Movement were not as concerned about socioeconomic factors impeding
conversions and pushing society away from religion. Impressed, others in
attendance agreed to hold a preliminary planning meeting, which con-

vened at Geneva in 1920. A letter came from the ecumenical patriarch in Constantinople recommending the establishment of a "league of churches." Söderblom thereupon urged that all Christians, not only Protestants, should be invited to join. The conference consented, and thus began Orthodox involvement with the non-Orthodox. Confident that the path to Christian unity lay through joint action rather than doctrinal debate, the conferees declared, "Doctrine divides, but service unites." The Americans returned home in a triumphant mood, ready for a crusade that promised to extend their theological liberalism worldwide.

America's Protestant leaders had taken their first steps in concerted international engagement. They had all aligned now—the liberal theologians in prestigious seminaries, nationally known preachers, denominational leaders and their peers heading such extra-denominational organizations as the Laymen's Missionary Movement and the YMCA, and those leading the nascent ecumenical movement—all were pressing forward an agenda of progressive reform and international expansion. Their aims squared with those of a number of statesmen and businessmen like John D. Rockefeller, Jr., and J. P. Morgan to set America's moral course at home and abroad. Confident they were ushering in the Kingdom of God, this Protestant elite coalesced in a chain of relationships and occasions professing Christ, America, and modernity.

Missions likewise received a boost from the exalted wartime mood in America. To many, Christianity and American democracy were indistinguishable, and they saw themselves at the forefront of a colossal event, spreading Christianity around the world while building the world order envisioned by President Woodrow Wilson. As a result, membership in the SVM soared, with the number of missionaries going abroad more than doubling.[31] Going out on the tide of progressivism and wartime solidarity, the young volunteers sailed to Asia, Africa, and the Middle East filled with high expectations for the League of Nations and for winning the world to Christ.

Their generation, with few exceptions, had not questioned the optimistic underpinnings of American society. But now the horrors of the war in Europe came home with the shiploads of returning soldiers, profoundly disillusioning the rising student generation, among them those who would shortly become the Protestant elite and leaders of the new ecumenical movement. Having entered college with all the optimism of their graduating elders, taking progressive Christianity "on faith," they would soon rebel and challenge it.

TWO

The Found Generation
1890–1924

"YOU'RE ALL A LOST GENERATION," said Gertrude Stein to Ernest Hemingway in the early 1920s.[1] Her remark stuck to the young American writers around her in Paris and by extension to people like them back in the States. But for many others of the younger generation born between 1888 and 1902 it was wrong; thousands not only were not lost but knew they had found themselves and salvation because of their upbringing and involvement in the intercollegiate YMCA and the Student Volunteer Movement (SVM). To them it was the world that was "lost" (or well on the way), and they saw themselves as the ones to save it.

Family, College, and Faith

How these people came to see themselves as "found"—both as "saved" individuals and as a generation set apart to save the world through missions and social reform—was a process that began with their upbringing. The religious commitments and reformist sympathies held by their parents predisposed them to develop beliefs along theologically liberal and civically active lines. Like their literati peers, these young men and women had a middle- or upper-middle-class background that exposed them to the matrix of ideas underlying the progressive outlook. They grew up on the East Coast or in the Midwest and came from families that steered them toward higher education.

Several had fathers who were clergymen with tendencies toward lib-eralism. Gustav Niebuhr, the father of Reinhold and H. Richard, was a midwestern pastor of the German Evangelical Synod who accepted some tenets of liberal theology. While holding to the divinity of Christ and the veracity of New Testament miracles, he accepted biblical interpretation based on historical and literary analysis of the texts and believed the gos-pel had direct application to society as well as to the individual.[2] Francis Miller's father, a Presbyterian minister serving a small western Virginia resort town, subscribed to the *Atlanta Constitution* and the *Baltimore Sun* because he distrusted the conservative Richmond papers. Miller recalled that his father "leaned to the liberal and progressive side."[3]

Such parents typically were active in local politics. Henry P. Van Dusen identified his father's participation in local reform as an important influ-ence in his childhood and youth.[4] The Niebuhr brothers had a model in their father, who took the unpopular stance of fighting the saloon in his German-American community.[5] Georgia Harkness's father, a prosperous farmer in upstate New York, was committed to civic service and was an active layman in the church, teaching Sunday school for many years.[6] He pushed for the establishment of a state teacher's college at the county seat, organized a Grange society, brought rural free delivery of the mail to the area, started the local telephone company, and served as the local notary public. Likewise, Samuel McCrea Cavert's father was a leading citizen of his town in upstate New York, serving as a member of the county board of supervisors.[7] These parents, moreover, expected their children to go to college, be liberally educated, take their degrees at the strongest schools—Amherst, Cornell, Princeton—and choose a career that would both dignify them and enable them to contribute to society.

When they went to college, usually far from home, they had the same educational experience as the literati. There, they underwent an educa-tion designed to make them cosmopolitan citizens of the world. As the writer Malcolm Cowley recalled the ethos at Harvard: "We were not being prepared for citizenship in a town, a state, or a nation; . . . instead we were being exhorted to enter that international republic of learning whose tra-ditions are those of Athens, Florence, Paris, Berlin and Oxford." They went aiming to prepare for a higher order of life. "What we were seek-ing," he remembered, was "a key to unlock the world, a picture to guide us in fitting its jigsaw parts together."[8]

The future theologians, having had highly religious upbringings, natu-rally joined the campus religious movement that flourished in the YMCA and SVM. Several had profound experiences that gave them a sense of being "found" in faith and at the same time a framework for "fitting the jigsaw parts together."

For Samuel McCrea Cavert it happened through the YMCA. Devoting himself to study at Union College in Schenectady, he limited his extracurricular activity to the campus Y. In the summer between his freshman and sophomore years he attended a YMCA conference at Northfield, Massachusetts, and fell under the influence of such dynamic Protestant leaders as John R. Mott, Robert E. Speer, Sherwood Eddy, and Harry Emerson Fosdick. He then assisted a fellow student YMCA leader in an evangelistic trip to the Catskills in New York, where he worked and played with teenagers as well as preached. This led him to be "fully committed to Christian service, in some form" by the time he graduated.[9] Cavert then became president of the Union College YMCA and stayed an additional year as its director before going on to seminary.

Henry P. Van Dusen, who grew up in a blue-blooded Philadelphia family of lawyers, experienced "personal religion" as a member of the Princeton YMCA and for the first time perceived "living possibilities in the church." This moved him to question his original plan to follow his father's, grandfather's, and great-grandfather's footsteps into law. "I saw," he wrote, "that the springs of action lie deeper than intellectual conviction or even a high ethical ideal, and I came to suspect that the kind of motivation which the highest forms of religious faith and religious experience can create were needed." He decided to pursue theological study rather than "conventional success."[10]

For Georgia Harkness at Cornell, the Christian Association and the SVM were her "real home and greatest satisfaction."[11] She joined in her freshman year. At an SVM picnic, after singing around a campfire on the edge of Fall Creek Gorge, she fell off a twenty-five-foot cliff, but instead of hitting the rocks as she expected, she landed in water twelve feet deep. She did not know how to swim. She remembered praying with an intensity she had not known before, and then suddenly felt buoyant as the current carried her to shallower water where a rescuer waited. She interpreted this "miracle of deliverance" as God's call for special purpose in her life, as either a missionary or a teacher of religion.

Francis Miller, at Washington and Lee College in Virginia, experienced similar confirmation through his involvement with the YMCA.[12] He went off to college at fifteen years of age and was immediately attracted to the weekly YMCA meetings and study groups. More powerful still were the summer conferences he attended as a representative of his Y. He fell under the sway of the evangelists who preached there, particularly Robert Speer and John R. Mott, and recalled those events as times "for thinking deep thoughts and dreaming great dreams." Miller became aware of racism, reading *The Negro in the South* (1909) by W. D. Weatherford, secretary for student YMCAs in that region. The book opened his eyes and sustained his lifelong fight against racism at home and abroad. In his senior year he attended the quadrennial SVM convention, where, in the "air of invincible confidence and optimism," he had "a vision of a new heaven and a new earth." Upon graduating Miller accepted an invitation to join the staff of the student YMCA as secretary for colleges in New England and prep schools from Maine to North Carolina. He traveled throughout the area, reinvigorating Associations that already existed, organizing new ones, and speaking in college and school chapels. On these visits he became acquainted with the boys and young men who would become Protestantism's leaders: among them, Henry P. Van Dusen, future president of Union Theological Seminary; Alexander Zabriskie, future dean of the Virginia Theological Seminary; and Charles P. Taft, the first lay president of the Federal Council of Churches.

Miller enlisted in the army when America entered the war in 1917, and an experience in France turned his thoughts toward ecumenical possibilities. On Easter Sunday, 1918, an Episcopal bishop celebrated the Eucharist in the village where Miller's battalion was billeted a few days before going to the front. Miller, though a Presbyterian, received communion and had a poignant perception of the transcendent nature of the church. "As I knelt to receive the sacraments," he recalled, "[the bishop] did not ask me what I believed or to what church I belonged. It was sufficient that I asked to receive them. . . . I have always cherished the memory of that communion service as my first vivid experience of the meaning of the Church Universal."[13] Later Miller learned the bishop was Charles Brent, the founder of the Faith and Order Movement.

The family backgrounds and religious experiences of Miller and his peers predisposed them to view Christianity as both a personal and a public matter. Their parents' faith and civic action inclined them to believe Christianity held the solution to all social problems. Their involvement in the YMCA and SVM reinforced this at the same that it deepened their beliefs and gave them an expanded vision of Christianity's role in the world. The Y's and the SVM's promise of personal fulfillment and social salvation led them to believe it was indeed necessary to spread the gospel around the world, so that "making disciples of all nations" was the way to improve human existence spiritually and materially. This extended their conceptualization of Christianity's public scope to the national and international spheres. It also dovetailed with the prevailing liberal ethos arising from the political campaigns of populists and progressives and America's international expansionism through the Spanish-American War and business in Asia. The Y and SVM also steered these men and women to religious vocations in higher education. In contrast to popular revivalism, these organizations led them to profound experiences of God while allowing them to continue their intellectual inquiry. In the liberal religious milieu, equal value was given to the experience of grace and the exercise of reason. Christianity's relevance meant cultural adaptability. After the war, however, they began to think Christianity was relevant more for the critical perspective it could offer than for its flexibility.

Forming a Generational Identity

Immediately after the war these young people came together through their involvement in the YMCA and the SVM. Their sharing of concerns at various Y and SVM functions stoked a collective passion to abolish war and determine Christianity's role in the struggle against the tangle of spiritual root causes, chiefly racism and nationalism. Critical of the religious establishment, which they viewed as having abetted the war, their antiwar agitation was also the way this student generation marked itself off from the preceding one.[14] The optimistic view of human nature they had absorbed as adolescents clashed with their profound disillusionment from the war, its carnage no longer justified but rendered obscene by the "peace arrangements" that amounted to the victors' vindictive wrangling at Versailles. The Senate's rejection of the League of Nations Treaty depressed them even more. Frustrated, the young Protestants lost the optimism of the progressivist outlook but held onto the promise of international cooperation. While many of their generation expressed rebellion by conspicuous smoking, dancing, drinking, and whatever else flew in the face of their elders' public virtues, the more serious among them flung themselves into the campus peace movement to correct their elders' grossest public vice.[15]

They joined and often led the students opposing compulsory Reserve Officer Training Corps (ROTC) instruction. The ROTC had declined during the year America was in the war—owing to the mobilization of its recruits and a change in government policy—but was revived with the Defense Act of 1920. While that act did not require ROTC participation, the War Department construed it that way, citing the Morrill Act of 1863, the legislation founding land-grant colleges, particularly the provision that courses in military tactics be offered. Colleges complied, wanting neither to jeopardize the subsidy an ROTC program brought nor to be seen as un-American in the wake of the Palmer Raids. By 1921, 124 ROTC units were active on campuses.[16]

Opposition sprang up immediately that year. The YMCA lent support by reporting anti-ROTC arguments and action in the *Intercollegian*, its monthly journal for students. The most common tactic was to object to the educational worth of military courses and the fact that even "conscientious objectors" were required to take part. Compulsory military training, its critics argued, perverted the educational enterprise, bred the spirit of war, and undermined the development of intellectual integrity of students by indoctrinating them rather than teaching them to think for themselves. Worst, to the Christian idealist, the ROTC made war seem an acceptable means of settling international disputes. It tended to make the male student "discount all effort to question war."[17]

Opponents of ROTC waged their campaign using a variety of tactics, among them campus rallies and the distribution of handbills. They shrewdly focused on the compulsory aspect—the student delighting in the freedom of college life did not like requirements of any kind, much less one that kept him on the drill fields during what would have otherwise been leisure hours. Opponents ridiculed the lures with which ROTC was baited: championship polo teams for cadet cavalry and attractive "honorary co-ed colonels" dressed in officers' uniforms.[18] Debates were held with ROTC's defenders. Potential conscientious objectors were identified, coached on how to boycott drill, and then helped to fight in the courts when they were suspended for doing so.[19] The *Intercollegian* reported the cases of conscientious objectors losing their diplomas and being "vigorously denounced as unpatriotic." It noted the majority of them argued on religious grounds.[20] By mid-decade the agitation had produced an anguished mood on many campuses. The Department of the Interior, which administered the grants, upheld the University of Wisconsin's decision to make ROTC an elective. Other schools gradually followed suit.

For most anti-ROTC activists all of this expressed their antiwar sentiment in collective opposition to the older generation. But for the several thousand students who belonged to the YMCA and the SVM, anti-ROTC activism was insufficient. The campus rally offered too shallow an understanding of the causes of war and far too limited a means for eradicating it. The Christian students' passion was fed by their double aim of world salvation and their desire to take over from the adult establishment whose jingoism, they believed, had driven the nations to war. Owing to their college education and wartime service, they presumed the authority to speak for the nation. They believed themselves to be the true citizens of the world and consequently better equipped than the older generation to deal with international problems.

Though these young people did not articulate a causal connection between evangelization of the world and world peace, they believed that *as Christians* their generation's mission was to prevent another world war. One veteran who had joined the YMCA wrote that because their battle-field experiences had taught his generation the essential incompatibility of Christianity and war, they "agreed on the desirability of eliminating war" and thought the task facing them was "to show how it is to be done."[21] Robert P. Wilder, the SVM general secretary, confirmed the prevalence of this attitude. "The elders have failed," he reported students saying, "otherwise the world war would not have come. Turn out the old, bring in the new. . . . [T]he youth alone can bring in the new age which must come or humanity will perish."[22] Though the students accepted the SVM watchword "the evangelization of the world in this generation" and maintained that work leading to conversions and Christian living was important, their hearts were set on preventing war. For them this mission was a crucial step in converting the world to the gospel.[23]

It also gave the students a critical perspective on the older generation running the American Christian student movement, which they promptly turned into action. To transform the world, they would have to start with the average American student. They began "at home" by trying to democratize the SVM and the intercollegiate YMCA. Neither a crude power grab nor mere rebellion against their parents' generation, these young people believed this was how to begin dealing with the sociopolitical problems of the postwar world. Organizations' means, they thought, must correspond to their desired ends.

The SVM was the first to be hit with members calling for reorganization and an overhaul of campus programs. The adult leaders were the targets of an "insurgent revolution" at the quadrennial convention on overseas missions at Des Moines during the 1919–1920 Christmas vacation. Nearly seven thousand delegates attended, representing 906 colleges.[24] The young participants raised complaints about the organizers' neglect of sociopolitical concerns and the exclusion of young people from the conference planning. Registering their dissatisfaction with old-style missions, the insurgents blamed the organizers for failing to address the relation between industrialism in North America and the conditions it fostered in other countries that made relief work abroad necessary. George Coe, a prominent religious educator attending as an observer, remarked that students frequently responded to appeals to become missionaries by asking, "What are missions for, and particularly how are they related to the present social chaos?"[25]

The students were right; the conference agenda had not integrated social concerns and international missions. This was obvious to anyone who viewed the arrangement of the convention exhibit hall.[26] Booths on the left side of the room depicted village life and missions in Asia, Africa, and South America. Displays on the right told about the SVM's relation to education, industry, and the YM-YWCA. In the center was a "Court of Religions" informing conventioneers about world faiths. It was ringed by a horseshoe-shaped arrangement of displays detailing SVM operations. The lone one labeled "social conditions" with the slogan "Every Mission Is a Social Settlement" stood at the end of the row on institutions—as far as possible from the center. Though it linked urban problems in foreign lands with the settlement houses in North America, it did not show them both arising from the social and spiritual derangement of industrialism.

The insurgents injected their own views into the convention proceedings by passing resolutions dedicating the SVM to remedy poverty, racism, and injustice in North America as well as abroad, and to supply home missionaries in addition to foreign ones.[27] They also criticized how the SVM was run by the older generation, objecting to the lack of student involvement in planning the convention. They demanded representation in the preparations for the next one and urged the SVM to put more student representatives on its governing bodies, especially its executive committee. This, they thought, would enable them to put more relevant issues on the agenda. The older SVM leaders complied, establishing a student council for determining the movement's policies and enlarging the executive committee to make half its membership students.[28] One observer commented that because students could now steer the SVM's course, a "new era" had begun.[29]

The younger generation's search for ways to prevent war by addressing its underlying causes reached into the field of religious education. This interest was not unique to the SVM. A small group of Christian educators in New York and Chicago were seeking new methods to promote world fellowship through missionary education.[30] They crusaded against "imperialist" rationales for mission work, congratulating missions boards for teaching future missionaries about the cultures, including the religions, of the peoples they would serve. They hoped that by infusing Sunday school curricula with this changed perspective congregations would become centers for developing an international outlook.

Milton T. Stauffer, the SVM educational secretary, was committed to this viewpoint. Having lately served as a missionary in China for six years,

he knew firsthand the challenges facing missions in a country with a developed civilization of its own. He pushed four changes in the SVM's
education program: that it give attention to the cultural factors affecting
natives' lives; drop paternalistic methods of assessing mission needs; develop an international perspective on all topics, regardless of how local
the actual subject; and emphasize extensive reading about the sociopolitical matters related to missions.[31] In effect he was encouraging the
younger generation to view the world through the lenses of Christianity
and politics simultaneously, with the result that they would think about
international affairs in theological terms.

By the fall of 1923 Stauffer had led the SVM through a successful year
of educational experiment in using "discussion groups," a method that
encouraged the sharing of opinions and ideas among participants in a
review of a subject. This mode of teaching accorded with the students'
demands for Wilsonian "self-determination" in the movement. The tech-
nique held such appeal that within two months a joint committee of the
SVM, YMCA, and YWCA endorsed it.[32] The planning committee for the
next SVM convention incorporated the discussion group method in its
proceedings. A separate committee was formed to assign delegates to small
discussion units and integrate each group's findings into the program
during the convention. It recommended that discussion group leaders be
"of or near" student age, receive leadership training in advance of the
convention, and include women. It also chose three educators widely
respected in their fields and well-known in YMCA-SVM circles as the
trainers. One, Harrison Elliott, was commissioned to write an instruction
booklet.[33]

Elliott was no stranger to missionaries, students, or religious educators,
having been the secretary to a Methodist bishop in China, a teacher at
the YWCA National Training School, the editorial secretary of the YMCA
publishing house, and a professor at Union Theological Seminary.[34] His
booklet, *The Why and How of Group Discussion*, served as both a philosophical statement and a how-to manual. A liberal like John Dewey, Elliott
thought that knowledge came from experience and that discussion groups
taught democracy by giving people participatory experience. "Group thinking," he wrote, "is essentially the instrument of democracy."[35] He offered
concrete advice for discussion leaders: continuously clarify the analyses
of the members, keep discussion to the point, seek to involve everyone,
and move the group through a five-step problem-solving process. Elliott
recommended that leaders use blackboards to keep the discussion from
wandering, prevent arguments, and hold participants' attention. Most
important, the discussion group method promised to elicit the comments

of many delegates because it aimed to be "a process for all," a model of the nonprejudicial, inclusive, enfranchised society they hoped to build.[36] It would make SVM conventions more participatory, allow students to set the agenda, and make the program educational rather than triumphalistic. To the students' way of thinking, it was a method that would develop democratic structures and processes, and thus, by extension, serve their goal of preventing war by transforming the old authoritarian, oligarchical ways of their elders.

Opposition to Racism and Nationalism

Between 1920 and 1924, at the same time that the SVM leadership was preparing the next quadrennial convention, the students were defining their mission to prevent war, targeting racism and nationalism as the two chief causes that had to be eradicated immediately. Their college education, having divested them of their allegiance to local peculiarities, predisposed them to oppose prejudice, particularly the kinds rooted in either local or widespread tribalism. Combining with events at home and abroad, this outlook led them to sound the mission theme in a new register. Moreover, the older generation of leaders had avoided the issues of racism and nationalism, providing the younger one with the opportunity to challenge them and eventually question the theology that had permitted such negligence.

A rising fever of race hatred in the United States and other countries alerted these young people. Race riots in Chicago, Ku Klux Klan demonstrations in the North, and a wave of lynchings in the South made it obvious the United States was not free of the disease. Some Christian organizations tried to respond constructively. Between 1921 and 1923 the Federal Council of Churches established a special commission to deal with race relations and sponsored its first Race Relations Sunday, promoting pulpit exchanges between black and white pastors. Methodist women in the South adopted a resolution condemning lynching and publicly confronted law enforcement officials, challenging them to take an anti-lynching pledge. Meanwhile in China, antiforeign rioting targeted missionaries, who in turn blamed the violence on xenophobic propaganda of the Nationalist revolution. Students drew the conclusions that racism was a worldwide epidemic and that religious leaders had avoided it far too long.[37]

One person responsible for bringing these issues to the attention of the rising Protestant leaders was Sherwood Eddy, a much-beloved YMCA evangelist. Independently wealthy, he had been an unpaid evangelist for

the SVM and YMCA in Asia since 1896 and served as the YMCA's regional secretary from 1911 until the war broke out in 1914. At the invitation of the British YMCA, he ministered to soldiers in the camps and at
the front, even going to the Verdun battlefield. The carnage he witnessed
changed his life. War, "one of the supreme moral problems," made him
undertake a "pilgrimage of ideas" to "find what was radically wrong with
the world," leading him to become a passionate advocate of pacifism and
social reform.[38]

Eddy's crusade produced the American Seminar, an annual study trip
to Europe for a select group of public speakers, writers, and educators.
He conceived it while in Britain in the summer of 1920 studying industrial relations. Helped by his friend J. J. Mallon, warden of the pioneering
settlement house Toynbee Hall, Eddy met with British labor leaders to
discuss solutions to the world's problems. In the course of this discussion
the idea of bringing over American opinion makers to observe European
politics and talk with Europe's prominent people "flashed" into his mind.
Mallon encouraged him to do it. Eddy, however, did not want it to be yet
another "annual invasion of tourists"; he aimed to sensitize the groups to
the economic, political, and religious problems of Europe. He hoped the
exchange of ideas "would be one avenue to international understanding
and peace."[39] The seminar began the following summer, 1921, and was
repeated every year until 1939. The group took a ship to Britain, crossed
over to the Continent, and went to Soviet Russia. There were interviews
with British Prime Minister Ramsay McDonald, German Finance Minister Walter Rathenau, and Pope Pius XI, among others.

Eddy also used the seminar to introduce the rising generation of Protestant leaders to one another. Henry P. Van Dusen and the future Methodist bishop G. Bromley Oxnam were on the first trip.[40] Reinhold Niebuhr
and Georgia Harkness went in 1924.[41] These people already knew of each
other through the YMCA or SVM and their publications in the *Christian
Century*, but on Eddy's summer-long trips they had time to become fully
acquainted. In 1922 Eddy and fellow pacifist Kirby Page founded the
Fellowship for a Christian Social Order. One of their first recruits was
Samuel McCrea Cavert, the young general secretary of the Federal Council
of Churches.[42]

Eddy worked tirelessly to reinvigorate the YMCA and the SVM, and
in doing so he fostered many more personal associations among the
younger generation. He drafted them as evangelists to tour the colleges
and speak about their commitment to "social" Christianity.[43] In January
1924 he intentionally brought Niebuhr and Van Dusen together with
another student leader, Sam Shoemaker, to form the nucleus of a speak-

ers' group. Niebuhr and Shoemaker clashed, but Niebuhr and Van Dusen developed a lasting relationship. Eddy briefly revived the student movement but, more important, mentored the emerging leaders.

Another man who focused their attention was Francis P. Miller. He was well-known and liked from his tours of East Coast colleges and prep schools as YMCA secretary before the war. Following this, he attended Oxford as a Rhodes Scholar and there became deeply involved with Britain's Student Christian Movement (SCM).[44] In 1921, after graduating with a bachelor of arts degree in history, he worked for the SCM as international relations secretary, participating in the World's Student Christian Federation (WSCF) European Discussion Conferences, occasionally leading groups of students in studies of international issues. These episodes brought Miller into contact with the future leaders of the European ecumenical movement, and conversations with them gave him insight into nationalist passions. He was convinced the cure lay in unity of the churches. As he recalled:

> It was growing upon me that the curse of European civilization and of the Protestant churches in Europe was the type of nationalism that had developed there during the nineteenth century. It seemed to me that the only way to counteract this false religion of nationalism was for men to be reminded that they had an ultimate loyalty beyond the nation. For me loyalty to the Kingdom of God was the ultimate loyalty and that could only be expressed through the Church Universal.[45]

Unlike the older social gospel advocates who put loyalty to the Kingdom of God at the center of their thought but rarely mentioned the church, Miller saw the church as a transcendent entity, not a mere association of like-minded people gathered here and now, as the essential agent for transforming the world.

In 1922 Miller attended a WSCF General Committee meeting at Peking, where these issues became clear to him and the other Americans there. For the first time in the Federation's history, all the delegations included natives of the countries they represented. There was the usual prolonged and prayerful discussion, then the WSCF declared its unanimous opposition to war and its causes, particularly nationalism and racism. But what was new was an affirmation of the centrality of Christ in bringing the delegates together to overcome those ills. As one observer put it, "the unity of the human race is discovered and realized only through Jesus Christ."[46] The experience pushed the students toward the idea that nationalism and racism, when viewed from a Christocentric perspective, were not only politically perilous but also profoundly corrupting, undermining the moral basis of society.

Miller returned to Oxford in 1922 to study theology, and after taking his degree in 1923 headed back to America determined to pursue his new objective through YMCA work. From the fall of 1923 he was associate executive secretary of the YMCA for student work and a member of the SVM executive committee. He arrived just in time to work on the upcoming SVM quadrennial convention. He brought to the planning sessions the conviction that racism and nationalism were threatening to lead Christians astray around the world, and that there were potential "common bonds" among Christians that should transcend national loyalties. Before going to Oxford, Miller had recommended the WSCF conduct a serious study of Christian internationalism.[47] Now he urged it to lead in that direction. The WSCF stood at the threshold of a new era, he wrote to Mott, a new stage in which it could exist more as a worldwide fellowship than as a collection of national organizations.[48]

In the WSCF journal the *Student World* Miller wrote of the transcendent church, saying that the only hope for the future of the human race lay "in the emergence of a truly Universal Church of Christ."[49] A united church would advance evangelism much more effectively by exhibiting the spiritual kinship of people who lived in awareness of salvation through Christ. Miller was just beginning to realize the implications of the idea. At this point he could only put it in the most general terms, a rhetorical appeal.

The influence of Eddy and Miller on the Americans became apparent in the preparations for the upcoming SVM quadrennial convention. The program committee echoed the WSCF Peking conference, declaring the Christocentric principles that informed their planning: "[T]he contributions of all races to the interpretation and embodiment of Christ and to the upbuilding of the Kingdom should be recognized, and that of the white races not duly stressed."[50] Half of the preconvention study topics were a continuation of the issues raised at Peking, "Race Relations and the International Ideal" and "International Problems and the Christian Way of Life." The student YMCA magazine commented that racism and the need for international goodwill were "pressing" and "painfully distressing" matters.[51]

The discussion group method and internationalist content made for a predictable convention held the week after Christmas 1924 at Indianapolis. As planned, the discussion groups provided students a "democratic" way to relate the substantive messages of the leaders to their generational mission of preventing another world war. The resolutions that came back from the discussion groups registered these views.[52] Forty-nine groups, each of about one-hundred people, met twice for two hours. Standing at "democratic" blackboards, the leaders guided the discussion over potentially relevant subjects, from fraternity social life to the nature of God, before focusing on racism, nationalism, and war.[53] Students ventured opinions on North American "attitudes" toward "the imposition of western civilization" on other peoples.

They singled out racism as the main source of international conflict and the major challenge facing Christian missions. The evangelist Robert E. Speer set forth the analysis and issued the call:

> Great forces are weaving once again the war patterns. . . . There is the rejection with open eyes of the ideals of brotherhood and of humanity, and the assertion of the right of the white race to dominate the rest of mankind and exploit the colored races. . . . There can be but one result of such a doctrine—the same result which came in 1914 on a wider and more deadly scale. . . . Again and again we have heard quote those old words of St. Paul about there being in Christ no foreigner and no citizen. . . . [H]e had the solution of the problem of the relationship of race to race in the wiping out of all cleavage in the unity of Christ, . . . the solution of the problem of the relationship of nation to nation, in the building up . . . of Christ's body throughout the nations.[54]

This announced focus on Christ hinted at the new line of thought about the church's potential competitiveness with racism on an international scale. But Speer was an older-generation liberal evangelical who uncritically embraced his optimistic outlook. Though he declared worldwide Christian unity could overcome international hostility, he did not say how this would happen in concrete terms. Because much of the discussion groups' time was spent on American manifestations of racism, the resolutions that came up prescribed ways to fight it in their own society. One resolution said it was essential to eliminate the "white superiority complex" inculcated from primary school onward. Another had the delegates pledging to develop friendships with "people of color" even if it involved going into segregated communities. Yet another had them promise to work with people in other countries who opposed organizations advancing attitudes of racial superiority. These resolutions were well intentioned but lacked any realistic sense of what was involved.

The groups' treatment of nationalism was similarly superficial, stemming from discussion over whether the SVM should endorse pacifism. When the debate started to become divisive, the leaders steered it to the causes of war, calling for the college SVM groups to study other nations' histories and to support student and faculty exchanges as a means of reducing nationalist prejudice.[55] They asked SVM members to put their beliefs into practice by contributing to the Student Friendship Fund for European student aid.

Despite the lack of depth, the principle underlying these resolutions was representative of the emerging generational shift in attitude: "unity in Christ" was superseding consideration of racial and national differences, a view the SVM now shared with the WSCF. The contrast with the Des Moines convention four years earlier, which had highlighted the territorial diversity of SVM mission work, was graphically clear from the arrangement of exhibits in the convention hall.[56] Indianapolis had a "Court of Life" display depicting famous missionaries joining with native Christian leaders *around* Jesus. Surrounding the Court of Life were exhibits entitled "Problems at Home," "Problems Abroad," "Evils at Home," and "Evils Abroad." Three booths presented the ministries of teaching, preaching, and healing, linking the Court of Life with displays about native leadership, native churches in action, and native Christian contributions to Christianity as a whole. Issues and solutions were ranged around Christ. The thematic unity imposed the idea that the ultimate goal was a Christocentric all-inclusiveness; geographical distinctions belonged to a bygone day.[57]

But the theology implicit in the displays of Christ-centeredness was shallow and ambiguous, and this irritated some of the more intellectual delegates. The "discussion" sounded to them like the social gospel being applied to the international arena, with "solutions" no more practical than "doing as Christ would do." The unarticulated implications of the new "unity in Christ" concept incited the budding theologians to fill it with metaphysics, and this gave purpose to their involvement: they saw the possibility of modifying the movement's emphasis on the churches' *acting* in concert for evangelization to *being* a united witness of salvation. Such conceptualizing was beyond the masses of delegates, but the intellectuals found the absence of any attempt at it a deplorable lack of theological probity. One of them—Van Dusen—registered his opinion, writing in the *Student Volunteer Movement Bulletin* that for all the merits of the discussion groups, they did not reach a depth commensurate with the magnitude of the problems they pledged to solve. "The atmosphere of Indianapolis was healthy," he said, "but not very profound."[58]

Yet in a larger sense Indianapolis was a turning point, particularly in the life of the young intellectuals. Attending gave them an actual experience of Christian unity while clarifying their thoughts about integrating the social and personal aspects of their faith. For the movement it brought a theological viewpoint, Christocentrism, to bear on racism and nationalism, and talking about it in the groups gave everyone the experience of "discovering" it at the same time. For the future theologians Indianapolis was a defining moment in their careers.

Like the expatriate literati of the "lost generation," the young religious intellectuals went abroad to study theology and see the world from the vantage of another country. Cavert went to China, Bennett to Oxford, and Van Dusen to Edinburgh. Some went to Europe on Eddy's American Seminars. Others stayed in the States to pursue postgraduate degrees. Wherever they were, they all probed deeply into the liberal theology that underpinned the Protestant world. Van Dusen at Edinburgh studied Kant and Schleiermacher and wrote his dissertation on Baron Friedrich von Hügel (1852–1925). He was mentored by Henry Sloane Coffin, the already well-known liberal pastor of Madison Avenue Presbyterian Church and future president of Union Theological Seminary. At Boston University Georgia Harkness studied with Edgar S. Brightman, the leading proponent of a variant of liberal theology called "personalism." Reinhold Niebuhr had studied at Yale under D. C. Mackintosh, the modernist Canadian theologian who emphasized human experience as the starting point of systematic theology. From such training came easy use of the liberal theologians' critical methods of inquiry as well as detailed knowledge of the substance of their work.

On completing their degrees and returning from abroad, the young theologians gravitated to New York and the metropolitan heights of the Northeast to take their stand. Van Dusen and Reinhold Niebuhr wound up at Union Theological Seminary in New York City; Cavert, as general secretary of the Federal Council of Churches, was also a New Yorker; John Bennett accepted a position at Auburn Seminary not far away; Georgia Harkness taught at Elmira College, also nearby; and Francis P. Miller and H. Richard Niebuhr landed at Yale. Unlike the experiences of the *deracine* literati who went overseas and became expatriates, the young theologians' ventures abroad had been a detour that routed them back to the United States. Now they were firmly convinced that unity in Christ was essential to cure the world's sickness and that it was their mission to apply it. To borrow Gertrude Stein's observation about the literati, it was the world that was "lost" in their generation; they had "found" themselves and were going back, prepared to make the radical diagnosis that had to precede deliverance from the evils of racism, nationalism, and war.

THREE

Age of Negativism
1925–1933

ASSESSING THE AMERICAN Student Christian Movement in December 1927, Henry P. Van Dusen, now a lecturer at Union Theological Seminary in New York, characterized the years since Indianapolis as "the age of negativism." He and his peers, no longer students, returned from their travel abroad and took up academic appointments at prestigious schools in the Northeast—Union Theological Seminary, Auburn Seminary, Yale. Collectively they knew what they had rejected—liberalism—but had little to offer as an alternative. "We have been clear about the weakness and failures of the Christian Church," Van Dusen wrote: "[W]e have been quite hazy about any necessary place for the Church in the modern world. We have recognized that the day of old-fashioned missions was past; we have had no conception of what missions in the new day might be."[1] Such criticism marked the first groping steps toward a theology of international engagement.

Though Van Dusen had his student generation in mind, his comment was true of mainline Protestantism as a whole. In the mid-1920s it was apparently losing its influence in public life.[2] Church attendance dropped; support for overseas missions fell off; the social status of clergy sank in comparison with that of sports heroes, movie stars, and businessmen. Liberal theology, the dominant ideology in America for nearly half a century, lost its hold among the thinking public. At the same time, the fundamentalist-modernist controversy put mainline Protestantism on the defensive, pressing it back into a corner as an institution and as a theological standard.[3] Fundamentalists criticized such extradenominational bodies as the SVM and YMCA for casting off their evangelical legacy, impugning and thereby undermining—in the public's mind—their credibility. The shift was perceptible first to religious educators. One remarked: "There is the conscious recognition that the church has lost its vital force, so far as the thinking of the populace is concerned."[4]

The mid-1920s were a particularly difficult time for Van Dusen. He momentarily became the focus of the fundamentalist-modernist struggle among Presbyterians in New York when, in seeking ordination, he refused to affirm a literal understanding of the Virgin Birth.[5] His admission to the New York Presbytery in October 1924 was opposed by fundamentalist elders and clergy, and when their complaint was dismissed they filed their objection with the General Assembly, the church's highest authority. Defending Van Dusen in that process was a bright young Presbyterian lawyer from the firm of Sullivan and Cromwell, John Foster Dulles. Van Dusen was eventually exonerated, but such bludgeonings became common and reduced the liberals' public stature. To young theologians like Van Dusen the contest was something they kept in the back of their minds. John Bennett, then teaching at Auburn Seminary in New York, later recalled they were "always concerned about fundamentalism."[6] The gap was widening between the extremes of fundamentalism and modernism, with nothing appearing immediately on the horizon to fill it. Bennett and his friends were about to change that.

Decline of the Student Movement

Adding to the decay in mainline Protestantism was a waning of moral zeal within the student movement. College students whose adolescence occurred during and just after the war still joined the YMCA, YWCA, and SVM in droves in the middle to late 1920s, but they were not totally swept up by the idealism of the prewar generation, nor did they have the same sense of urgency for reform as the wartime generation. The national mood had changed. Prosperity, a swing of attitude to the political right, and a desire for what President Harding dubbed "normalcy," all cooled the campus climate by the time they arrived. These trends contributed to the young theologians' negative outlook, producing in them a sense that something had gone seriously wrong in American life.

Three intercollegiate conferences reflected the trend. The first met at Evanston, Illinois, during the 1925–1926 Christmas vacation to discuss current social issues and the possibility of creating a united Student Christian Movement similar to ones recently formed in Europe and Asia. Observers and participants alike remarked how tepid the criticism of society was. The well-known religious educator George Coe pointed out the contrast. He reported that conference organizers had directed students' attention to the church's complacency on social problems, but, contrary to expectation, the younger students defended it, while those just a few years older delivered the stirring condemnations.[7] Seizing on these few critical remarks, local newspapers sensationalized the conference, making it out to be a "Bolshevik" assembly. Reinhold Niebuhr, who as a socialist knew what Bolshevism was, found the speeches were "anything but radical," tending instead to skate over subjects that required more profound treatment.[8] A student delegate from Mount Holyoke College put it bluntly in the *Intercollegian*: "[W]e spent our time dabbling around at big social questions."[9]

In fact, a shift away from social concern had occurred among the undergraduates just after the leaders of the previous student generation graduated and went into seminary, business, or full-time religious work. Carried away by the giddy, newfound prosperity of the 1920s, young people embraced the consumption ethic that glamorized the individual's satisfaction rather than society's.[10] For religious students this was manifested in the greater attention they gave to personal aspects of faith. SVM General Secretary Robert P. Wilder reported that a significant change in attitude had set in immediately after the Indianapolis convention in 1924, a "swing of the pendulum" to interest in Christ and personal salvation. Students still sometimes thought about overseas problems and race but were more interested in their own individual spiritual growth. The questions claiming their attention were "What is the meaning of prayer?" and "What is the life of victory, and can I live it?"[11]

This attitude dominated the next conference a year after Evanston, in 1927 in Milwaukee, again organized jointly by the YMCA, YWCA, and SVM.[12] Many attending frankly divorced the social aspects of faith from the personal. Francis Miller, one of the organizers, observed that few students considered social problems to be religious challenges. They tended to "hold in their minds a definite separation between the social and the personal."[13] This dichotomous thinking left the leadership uncertain where to focus its efforts. Though they did not put it in so many words, they sensed the movement was losing momentum.

The students' preoccupation with personal piety had a dampening effect on what the organizers planned for the discussion groups at Milwaukee. They had hoped the group experience would infuse social concerns into the conference as a whole; it turned out to be an imposition. Because the group leaders imposed their own socially minded questions on their groups, questions that did not address the personal concerns of the rank-and-file delegates, the groups were lifeless and the conference lacked vitality.[14]

The third disappointing episode came at a student-faculty conference sponsored by the YMCA and YWCA in Detroit in 1930. Here the organizers were shocked by the students' attitude toward a flagrant display of racism. Several months before the convention, Channing H. Tobias, senior secretary of the YMCA Colored Men's Department, assured the organizers that the Book-Cadillac Hotel had promised to open several dining rooms to all delegates and not discriminate in room accommodations. But when they arrived all of the blacks were assigned to one floor, and the hotel coffee shop refused to seat them together with the whites. Most of the delegates went along with these "separate but equal" arrangements. The older-generation leaders saw in this compromise a drop in the moral zeal that had previously impelled the movement.[15]

While decline occurred at these conferences, a few of the leaders from the wartime generation were highly visible, breaking away from the complacency of the students just as they had earlier broken away from their idealistic elders. Starting with the Evanston conference of 1925–1926, they were the ones who had constructively engaged the delegates and impressed members of the founding generation who were there. George Coe wrote glowingly in the *Intercollegian* about how they deftly summarized others' statements, quickly mastered large amounts of material, capably organized large numbers of people, drafted the resolutions, and expressed commitment to historic Christianity.[16] But this virtuosity in procedure did not save the conference. Coe noted "a rather wide gap" between the undergraduates and recent graduates. At Milwaukee these same people were starting to bridge the gap. They succeeded in reaching the students by theological innovation that simultaneously addressed the contemporary situation and acknowledged their personal, spiritual thirst. Reinhold Niebuhr delivered an outstanding speech, "Our World's Denial of God," which made students flock to him afterward for informal discussion. Van Dusen led a popular session on prayer and "the resources of Jesus for the world today." The YMCA endorsed Van Dusen's *In Quest of Life's Meaning* and Francis Miller's book *The Church and the World* as the official conference follow-up materials.[17] An *Intercollegian* editorial lauded these men's leadership, noting they were "out of college or graduate school only two or three years."[18]

The new stars were also becoming professionals, gaining even more prominence as they got appointments to seminaries and religious organizations. Research and writing for publication focused their thinking, and they took pride in it. Niebuhr, pointing out the students' indifference to the moral and theological dimensions of social issues, contrasted it with the older ones' intellectual discipline. Detachment from conventional viewpoints was not an inherent gift of rebellious youth, he argued, but "the reward of painstaking study."[19] His peers were devoting themselves to rigorous inquiry, writing, and public speaking, and they recognized each other in this.

While these young theologians matured, the SVM went into a decline from which it never recovered. Aimless and uncertain about relations with the YMCA-YWCA and mission boards, the SVM staff suffered inner prostration over the current student generation, the decreasing number of recruits, and chronic financial trouble. An internal Committee of Inquiry formed in 1925 to examine the SVM and make recommendations for future policies. Its report, issued in January 1926, prescribed only palliatives: remain independent but in close contact with the YMCA and YWCA; maintain good relations with the denominational mission boards; and nurture and emphasize the evangelical character of the movement.[20] Nine months later, General Secretary Wilder reported that membership was still dropping. He attributed it to students' confusion between the SVM's education for foreign missionary service and the general membership education program of distinctly Christian approaches for promoting internationalism and improving race relations.[21] So another committee was appointed to design an appropriate clarification for the institution's profile. Finding that students wanted emphasis on the movement's religious heritage, the committee recommended making evangelism the centerpiece of programming and publicity.[22] But the membership hemorrhage went on, and the SVM set up yet another committee to define evangelism, particularly for use among campus groups in which conservative factions had a divisive influence.[23] After many hours of wrangling, the committee gave up and did not issue a report. Siding neither for nor against the "jazz age" trends that were secularizing American life, the SVM stood pat, a mastodon stuck in the tar pit of its prewar liberal evangelicalism. By the fall of 1927, four college chapters had withdrawn on the grounds that they feared the movement "was becoming too liberal theologically."[24]

Decline within the student movement also had grave implications for the coalition of Protestant groups that had dominated American religious life. From the early nineteenth century through the Great War, the denominations and such extradenominational associations as the American Sunday School Union, YMCA, and SVM had had a shared ideology and an overlap of personnel, all the while politely avoiding doctrinal differences. In concert they spread American Protestantism and its values across the continent and around the globe. Then, in the 1920s, the denominations started doing for themselves what the extradenominational organizations had been doing for them, as it were. Episcopalians, Methodists, and Presbyterians launched their own campus ministries, making the college Ys and the SVM redundant.[25] Denominational missions boards expanded, came under the direction of professional lay administrators, and had little difficulty recruiting candidates for mission without suffering the same qualms over institutional identity that afflicted the SVM. Having grown so "vertically integrated" like the great business conglomerates of the day, the churches no longer needed the extradenominational agencies to deliver nationwide support. As a result, the extradenominational associations slipped out of the alignment, falling into financial difficulty and other internal problems of their own making. To those able to see it, the decline of the student movement signaled the need for a new theological and institutional reconfiguration if mainline Protestantism were ever to reassert its cultural authority.

Theologians' Departure from Liberalism

At the same time, adding to the upheaval, the liberal Christianity that had dominated American Protestantism for thirty years suddenly lost its appeal. The rising young theologians in particular found it distasteful, and their criticism engendered a negative climate of opinion about it that became more widespread as their work more and more often appeared in print. They had soured on liberal Christianity's celebration of God's immanence in natural processes and in all progress.[26] Such a theology, they thought, ignored the traditional doctrine of original sin, insisting, with liberal philosophy, that nothing was really wrong with human nature that education could not change. The liberal theologians had avoided commenting on the divinity of Jesus while making him the ethical exemplar. They taught that by following his model modern-day disciples could hasten the coming of God's Kingdom. To them the church was practically a voluntary organization toiling in the vineyard. They were apologists, trying to present Christianity in the language and ideas of contemporary culture. All of this had fit the progressive, reformist temper of prewar America. Now, after the war, people wanted a Christianity that spoke about God intervening directly in the world.

Fundamentalist attacks and a reactionary theological turn in postwar Europe, "neo-orthodoxy," pointed out the shortcomings of liberal theology, putting liberals on the defensive. Fundamentalists charged them with apostasy; humanist agnostics accused them of having cold feet in press-

ing out the implications of their views. The theologian William Adams
Brown lamented the "pathetic plight" of the "homeless liberal . . . held in
contempt by both reactionary and radical."[27]

A theological shift had already begun in Europe with the publication of
Karl Barth's *Commentary on the Epistle to the Romans* in 1918. Barth, having given up his liberal optimism during the war, undertook a systematic
examination of the Bible, beginning with Paul's Epistle to the Romans, using
the most recent biblical scholarship. He "caught a breath from afar" of "something primeval . . . indefinably sunny, wild, original" hidden behind the
sentences.[28] His admiration for Paul soared, and beyond Paul ("what realities . . . that could excite the man in such a way!") he found a God radically
different from what liberal theology made of him, a transcendent God
"wholly other" than humankind. The implications served as a basis for a
critique of culture and politics. Barth was unsparing with modern Protestantism. He thought all Christian groups and movements of that time were
flawed by their emphasis on God's immanence. It had led them not just
to lose a sense of God's transcendence but to make the facile assumption
that God accepted whatever they did. He explained: "God was always
thought to be good enough to put the crowning touch to what men began
of their own accord. The fear of the Lord did not stand objectively at the
beginning of our wisdom; we always attempted . . . to snatch at his assent
in passing."[29] Barth's transcendent God judged, and because of this, he said,
a crisis occurs in each individual when God confronts him or her with the
possibilities of death or new life. This "crisis theology" quickly gained
adherents and spread to America. Detractors called it "neo-orthodox" because its partisans did so much talking about the old-fashioned doctrines
of original sin, creation ex nihilo, and the divinity of Jesus.

The young American theologians were attracted to the radical cultural
criticism in Barth's commentary.[30] Though they still credited science and
reason with having a role in acquiring religious knowledge, because of the
war and their involvement in the Student Christian Movement they
had become more interested in transcendent aspects of reality, renewed
attention to the deeper reality of the church, "Christocentricity," and
serious theology itself as "queen of the sciences." Not just any theology,
either. Expressing themselves for the most part in negative terms, they
judged theological liberalism too optimistic about human nature, wrong
for having identified God too closely with the progress of society, and worst,
for practical purposes, morally impotent in its response to such evils as
gross social inequities, imperial colonialism, and unrestrained racism.

Francis Miller signaled the change with *The Church and the World*
(1926), an anthology on missions.[31] In his essay Miller returned to the

nature of the church, challenging the liberal view that it is merely an association of fellow builders of the Kingdom. He redefined it as a Christ-centered body with both divine and human aspects created by God to help save the world from sin. He identified the church as the people who, in their "fellowship" as representatives of Christ Jesus, already participated in the divine life because they acknowledged God's claim on them and subscribed to his transcendent values. The church's task was to make every aspect of human relations Christian. Consequently, missions meant more than the mere territorial expansion of Christianity characteristic of the prewar era.

Miller called on the church to lead the way in developing a critical perspective on contemporary society, beginning with itself. He faulted the American churches for aligning themselves with the dominant culture. "Our religious ideas and ecclesiastical policies," he charged, "have assumed far more completely than we realize the complexion of our national self-interest." The church needed to subject itself to an unsparing self-examination, a "dramatic scrutiny." In this way the church would rediscover its unique nature and mission. Though sounding hopeful, Miller was no naive idealist. Such an undertaking would be "extraordinarily difficult" because of the self-detachment required and the temptation to self-delusion. He hinted that for the church to reclaim its public influence it would have to offer society criticism, not conciliation. The title of the book itself suggested Miller's differences with the liberal view, making the church and the world distinct entities, associated but not coextensive.

That same year saw the publication of Henry P. Van Dusen's *In Quest of Life's Meaning*, based on vespers meditations he gave at the YMCA's Ozark Mountain Student Conference in 1926.[32] He assaulted the liberal emphasis on Jesus as the morally perfect man. He said that notion might have satisfied the modern intellect for a while, but it had not been the appeal of Christianity through the ages and it was not attracting believers now. Following a moral exemplar was fine, but the life of Christian faith involved more: it meant seeing the supremacy of Jesus as "*the giver of the power of life*" (emphasis in original). This belief was what built the early church and made converts century after century.

Van Dusen argued the value of theology in the face of challenges to Christianity from modern science and philosophy. Against the faddish faith in science he asserted that theology was supreme because it gave a higher vantage for discerning truth. Opposing the trend in philosophy and theology dating from the Enlightenment, Van Dusen said that the quest for meaning must not begin anthropocentrically. "The starting point in the discovery of truth," he wrote, "is genuine humility. . . . Nothing but the most consummate and childish egotism has led us to consider the Universe anthropocentric." Religion had to take modern thought into account but also had to keep a critical distance.

Finally, Van Dusen also meditated on eternal life—a sure indication of departure from liberalism. He did not exclude the possibility of a sharp division between the saved and the damned in eternity. Sinners who lived evil lives would not find themselves a final home anywhere other "than in a hell of some kind." The book was favorably received, and it added to Van Dusen's growing reputation both in the YMCA and in influential New York ecclesiastical circles.[33]

Reinhold Niebuhr launched a full frontal attack on liberalism in his first book, *Does Civilization Need Religion?* (1927), reiterating what he had already broached in several articles for the *Christian Century*.[34] Niebuhr charged liberalism with clinging to an optimism that nature and history belied. Its moral complacency, relying on "eighteenth-century sentimentalism and nineteenth-century individualism," was the main obstacle to a potent Protestantism. Like Miller and Van Dusen, Niebuhr abandoned the apologetic approach of liberal theology toward popular culture and challenged Christians to take a more critical stance: "Religion can be healthy and vital only if a certain tension is maintained between it and the civilization in which it functions." Alluding to Jesus' Sermon on the Mount, he compared religion that feels at home in the world with "salt that has lost its savor." He objected particularly to liberal ideas about Christ that sapped Christianity's strength. Jesus was not only the highest model of individual conduct, "the most perfect personality," he was also the victorious Christ who triumphed over the forces of evil. Niebuhr regarded this Christ as central: "a potent . . . yet suffering divine ideal which is defeated by the world but gains its victory in the defeat" was essential to "any morally creative worldview."

Rejecting a major assumption of the social gospel, he argued that institutions and social structures could not be redeemed by Jesus' victory in the same way as individuals. Groups were harder to affect. Because groups originate in loyalty to something beyond the individual but also serve their members' self-interest, the individuals forming the group abdicate their moral responsibility. Indeed, social groups are disinclined to take risks that threaten their existence; they aggrandize themselves by appealing to the members' self-interest, encouraging a grab for power at the expense of ethics. Nationalism existed because nation-states were the groups with the greatest power potential and as such engaged in the most unethical conduct. Because Christians were called to uphold the ethical standard, they were obliged to chastise nations for their recalcitrance. Religion "must find its social function," Niebuhr wrote, "in criticizing present realities from some ideal perspective and in presenting the ideal without corruption, so that it may sharpen the conscience and strengthen the faith of each generation." For the sake of civilization, religion had to confront, not accommodate, the secular culture, even if it meant discord. The book went through a printing of five thousand copies in less than three months, a remarkable number for a serious work on religion. The Federal Council of Churches identified it as one of the "Best New Religious Books."[35] Niebuhr's concerns had begun to resonate among thoughtful Americans.

Travails of the Ecumenical Movement

Sounding as another strain in American religious life, albeit for now a faint one outside the walls of its prestigious schools, the international ecumenical movement had similar but even more severe trouble that threatened its very existence in the mid-1920s and early 1930s. For it, too, this was an age of negativism. Trouble within the organizations known as Life and Work, Faith and Order, and the International Missionary Council ranged from leadership crises to financial insecurity. Such pressures forced the movement to streamline operations, distance itself from the liberal theology that had dominated it, and, most important, choose new leaders, many of whom belonged to the younger generation and were American. Though peripheral to American Protestantism at the time, these changes initiated a refashioning of the movement that would position it to play a central role in making international engagement a priority for American thought—and action.

Life and Work began having difficulties after its 1925 world conference in Stockholm. Samuel McCrea Cavert, general secretary of its American pillar, the Federal Council of Churches, called this period "years of floundering."[36] Inadequate financial support brought the malaise to the surface. Over half the organization's budget came from the United States, but because its work overlapped with that of the Federal Council, American donors had difficulty understanding why it needed additional funding.[37] Disagreement arose among participants over the nature of the movement—whether it aimed at the renewal of church life or was the practical manifestation, through cooperation, of a vitality already present.[38] Underneath it all, though, Life and Work suffered from being a reformist camp in the midst of the postwar disillusionment over progress. A collective letdown set in after Stockholm.

The conference had decided to establish a Life and Work International Christian Social Institute.[39] The leadership supported the proposal because they thought that for the movement to promote Christian unity it would need an agency to educate the churches about each other as well as the ecumenical idea. It would also strengthen international ties among theologians and examine the social and industrial conditions in the countries of member churches, especially in Europe and the United States. But when the institute opened it caused confusion. Its theological studies duplicated what Life and Work's Committee of Theologians had been doing for some time.[40] Chronic insufficient funding hampered it, especially once the depression spread from Europe to America, hitting with full force in 1930.

The leadership, meanwhile, decided to economize by streamlining the entire organization. European offices were consolidated, the London office merged with the one in Geneva, and a committee was formed to recommend additional changes for efficiency.[41] The American branch consolidated its structure, too, with three related but separate divisions in the Federal Council merging to form the American Section of the Life and Work Movement.

Three years later the movement showed signs of recovery. Fresh blood from the younger generation revived it. Two from the founding generation resigned in 1932: Henry A. Atkinson, the American secretary, and Adolf Keller, the general secretary.[42] Selected by the American branch as the new American executive secretary was Henry Smith Leiper, a former SVM missionary who had been Federal Council liaison to Life and Work for several years.[43] The new general secretary was Henry-Louis Henriod, former secretary of the World's Student Christian Federation. The biggest change came at the death of the movement's founder and chairman, Archbishop Söderblom in 1931. The executive committee replaced him with Dr. G. K. A. Bell, bishop of Chichester, who though older than the wartime student generation shared their views. At the same time the executive committee teamed him with an old-line liberal, William Adams Brown of Union Theological Seminary, as program chairman for the next international conference. In the middle of another consolidation in 1932, Brown emerged heading a new committee for overseeing the policy of the organization between meetings.[44] Brown, however, was never accepted by the new generation owing to his theological liberalism and a personality they did not find congenial.

The Faith and Order Movement faced similar difficulties after its international conference at Lausanne in August 1927. Though the press portrayed Lausanne as a harmonious event, those who attended knew there had been so much discord they feared it might break up, creating lasting divisions rather than new concord.[45] William Adams Brown, chairing the section on the nature of the church, got so caught up in its conflicts that he had to drop plans to join his wife for the weekend in Geneva, excusing himself in a letter saying that "all sorts of difficulties & questions" had arisen "at the eleventh hour," and he "dared not risk being away."[46]

Six of the seven working sections had this trouble. In the one on "The Church's Common Confession of Faith" there were two factions, one arguing for the primacy of the creeds, the other for Scripture.[47] There was another split over the authority of church tradition—an important doctrinal point for the Eastern Orthodox. But in the section on "The Unity of Christendom and the Place of the Different Churches in It" the most divisive debate arose when the draft statement said Life and Work complemented Faith and Order, and then called for collaboration among the churches.[48] Anglo-Catholics objected that this would mean going ahead with interchurch cooperation at the expense of efforts to achieve doctrinal unity, the drive for church federation replacing the goal of "organic," institutional unity in violation of Faith and Order's primary mandate. The Orthodox expressed reservations about the ultimate form of church unity, appending a four-point clarification of their views to the section's report. After vigorous debate they did not reach a consensus, and the report was sent back to committee to be revised after the conference. In the end the only statement adopted unanimously at Lausanne was "The Message of the Church to the World—The Gospel," an uncontroversial declaration that a common, unifying tradition ran through the history of Christianity despite the multiplication of churches.[49] This was nowhere near the longed-for reconciliation that would permit intercommunion.

Faith and Order faced a turning point like Life and Work when its founder and guiding light, Bishop Charles Brent, died in 1929.[50] A chairman as capable had to be picked—the more so since Faith and Order was by then suffering the same collapse of financial support that afflicted Life and Work. The choice fell on William Temple, archbishop of York, with J. Ross Stevenson, president of Princeton Theological Seminary, as vice chairman. Both were in their middle to late forties, about ten years older than the rising American theologians, but their outlook was similar. Through Temple's vigorous efforts the organization regained some financial ground, but in 1931 the full onset of the depression left it in deeper trouble than before. Faith and Order took drastic measures to economize.[51] The Geneva office was closed, depriving the staff of a point of contact with other international organizations. The office of the general secretary underwent consolidation; its staff was cut. One happy development was the arrival of Leonard Hodgson, canon of Winchester Theological Seminary, to serve as general secretary. Hodgson was a skilled administrator and respected theologian with contacts among influential people in the United States, formed while teaching at General Theological Seminary in New York.[52] Backed by Archbishop Temple and ably assisted by the American secretary, Rev. Floyd W. Tomkins, Jr., Hodgson brought Faith and Order through its crisis.

By now the next world conference was approaching. Since the last one, Faith and Order had engaged a committee of "theological experts" to come up with answers to the critical reaction that poured in.[53] The committee's task was to address "a number of crucial questions." Dominated by Europeans, it focused first on the issue of "grace," and in 1931 published a volume of essays typical of the theological departure from liberalism that was under way. The book showed the influence of Karl Barth's dialectical method, bringing out differences in such a way as to illumine a synthesis leading to Christian unity.[54] Taking an historical approach, the authors identified four sources of the contemporary division over the doctrine of grace. First, not surprisingly for Barthian "crisis theologians," the committee singled out transcendence as the main point of contention. One side held that God so completely transcends nature that any entrance of God into creation—any act of grace—is miraculous; the opposing view held that an element of kinship exists between God and creation, making God's entrance continuous in natural processes. The other three issues were corollaries. First, through the centuries theologians had parted company over the nature of God's "gracious" self-revelation: Does it occur through the contact of God's Spirit with the human spirit, as if there were a special religious sense, or do emotion and the mind play the essential part? Second, the mode of revelation: Does it happen primarily in a personal way, or is it socially mediated? Third, the completeness of revelation: Was it given all at once, or in portions as humankind matured? These opposing lines of thought persisted through the whole history of Christianity, the authors concluded, and no adequate account could omit the types of religious experience from which they grew. The authors did not suggest a reconciliation; on the contrary, they asserted that both were valid and necessary to the faith, sidestepping the increasingly apparent differences between liberal theology and the emerging challenge to it.

This Theological Committee also undertook to clarify its relation to Life and Work's Committee of Theologians. Some served on both, which was a problem when financial stringency dictated cutting redundancy. Faith and Order's theologians, however, held out, insisting they only studied subjects arising from discussions about doctrine and church polity, while the work done for Life and Work addressed all issues that would promote cooperation.[55] The distinction, however, would not last, and the two movements drew closer together through their overlapping theological projects.

Meanwhile, the ecumenical missions movement was also experiencing a malaise. Signs of trouble appeared at the expanded meeting of the International Missionary Council (IMC) at Jerusalem in 1928, considered by the older generation of leaders to be the movement's high-water mark. Already in 1925 the IMC leaders had sensed the movement was losing momentum, discernible in a negative attitude toward missions among the churches. They hoped a large international gathering would stimulate a revival. An expanded session of the council was planned to meet at Jerusalem in the spring of 1928.[56] The regular council members, leavened with native representatives from Asia and Africa, would meet with select theologians and student representatives—all to reorient Christian missions to a world much changed since the last conference in 1910.[57] The preparations were handled personally by IMC chairman John R. Mott out of New York, secretary J. H. Oldham in England, and American secretary A. L. Warnshuis. They chose the subjects and authors of the preliminary conference papers.

The work initiated a modest international study of the relation between Christianity and other religions. The most influential paper of the lot was by the Quaker Rufus Jones, a professor at Haverford College active in both the Federal Council of Churches and Faith and Order. Mott and Oldham decided on him when they met in London for a planning session. They discovered they had the same instinctive conviction that a new "religion" with no place for God in it was threatening Christianity *and* civilization. Unable to define it, they provisionally called it "rationalism" and "materialism."[58] Mott, who was familiar with Jones's work, suggested asking him to develop the idea. Jones named the rival "secularism."[59] Appearing in the preconference papers, this notion signaled a shift in the concept of missions similar to Miller's ecclesiology in *The Church and the World*. Missions meant more than the geographical spread of Christianity; now secularist "civilized" society was as great a mission field as any.

For three weeks in the spring of 1928, Jerusalem was the spiritual focus of Christians all over the world while the IMC conference met at a sanitorium on the Mount of Olives.[60] An adjacent tent city served as housing for the 231 delegates, one-quarter of whom were African and Asian natives.[61] The most important task, everyone agreed, was to answer the question: What distinctively Christian word must missionaries proclaim? There were apparently irreconcilable differences between the liberal Anglo-Americans and continental Europeans, the latter holding that the gospel was uniquely valid and that consequently converts must completely renounce their former belief. The Anglo-Americans maintained that commonalities existed between the faiths; Christianity "fulfilled" truths the others anticipated. Arguments broke out. A particularly nasty exchange over miscegenation ended the discussion and prevented adoption of a statement condemning racism.

To stop the fractiousness, cochairmen Archbishop Temple and Robert E. Speer drew the conference together around a consensus principle that became the heart of the conference "Message": "Christ is our motive and Christ is our end."[62] Temple, the principal author, patterned it after the "Message" adopted by Faith and Order at Lausanne the year before, and worked in Jones's "secularism" as the negative goal to be countered by Christ. The Message declared a tenuous synthesis of the personal and social aspects of salvation: "Those who proclaim Christ's message must give evidence for it in their own lives and in the social institutions which they uphold." That affirmed Christocentricity without forcing the issue of missions philosophy and strategy.

Criticism came quickly from several quarters afterward. Muslims, belittling the new crusade against secularism, denounced the conference as Christianity's preparation for a final assault on Islam. Theological conservatives, especially the continental Europeans, charged that the Message had a modernistic cast, that focusing on secularism opened the door to syncretism with any non-Christian religion opposing it, expediently passing over the uniqueness of Christianity.[63] Frederik Torm, a professor of theology at the University of Copenhagen, tried to offset the weight some Anglo-Americans assigned to social salvation, arguing that the church and its missions should not assume responsibility for social problems but concentrate on conversions that lead to more communities of the just. Hendrik Kraemer, a Dutch theologian, thought a Barthian critical perspective would have helped by sharpening the contrast between Christianity and secularism, which he thought the conference only obscured.

Like the other two ecumenical organizations, the IMC floundered through the rest of the decade and into the next one.[64] Jerusalem failed to reverse the IMC's ebbing strength. The depression hit the following year. The IMC was particularly vulnerable because its funding mechanism for getting money from the contributing countries to mission lands went through the Austrian Credit-Anstalt, the first major financial institution to fail. In 1931 the Japanese invasion of Manchuria put the IMC steering committee in an embarrassing moral position. To condemn the aggression by withdrawing personnel and financial support for the missions in Japan would have doomed them. The IMC vacillated, and the missions of China began to be lost in Manchuria.

Despite its wavering, the IMC had turned a corner. It had begun to face the winds of theological change, and it had a capable helmsman in its chief executive officer, J. H. Oldham, who though considerably older than the rising generation shared their outlook. This put him in league with the new leaders of the other two ecumenical bodies, Bishop Bell of Life and Work and Archbishop Temple of Faith and Order. In the immediate years ahead, their collegiality and like-mindedness went far in advancing the movement. Through them, their associates formed a collegial, routine working relationship. Standing out among that association was the cadre of young American theologians who continued doggedly to distinguish themselves from the older generation and its theology.

Theological Assault on Liberalism

Between 1928 and 1932 the theological tide in American Protestantism turned even more sharply from prewar liberalism as the neo-orthodoxy of Karl Barth and Emil Brunner pushed the younger-generation theologians in the direction they were already moving. Continental theology became increasingly accessible to Americans through English translations and commentaries. In July 1928 the World's Student Christian Federation journal, the *Student World*, featured one of Barth's sermons that sounded some of his main themes: the profundity of sin in human nature; the transcendence of God; the essential difference between God's Word and any human expression or institution; and the crisis that happens to an individual when confronted by God.[65] A translation of Barth's *Word of God and the Word of Man* was published that same year, and two books about him were not long in coming: John McConnachie's *Significance of Karl Barth* and Wilhelm Pauck's *Karl Barth, Prophet of a New Christianity*.

Emil Brunner did much to popularize the new theology, lecturing in the fall of 1928 at the Theological Seminary of the Reformed Church in Lancaster, Pennsylvania, then at Princeton, Harvard, and Union Theological Seminary in New York, among others.[66] Many of the younger-generation Protestant leaders got to know him, and at the request of several American friends he published the lectures as *The Theology of Crisis*.[67] Brunner's language translated well into English, and the book received enthusiastic welcome as an alternative to the unpalatable choice of reactionary fundamentalism or the naïveté of liberal theology. Jesse Wilson, the newly appointed SVM general secretary, hailed it as "an orthodox theology adjusted to . . . modern science without . . . the relativism of modern liberalism."[68]

The appearance of Walter Lippmann's *Preface to Morals* in 1929 added fuel to the antiliberal bonfire. Lippmann sought to understand how industrial society was rapidly eroding the old religiously based moral code. Searching for an adequate basis of morality for unbelievers like himself who experienced distress and emptiness over their loss of belief, he found it in rational inquiry and disinterested service. Well-received throughout America, Lippmann's book was also favorably reviewed by the Protestant theologians as an accurate expression of the state of mind of the educated laity. Lippmann's sounding of the death knell for traditional religion, however, begged for a response.

Reinhold Niebuhr rose to the challenge first. He had anticipated Lippmann's diagnosis by two years.[69] But, unlike Lippmann, he thought ethical behavior involved more than the individual's relation to society; it extended to relations between social groups. In 1932 Niebuhr elaborated this point in *Moral Man and Immoral Society*. He argued that because social groups are inherently more selfish than individuals, societies must use coercion—even though it violates the ethics appropriate for individuals—to restrain the destructive egoism of races, classes, and nations.[70] He refuted the idée fixe among liberals that the key to social harmony lay in progressively moderating egoism through moral education. As America's opinion makers they failed in not recognizing the ethical result of the power relations permeating group interactions and the consequent need for political action rather than individuals' ethical improvement to control them. Niebuhr chided the sociologists for assuming that conflicting parties had equal claim to being right and that conflict was merely a transitory phenomenon, lasting only until sufficient education brought about social cooperation. This denied sinful selfishness as the root of social strife. He criticized these thinkers for regarding "ignorance rather than self-interest as the cause of the conflict."

He was particularly harsh with John Dewey, the dean of liberal educators, for overlooking collective egoism, especially that of nations. He pilloried Dewey's ideas about democracy and education as being hopelessly rosy, an offspring of the American middle-class perspective. Against the Deweyites' claim that education does not use force, Niebuhr retorted that not every exercise of force takes physical form. Propaganda was a prime example, and all education involved an element of it. In the same vein Niebuhr flayed liberals in general for abjuring coercion. They failed to acknowledge that injustice and coercion existed in peaceful society: the "coercive elements are covert, because dominant groups are able to avail themselves of . . . economic power, propaganda, the traditional processes of government, and other types of non-violent power." Liberal moralists wrongly distinguished between violent and nonviolent methods of coercion based on whether any significant destruction resulted. Niebuhr argued that the real difference was what their agents intended, not the magnitude of the consequent destruction. Nonviolent resistance to evil sometimes involved much bloodshed, but it begat social change that made the sacrifice of lives worthwhile.

Niebuhr also criticized liberals for clinging to outmoded progressivism and obscuring the cruel reality of power relations in the functioning of nation-states. Such beliefs bred sentimentalism. He complained that in spite of the disillusionment that followed from the war, "the average liberal Protestant Christian is still convinced that the kingdom of God is gradually approaching" and "that the conversion of individuals is the only safe method of solving the social problem." This "counsel of accommodation" had public consequences. It led to denying absolute standards of justice and keeping the door open to the exercise of gross prejudice, as was evident in America's treatment of the Negro.

Niebuhr concluded *Moral Man* with a prescription for living with the conflict between society's needs and the individual's conscience, drawing on Hegelian-Marxist ideas about the dialectical nature of reality to argue that ethics and politics must exist in constructive tension, informing and correcting each other. The most pernicious illusion in need of constant correction was that humanity could achieve perfect justice. Only by the strong exercise of reason could that attitude be prevented from spoiling public life. Niebuhr did not abandon social justice as a goal, nor did he suggest putting full confidence in reason; rather, each had a role in achieving the most just society possible at a given moment in history.

For all that, what attracted popular attention to Niebuhr's book was its repudiation of the pacifism that had dominated the intellectual marketplace since the war, especially coming from a socialist fellow traveler like Niebuhr. His defection made hostile reviewers his best promoters. Norman Thomas, the Socialist Party presidential candidate that year, called the rejection of pacifist idealism "defeatism."[71] A reviewer for the *Christian Century* condemned it as "cynicism" and "unrelieved pessimism."[72] Charles Macfarland, longtime leader of the Federal Council of Churches, cast Niebuhr into the Barthian camp for abandoning liberalism's two chief tenets, its benevolent view of human nature and its faith in education as the panacea for injustice.[73] Niebuhr dared to replace love with justice as the attainable goal of Christian action.

Even his immediate peers thought he went too far. Francis Miller circulated two lengthy critiques accusing Niebuhr of devaluing Christianity as a unique agency in transforming society and, more serious, lacking an ecclesiology, a theology of the church.[74] Niebuhr replied that Miller was right about the latter but argued that the book was not written for the church; it was for liberals in and out of organized religion. Niebuhr's younger brother, H. Richard, by then a professor at Yale Divinity School, assessed the book on its own terms as another voice in the open discussion of public morals Lippmann had provoked. "I continue to regard your book with Lippmann's *Preface* as the two most important religious books since the war," he wrote him. "But neither of them are finality. They are the death of the old and the harbingers of a new birth."[75] The Dutch theologian W. A. Visser 't Hooft, general secretary of the World's Student Christian Federation, a man of the same generation as Niebuhr, pointed out that *Moral Man* excelled in analyzing liberalism but had little to offer by way of prescription.[76] Yet the book's importance was in its timeliness, and for that Visser 't Hooft predicted it would have enduring significance.

Lippmann's *Preface to Morals* provoked Henry P. Van Dusen to write his own book, *The Plain Man Seeks for God*, against the type of liberalism he saw in Lippmann and the British philosopher-publicist Julian Huxley. He called it "Humanism," a view that advocated the ethics of Christianity but rejected the theological foundation.[77] Humanism's flaw was its contradictory ideas about nature and man: a pessimism about the cosmos, bordering on fatalism, yet a glorification of human nature. Such a philosophy begged criticism, Van Dusen thought, because the contemporary world was bringing a hasty demise to this "theological expression of the jazz age." A more profound understanding of life was needed.

But liberal Protestantism had no answers, having sacrificed evangelical fervor and personal experience in its effort to harmonize Christianity with science. By trying to appeal to thoughtful people through the use of scientific-sounding ideas, the liberals had become entangled in their nonreligious basis and succeeded in making Christianity "a pallid reflection of secular philosophy." On the personal level, liberalism's emphasis on the role of reason in religious life to the neglect of spiritual experience made God "the last term in an arduous and technical intellectual inquiry instead of the first fact of a vital religious experience."

Like Niebuhr, Van Dusen chafed at the ethical relativism the liberals had engendered. Aiming to overthrow the arguments of social evolution theorists, he analyzed how values really get exercised and asserted that both the existence of transcendent standards and their origin in a transcendent God are demonstrable:

[M]an's awareness of values, in its every aspect, points beyond itself to a supernatural objective reality as its source and the guarantor of its fulfill-ment. . . . On no account can the rise . . . of man's sense of the good, the lovely, the true and the holy be explained as due to "natural selection" or self-germination or some other purely naturalistic instrumentality. It can only have been brought to birth . . . through the touch and call of an in-finite Source of perfect value, God.

Echoing Barth on God's transcendence, he wrote: "We should not forget that [God] is very much more than personal and, in certain respects, very unlike a person. . . . He who is 'closer than breathing, nearer than hands and feet,' is also the Wholly Other." Van Dusen, too, appealed to dialec-tics, describing how God is known as personal and transcendent. He said that in "the fullest religious experience, one's thought moves constantly between these two poles by a process of alternation." The liberals' failure to perceive this led to their exaltation of reason, which virtually precluded the crucial acknowledgment of God's sovereignty, which in turn led to denying the profundity of sin. Sin, he thought, was the fundamental cause of social conflict: "The truth is there has been sin in our society—whole-sale, unabashed, ruthless sin. The sin of gluttony for money and for power . . . the sin of sharp and heartless business practice. . . . The agony of our generation is not the failure of ignorance; it is due to flaws in human character more blameworthy by far." Van Dusen saw thoughtful people substituting reasoned morality for God's principles, to their own and society's detriment. With Lippmann in mind, he concluded it was neces-sary to choose between the arguably noble but ultimately despairing resig-nation based on a metaphysics of indifferent ultimate reality, and a rea-soned religious faith, rooted in experience and based on belief in a God who is good.

Probably because, unlike Niebuhr's *Moral Man*, Van Dusen's *Plain Man* was apologetic rather than polemical the Protestant establishment's jour-nals reviewed it favorably. An advertisement in the *Federal Council Bul-letin* recommended it as "a searching diagnosis of the weakness of 'liberal' religions," a "simple and cogent presentation" of historic Christianity.[78] The Religious Book Club made it the book of the month for October 1933, which guaranteed it as much of an initial readership as Niebuhr's *Moral Man*.[79]

But again the most discerning assessments of *The Plain Man* came from Van Dusen's peers. Visser 't Hooft found inconsistency in the role of rea-son: Van Dusen seemed to reject the liberals' inductive approach to God in the first part of the book but later did not discount reason in making sense of religious experience. And despite its title, Visser 't Hooft remarked, half in jest, the book addressed an unusually highbrowed "plain man."[80] Francis Miller criticized it for what was left out: any treatment of the concepts of historical time, eternity, and the community of faith. Yet he thought the book important because it persuasively argued for a reorientation of thought about Christianity, exposing liberalism's degeneration into incipient moral relativism. He endorsed Van Dusen's call for renewed emphasis on God's transcendence as a source of hope for the challenges of modern life.[81]

Van Dusen and Niebuhr had shown up the deficiencies of liberalism, but their simple assertion of the reality of power and the way to religious insight was not about to remedy the malaise of mainline Protestantism overnight. It would be easier to exercise leadership—intellectual and organizational—operating from the high perches of academia and the Federal Council, exploiting their own experience in the international student movement and the personal ties they had developed there with the men now at the head of the ecumenical movement. It was a moment of high opportunity: the fate of the international ecumenical organizations hung in the balance. Life and Work, Faith and Order, and the IMC reorganized in hope of surviving the strains of the worldwide depression and the need to adapt their mission both to theological change and to the increased interdependence of nations. From the margin the American theologians would move to the center, where they could set the agenda for these international organizations and, through indirect channels, lay the groundwork for making international cooperation and antiwar projects a characteristic of mainline Protestantism in the years ahead. They would do this by bringing interdenominational associations into the Protestant alignment, in lieu of the cast-off extradenominational ones. Intellectually, meanwhile, they would offer a theology—Christian realism—to fill the void between liberalism and fundamentalism.

FOUR

European Upheaval, Theological Ferment
1933–1937

ADOLF HITLER'S THIRD REICH created a new political context for the American Protestant theologians. It also revived the struggling ecumenical movement by presenting the need for a new theology within which the Nazi rise in a country as civilized as Germany could be comprehended. The young American thinkers who provided the requisite insight were to become central figures in the ecumenical movement. Their very involvement in the movement gave them the perspective from which to discern the theological dimension of a problem that had never been the province of either Protestant or Orthodox churches—international politics—in effect, widening the public stage along with the substantive scope of their work. With the Christian internationalist vision from their student days and their criticism of liberal theology, these theologians banded together in articulating the theology that would speak to the new situation in Central Europe and its threat to Christians everywhere.

Nazi Seizure of Power

Attending an ecumenical study conference near Bonn in March 1933, William Adams Brown witnessed the swift opening of the Nazi New Order, the promulgation of laws disabling Jews and ending free speech. Henceforth churchmen preached at the risk of imprisonment if they criticized the regime. Brown wrote his brother it was a "Fascist Revolution modeled after the Italian plan" with "many of the disagreeable incidents" in

Italy "reproducing themselves in Germany—house to house visitation, people taken from their beds at night and beaten." Even more serious, he thought, were the "surprising number of good simple people who are enthusiastic Hitlerites."[1]

In April, Samuel McCrea Cavert, in Berlin on a fact-finding mission for the Federal Council of Churches, witnessed the Nazi takeover of the established Evangelical Church.[2] The same month there was a nationwide conference of "German Christians" (*Deutsche Christen*) whose neopagan tribalistic Nazi-Christian syncretism held that the Old Testament was superseded by the New and that Jesus was not Jewish but Aryan. An appearance by Hitler's crony, Hermann Göring, lent Nazi authority to the occasion. Speakers demanded that non-Aryans be barred from pulpits and refused marriage before Evangelical altars. There was talk of a "Reich" Church and racial conformity within it, and by the end of April the "German Christians" set a plan in motion to establish such a church. A few theologians welcomed this movement, thinking it might enhance the influence of the church in the New Order. All of this made a profound impression on Cavert. After returning to New York, he used the Federal Council's connections in Europe to keep abreast of the situation while he saw to it that the *Federal Council Bulletin* carried articles on Nazi oppression and the idiosyncratic theology of the Reich Church.

Then Dietrich Bonhoeffer and Karl Barth, theologians the Americans knew, came out in opposition to the Nazi regime. Their act was in protest to a synod of the Evangelical Church on 5 and 6 September. Many of the delegates wore outfits resembling the brownshirt uniform of the Nazi Party's paramilitary SA, prompting someone to call it "the Brown Synod." It voted to prohibit employment of non-Aryans and those married to non-Aryans.[3] A dissenting minority led by Bonhoeffer and Martin Niemöller held that with this step the synod had abandoned Christianity and was de facto schismatic, so they formed a Pastors' Emergency League to preserve the true church. Bonhoeffer told his fellow dissenters he planned to generate support by cultivating contacts in academic circles and the ecumenical movement. In May 1934 the Pastors' Emergency League issued the Barmen Declaration—a denunciation of the "German Christians" and the trend in Evangelical Church politics. Written principally by Barth, it called upon the Evangelical Church to return to the essential truths of Christianity. After waiting due time for a reply, the dissidents formed the Confessing Church, viewing themselves not as sectarians breaking with the Evangelical Church but as the faithful remnant defending the faith.[4] This invited more repression. On 7 July the regime muzzled church publications with the Church Law for the Evangelical Press. On July 9 a decree prohibited church disputes in the press or public assembly. A month later the National Synod of the Evangelical Church declared that pastors must swear a "service oath" to the state and to Hitler as its leader.[5]

Writing from Bonn in March 1933, William Adams Brown discerned that the Nazification of the German church would have a defining effect on the Christian unity movement, particularly Life and Work, though for the moment the ecumenical study conference gave him hope that Christians could still work together in mission and theological inquiry and for world peace.[6] He was soon disappointed.

Discord marked the annual executive committee meeting at Novi Sad, Yugoslavia, that September.[7] The head of the German delegation was Theodore Heckel, the Evangelical Church official responsible for German churches abroad. His report made no mention of the resolutions of the Brown Synod or the disabilities imposed on Christians of Jewish origin.[8] The Frenchman Wilfred Monod confronted him about these omissions, and a row followed. Meanwhile, Bonhoeffer, though not a committee member, pressed the case of the Pastors' Emergency League through proxies, particularly through his close friend, Life and Work chairman Bishop G. K. A. Bell. After heated debate the executive committee passed resolutions expressing "grave anxieties" about the laws aimed at people of Jewish origin and the muzzling of discussion. Bell was instructed to convey these grievances in writing to the German government.

The protest had limited effect. The German Foreign Ministry promptly forbade mention of the Aryan clause at the upcoming Evangelical Church national assembly, which meant there would be no discussion of repealing it.[9] Nazi subversion of the church went on. The party ideologists' popular "blood and soil" propaganda touted the racial superiority of the Aryan *Volk* as ordained by God.

The Novi Sad episode generated a sense of urgency among the younger-generation Protestant leaders around the world for a reexamination of church-state relations.[10] The Europeans put the matter in theological terms. Typical was the reaction of W. A. Visser 't Hooft, general secretary of the World's Student Christian Federation, who argued that the problem was as much ecclesiological as political, the essential issue being whether or not the church regarded itself as a supranational body entirely dependent on God and therefore independent of the state.[11]

The Life and Work governing council planned a meeting on the problem for August 1934. As it approached, the ecclesiological problem came to the fore in a diplomatic dilemma that arose over inviting Bonhoeffer's Confessing Church and hence recognizing it as a legitimate communion. It considered itself the true German Evangelical Church and not a second church alongside the Reich Church. But when Bonhoeffer requested an invitation as Germany's representative he was told the Confessing Church must first formally separate from the Reich Church.[12] Bonhoeffer appealed, and Bishop Bell, on his authority as Life and Work chairman, invited him and other Confessing Church members *as individuals* who could help clarify the situation in the emergency, not as Germany's delegation.

The meeting, held at Fanø in Denmark, dealt squarely with the Nazi policies. A drafting committee was formed to write a critique of them. Its members were the strongest supporters of the Confessing Church, among them Marc Boegner of France, American secretary Henry Smith Leiper, and Bishop Bell. Still, lively argument erupted over how offensive the text should be toward the German government. Five days later, when the conference adjourned, it presented a resolution condemning the regime of force being exercised against the German church, the racial disabilities, the service oath, and the restriction of public expression. As for the Confessing Church, the council assured "its brethren in the Confessional Synod" of "its prayers and heartfelt sympathy in their witness to the principles of the gospel, and of its resolve to maintain close fellowship with them."[13] The conferees exercised their prerogative to co-opt new members for special purposes, electing Bonhoeffer and Karl Koch, executive leader of the Confessing Synod.

The meeting also laid plans for a Life and Work world conference in 1937. Its members agreed on the theme—"Church, Community, and State"—aimed to deal with the new political and religious situation. They instructed the research department to dedicate itself exclusively to the theological preparation for it, and enlarged its advisory commission to accommodate the desire of the young leaders to be involved: Henry P. Van Dusen, W. A. Visser 't Hooft, and Leonard Hodgson, secretary of Faith and Order. To direct the study, they chose J. H. Oldham, secretary of the International Missionary Council, a prominent figure from the older generation (in his late fifties) who shared the younger men's "crisis" outlook.[14] Sensing the seriousness of the task, Oldham resigned from the IMC to devote himself to it.[15]

Along with theologians he enlisted laymen experienced in public affairs—among them John Foster Dulles and Charles P. Taft, son of the former president—to widen the range of concerns the conference would address. The theologians, Van Dusen, John Bennett, and Reinhold Niebuhr, among others, were to define the study topics and pick people to write papers on them.[16] The "terms of reference" they issued stimulated a vigorous discussion among Christian leaders around the world, creating an international, intellectual laboratory. Nearly 250 essays were received and sent out for peer review and refinement. (One member of Oldham's staff in Geneva later recalled suffering "intellectual indigestion" from having read them all.) The reports that emerged from this intensive exchange became a prime source on social ethics for Protestant writers over the next twenty-five years.[17]

The Theological Discussion Group

The German situation presented the younger American theologians a new focus for their inquiry and analysis, pushing them to formulate a positive, alternative theology. The liberal theology they had been criticizing for five years now allowed such German theologians as Gerhard Kittel, Paul Althaus, and Emanuel Hirsch to side publicly with Hitler because his regime promised to restore the national prestige and prosperity Germany had enjoyed under the kaiser.[18] Though not all of the American theologians made the same assessment of liberalism's responsibility for this, they now finally broke with liberalism over it. The heterodox theology that sanctioned the Third Reich and its expansionist ideology required correction by an orthodox theology equally as public and persuasive.

John Bennett, now professor at Auburn Seminary in New York, called for the countervailing theology in an essay in the November 1933 *Christian Century*, "After Liberalism—What?"[19] The very title proclaimed a new stage in American thought. Though the reign of liberalism had ended, its replacement had yet to be found and enthroned. "Whatever the new theology may be . . . ," Bennett wrote, "it will not be any of the other systems of theology which now have names." He thought several elements in liberalism should be retained. First, the method of inquiry, particularly the historical-critical method of biblical study, which had removed impediments to faith set up by biblical literalism. This allowed one to dwell on the essentials of Christianity and to criticize the doctrine of double predestination on moral grounds. Second, the liberal epistemology, which credited individual insight with a degree of competence to know God— though Bennett added that it did not occur in a vacuum but developed in relation to Scripture, the church, and others' convictions. Third, a Christology which insisted that the historical Jesus linked human existence and divine reality. And fourth, emphasis on the continuity between human reason and divine revelation, the antithesis of the atheists' perennial cynical charge that God is capricious, therefore untrustworthy, and by definition no God at all.

Bennett then set down four principles for an alternative theology. First, he argued, human nature is profoundly sinful. Second, he emphasized God's transcendent nature. Third—a borrowing from Marxism—he stressed the expectation that unjust socioeconomic systems would destroy themselves by failing to resolve internal contradictions. And fourth, he expressed the conviction that while nationalism was on the rise world-wide, Christianity is a historic phenomenon capable of uniting disparate peoples because it transcends national identities and loyalties. It was up to theologians to disclose its depth and sweep. Though Bennett's atten-tion to the traditional doctrines of sin and God's sovereignty sounded like "crisis" theology, his retention of and emphasis on the social thrust of Christianity and a high degree of confidence in the mind made it distinct. Bennett had reason to believe there was a ready audience for this new theology. Diminished confidence in science made way for Christianity to fill the need for a universal key. Moreover, the worldwide depression had forced the churches to think in terms of social morality.

Following the publication of "After Liberalism—What?" Bennett re-ceived congratulatory messages from his peers. Gregory Vlastos, a young Canadian philosopher, wrote him: "Your article in the *Christian Century* was grand. . . . I agree pretty much with the way [you] put the whole matter."[20] Walter M. Horton, a young professor of theology at Oberlin College, thanked Bennett for providing the outline for a lecture series that he, Horton, was to deliver at Andover-Newton Seminary.[21] Bennett's essay formulated what was on the collective mind of the younger-generation theologians, and did so appealingly, showing them they did not have to accept the whole cloth of European "crisis theology" but could fashion an appropriate one of their own.

Henry P. Van Dusen organized a retreat for them to mine this prom-ising vein together. After exploring the idea with several others, he ob-tained a travel grant from the Hazen Foundation and formed a commit-tee of six to select the participants who would bring a broad range of views to discuss Christianity and the complexities of the world situation. But Van Dusen rejected the list his "recruiters" drew up, complaining it rep-resented such diverse attitudes that the meetings would produce nothing but vague generalities.[22] He then solicited recommendations from three others who had expressed interest—Cavert, Bennett, and Douglas Steere—and their suggestions solved the problem.[23]

Between the end of October and mid-November 1933 the invitations were sent, stating that the purpose of the group was to pursue "a more collective attack upon the central issues of Christian thought" in a "more thorough, systematic and consecutive conference . . . than is ordinarily possible." The organizers, under Van Dusen's direction, planned to bring together a select group twice each academic year for a weekend retreat. They hoped the participants would grow together spiritually as well as intellectually from the experience and become a new leadership network with a shared theology. Van Dusen and his friends were deliberately aiming to set the terms of reference for a new theology that would move American Protestantism to hold a more global perspective. About two dozen accepted, a number that remained fairly constant over the years. Besides Van Dusen himself were Miller, Cavert, Bennett, Georgia Harkness, the Niebuhr brothers, Wilhelm Pauck, Edwin Aubrey, Walter M. Horton, Robert L. Calhoun, and church historian Roland Bainton.

The group promptly coalesced, conscious of having two defining characteristics: a generational identity ("the younger element in Christian thought" either "in age or in outlook"); and a common ecumenical vision (that in concert they would discover a "body of common convictions" greater than any of them currently recognized or had been able to articulate alone). Though they never would unite in a "school," they felt a sharp sense of collective difference from other theologians and church leaders, considering themselves "realists" as opposed to "liberals," "modernists," and "fundamentalists."[24] Like their contemporaries among the literati who regarded themselves as a "literary generation," this group banded together as a "theological generation."[25]

The inaugural retreat took place at the Princeton Inn in Princeton, New Jersey, on 2–4 February 1934, and set the pattern.[26] To foster cohesion, the participants lodged under one roof and ate all their meals together. To put them all on the same track for the first meeting, Van Dusen had sent out a reading list covering the current state of the search for a new theology. They read Paul Tillich's *Religious Situation*, D. C. Mackintosh's *Religious Realism*, and John Bennett's "After Liberalism— What?"[27] The theme for this first retreat was "What Is Essential and Distinctive in the Christian Gospel for Today?" Led by Van Dusen, the proceedings followed the discussion group model they all knew from the SVM conferences in their student days. But here their discussion was more truly democratic, and, among intellectual peers, focused and intense. Four members had prepared papers on preassigned topics that were circulated a month in advance.[28] Four others brought prepared responses to be read at the respective sessions, and a wide-ranging discussion followed each one for up to two hours. To round out the retreat, one participant was charged to lead devotions, another to be the rapporteur for the Sunday morning wrap-up session.

Van Dusen realized he had found the right formula, and the group agreed to continue. A second meeting was held at Drew University in Morristown, New Jersey, on 27–29 April. Initially Van Dusen had called the project the Younger Christian Thinkers, but after the Princeton and Drew retreats he started referring to it as the Theological Discussion Group, which seemed more appropriate since the participants were now in their forties and had established careers. From October 1934 to 1943 the retreats were held at the Yale Divinity School, arranged by H. Richard Niebuhr, who was a professor there.[29] The men stayed on campus, the women took lodgings outside. The sessions were in the faculty lounge, in the refectory building. In 1943 the group started meeting at the College of Preachers at the National Cathedral in Washington, continuing there until disbanding in 1965, owing to deaths and bad health.[30] New members were added when someone who was considered a peer came to the eastern United States or a member resigned.[31] In April 1934 the group welcomed Paul Tillich, exiled from Germany.

They stepped into the leadership of the ecumenical movement as a group in the winter of 1934–1935 when Van Dusen began helping J. H. Oldham run the study program for the Life and Work world conference. The theme—church, community, and state—represented their collective commitment to deliver a new theology. Oldham worked closely with both Van Dusen and Cavert, general secretary of the Federal Council of Churches. All three held mutually high opinions of each other. Van Dusen confided to Cavert: "We seem to be the only two in whom Oldham has reasonably full confidence."[32] Among the duties Van Dusen had was to serve Oldham as his appointments secretary, arranging interviews for him with influential churchmen when he would be in the United States.

The consensus of the three was to divide the responsibilities for the conference, putting the work with church agencies and laity under Henry Smith Leiper, Federal Council secretary for Life and Work, while Van Dusen was to lead the theological study that would be the source of principles for Leiper's talking points.[33] Van Dusen engaged the Theological Discussion Group to provide the substance. In December 1934 he issued the members an invitation to participate "both as a group and as individuals." The organizers, he explained, wanted to prepare the conference by making "a thorough examination of the three great theological doctrines which most vitally underlie the conference themes"—Christian anthropology, creation and redemption, and the Kingdom of God and history.[34] The procedure was to be the same as at the Princeton retreat:

It is proposed that on each of the three themes . . . papers be prepared by
some one person especially qualified . . . ; that these be submitted for thorough examination and rejoinder to men like ourselves in various countries; and that, as a result of the process, a volume on each topic be made
available for the 1937 conference.[35]

The group met at the Yale Divinity School in early February 1935 and
took the first step in formulating the new theology by turning their
thoughts to Christian anthropology.[36] Robert L. Calhoun, professor at Yale
Divinity School, opened with an overview from New Testament times to
trends in modern Catholic and Protestant thought as a way of exposing
the Achilles' heel in contemporary liberal theology. At the end of his
survey he faulted the "larger Protestant communions" for their "dilution"
of the doctrine of original sin: "Liberal Protestantism has swung far, once
more, toward the Pelagian confidence that nature and grace are one." As
if to acknowledge assent, he gave the last word to "dialectical theology"
and other "counter-reactions" that distinguished more sharply between
human nature and divine grace.

H. Richard Niebuhr, in "Man the Sinner," argued against the liberal
predilection for a moral theory of atonement. He maintained that sin is
not primarily a moral matter but a theological one having to do with
people's disloyalty to God. With sin so pervasive, people cannot extract
themselves from the problems created by their disloyalty; only God can
initiate the reconciliation on which the solutions depend. In practice this
meant society's restraint of sin is always the restraint of sinners by other
sinners and must be part of an overriding commitment by all involved to
be reconciled to God. Urging that sociopolitical action be subordinated
to the divine intention of reconciliation, he suggested theology was the
appropriate starting point for social analysis and, by implication, the appropriate one for the upcoming world conference that would be addressing social and political distress.

Wilhelm Pauck, a German émigré, put the case in positive terms, saying in Barthian fashion that redemption occurs in the crisis of repentance
when an individual's intentions undergo transformation from love of self
to love of God; such a change has a dynamic, dialectical character because of human finitude. Like Calhoun and Niebuhr, Pauck underscored
the importance of retrieving an acute awareness of humankind's fallen
nature. Taken together the papers pointed toward a theology akin to
European neo-orthodoxy yet with a distinctly American emphasis on the
ability of reason to apprehend divine revelation and the Christian imperative to attend to the social aspects of life.

Oldham timed a six-week speaking tour of North America to coincide with the next New Haven retreat in November of that year.[37] But first he attended a Life and Work Executive Committee session at Chamby, Switzerland, which scheduled the world conference for 13–25 July 1937 at Oxford. Everyone was talking about the increasing menace in Germany. Reaching North America, Oldham repeated what he had heard, remarking that the work of the Theological Discussion Group for the conference took on significance in light of the struggle between the heretical "German Christians" and orthodoxy.[38]

Over the 1–3 November weekend Oldham attended the Theological Discussion Group retreat. The theme was religious epistemology, "our knowledge of God."[39] The group brought this abstract subject to bear on the contemporary theological and political situations they believed had to do with the way people come to know God. Walter Horton opened by attacking the liberals' inattention to the supernatural. Because liberalism had neglected the supernatural aspect of revelation and because people inclined toward evil, the contemporary situation required a renewed emphasis on the role of revelation in human existence—not that it entirely substituted for reason. Staking out a middle ground between the liberals' overestimation of human reason and a reactionary "superstitious" embrace of revelation, he said that the present day demanded such a balance: "*It should be a primary concern of contemporary theology to reassert the full Christian idea of revelation in the clearest possible terms and reestablish its supremacy in Christian teaching, while at the same time making it plain that faith in revelation does not violate that reverence for all truth which liberal Protestantism . . . has made permanently a part of the Christian conscience*" (emphasis in original). He was trying to salvage some merit from the tradition that was being abandoned, combining liberalism with the strengths of traditional Protestantism.

The church historian Roland Bainton examined the state of world affairs in light of changing ideas about the relation between community and authority, especially regarding biblical interpretation. He made the case for reasserting the notion that the church is a distinct body with distinct claims, as opposed to the liberal view that saw the church as an amorphous mass of people called Christians. He began by describing how in earlier times religious authority was based on revelation, while the success of the modern substitutes, Nazism in Germany and fundamentalism in America, had roots in people's need for social authority in chaotic times. Surveying the historical differences between Protestantism and Catholicism, he pointed out that their different concepts of the church created

their different views of authority. Bainton noted that although early Protestants bowed to the authority of the Bible, they did not reject the context of community for interpreting revelation. The need in the present
day was to reaffirm the role of the social, ecclesial factor in discerning
revelational authority and to see it in interplay with individual insight,
each acting as a check on the other.

In the two remaining papers, John Moore probed for a relation between
the scientific method and the quest for religious knowledge, while Douglas Steere took the opposite side of the problem, examining the role of
mystical experience in religious knowledge and morality. The four papers
and the discussion they stimulated cautiously explored the relation between reason and revelation in a way that laid foundations for their larger
project. The new theology was beginning to take shape as a critical synthesis of liberal intellectual methods, a revival of classical Protestant doctrines, and attention to the political and ecclesial contexts in which the
gospel is received.

Later that year, three members of the Theological Discussion Group—
H. Richard Niebuhr, Francis Miller, and Wilhelm Pauck—brought out a
collection of essays, *The Church Against the World*, in which they criticized the pillars of liberal Protestantism and redefined the church and its
mission with the worldwide upheaval foremost in mind.[40] The book grew
out of conversations they had at the retreats, and it presented to a wider
audience the ideas they had been sharing.[41] As the title suggested, no
longer did the church *and* the world suffice; a sharper distinction needed
to be made for the sake of both the church and the world. In the introduction H. Richard Niebuhr wrote that their common task was to define
and defend the church's stance *against* the world. They would present an
"insider's" view that saw the church threatened by the lures of worldli-
ness from outside and compromise from within.[42] The problem was not
to identify the accommodations the church should make to secure its place
in society but to prescribe the adjustments people should make for the
sake of their souls and the world.

Pauck's essay, "The Crisis of Religion," analyzed the challenge in light
of larger social problems.[43] Because people were drifting helplessly in a
worldwide sea of meaninglessness and depression, they yearned for security and expressed it in extremist politics, drastic economic experiments,
and dramatic cultural ideologies. Of the three general philosophical solutions that promised to relieve people of this anxiety—humanism, modernism, and Barthianism—humanism gave no meaning to life and indeed
implicitly denied that people need meaning. Modernism assigned primacy
to social science and abandoned religious moorings in "feverish activism,"

having assumed the eighteenth- and nineteenth-century Enlightenment view of human nature as sufficiently independent of God. Barthianism, while theoretically the most promising solution, was of questionable usefulness because it called the church to return to itself—a dubious task apart from divine intervention—and it was too abstruse for the average person anyway. Pauck reminded the reader that he did not aim to provide answers but to present a clearer understanding of the contemporary crisis. He thought secularism had created the crisis, and expected the remedy for it would cause a crisis in secularism itself. By pointing to the promise of Barthianism at the same time that he criticized Christianity's drift into secularism, he called his readers to join him in practicing what he preached, to analyze contemporary sociopolitical problems in theological terms, and to reconceptualize the church so that it would be the solution it should be. The foundation for social action in the modern world was theological critique, not intellectual or cultural accommodation.

Francis Miller's essay, "American Protestantism and the Christian Faith," took as its point of departure the view that the religious crisis stemmed from the confusion liberal theology had created over the content of faith and its forms, essentially a concern about the relation between Christianity and culture.[44] Confusion of these made it easy for nationalism to subvert faith, as the German Christians did. Miller argued that Protestantism found itself in a world that had no universal frame of reference. But Christianity did, so the church's task was to instill belief in "Christendom" as the ultimate *and* universal frame of reference that would stop the erosion of faith and civil society. Drawing attention to the American scene as a case in point, Miller concluded that Christian cultural criticism would have a vital role to play in maintaining the welfare of the church and American society: "The Protestant churches will continue to merit confidence and support only if they choose the frame of reference supplied by the reality of Christendom. And paradoxical though it may seem, it will be only as they are faithful to that frame of reference that any culture worthy of the name will survive in America." According to Miller, Christianity had a very public role to play in modern life, at home and abroad: it had to stand against contemporary culture and offer its own culture, which was not only of human making.

The last essay in the book was Niebuhr's "Toward the Independence of the Church." Advancing Miller's point, he maintained that the church must free itself as well as contemporary civilization from perverted forms of worship and love—idolatry and lust.[45] The church, like the rest of society, lay in unquestioning bondage to capitalism, nationalism, and humanism because it believed in the power of wealth, the nation, and human self-sufficiency. Its task now was to move toward independence from society, acknowledging dependence on God.

The main danger in doing so, he wrote, would be the temptation to resolve the uncomfortable (but creative) contradiction of "living in the world" while "not being of it," as liberal Christianity had already tried to do. The way to maintain this creative tension was by renewing belief in the definitive nature of God's revelation in Christ:

> When this memory of the Christ, the crucified, comes fully alive it will not come as a traditional formula or symbol, reminding men only of the past, but as the recollection of a most decisive fact in the situation of men. The church's remembrance of Jesus Christ will come in contemporary terms, so that it will be able to say: "That which was from the beginning, that which we have heard, that which we have seen with our eyes, that which we have beheld and which our hands have handled concerning the Word of life—that we declare to you."

Niebuhr, like Miller and others in the Theological Discussion Group, was pushing to a new extreme the ecclesiological dimension of the contemporary crisis. Here he combined Christocentricity with an unsettling charge for the churches to recall Christians to their fundamental distinctness. Only by being genuinely Christ-centered could the church be true to itself and fulfill its mission of offering hope to the world. Repentance and faith, which set individuals and groups apart from the dominant culture, were the preconditions for this as well as for the subsequent achievement of the church's independence.

Collectively, the authors of *The Church Against the World* challenged Christians to view modern culture critically through the lens of a "realistic" theology. They assumed people's propensity to sin, individually and corporately. They counterposed faith in a transcendent God to the humanist outlook that relied on psychological, sociological, and economic analyses to gauge human welfare. They gave a vision of the church as being both divine and human, not just a voluntary association of ethical people. They did not make facile dichotomous distinctions between the righteous church and the unrighteous world but tried to depict the church's mission as a complex, often ambiguous matter. Samuel McCrea Cavert, addressing the denominations in his endorsement of the book as general secretary of the Federal Council of Churches, called it a "manifesto" of the new currents in theology, and warned that those who ignored it did so at their intellectual and spiritual peril.[46] Their call for an ecclesiology and traditional doctrine undiluted by cultural sympathies, their starting point for bringing religious conviction to bear on social and international conflict, gave a direction to proceedings of the Theological Discussion Group and, in turn, the Life and Work movement.

The Theological Discussion Group met again in February 1936, continuing preparation of the ground for the Oxford conference by probing the topic "a Christian philosophy of history."[47] They examined "progress," liberalism's axiom, a subject they thought neither liberal theology nor Barthianism had examined adequately. Though the group did not draw up a consensus statement of a Christian philosophy of history, it had begun to characterize it by reference to the competing views of liberalism and traditional Protestantism, tentatively positing a realist alternative, something between the overemphases on either God's immanence or transcendence. The theologians did not articulate this notion subsequently into a universal scheme of history; rather, it served to order their thinking on why Christians should be attentive to the terms of reference theologians and politicians used in addressing international developments.

At the end of October 1936 Oldham returned to North America to boost interest in the now-imminent Life and Work world conference. He met with several members of the Theological Discussion Group and select churchmen. Again he arranged the trip to coincide with a Theological Discussion Group retreat. Over the past year he had been thinking that the most important subject for the sake of the world and the ecumenical movement was ecclesiology. He wrote to Van Dusen: "[P]erhaps the fundamental question of all is `What is [the] Church'?"[48] Now, one of his reasons for coming to the States was to clarify his thoughts about it for his conference paper, "The Functions of the Church."[49]

The theme of the retreat over the first weekend in November was the church, precisely what Oldham wanted to address.[50] Pauck opened with a historical overview of the church's secularization as a way into critiquing the prevalent view that lacked a notion of transcendence. He emphasized that the Enlightenment had generated new understandings of the church as a corporate entity, particularly as John Locke's social contract theory exerted increasing influence, making the principle of church independence from the state the most widely accepted. This led to a theology of the church in which God's revelation in Jesus Christ was no longer the foundation of the institution but "an impulse" that endowed individuals with the principles of divine love of which Jesus was the exemplar. Though Pauck did not say so explicitly, this implied the liberal notion of the church as an association of morally like-minded people. This, in turn, undermined belief in the church's transcendent origin and Christians' sense of there being an overarching unity. "The idea of the unity of the church," he said, "in so far as it depends upon a clear revelation of the divine will, disappeared more and more." The contemporary result of this took two forms: emphasis on "a Christian philosophy of life," and on the church as an essentially educational, cultural enterprise. Pauck concluded by asking rhetorically whether such a church could withstand totalitarian regimes. For that a new ecclesiology was needed, one which reasserted the divine origin of the church and its mission to challenge contemporary culture.

Miller spoke on "The Church as World Community," developing his ideas from *The Church Against the World* by adding positive steps for the church to take in making meaning of the present time and giving cohesion to society. He said it was first necessary to reaffirm Paul's idea of the Body of Christ as the true description of corporate life; second, to raise people's consciousness of sharing in a worldwide fellowship; third, to train ministers to be conscious of their mission to build the Body of Christ; and fourth, to encourage participation in the increasingly church-oriented Christian unity movement. Proclaiming that the church was the genuine social answer, Miller waxed eloquent:

> The directors of the destructive forces are clever enough to know that since God has made man for *Community*, the only way they can destroy Community is to do it in the name of Community. Hence, they have rallied mankind's loyalty to a series of perverted and false communities. . . . They have said that Community is blood or Community is class or Community is state. So great is man's hunger for true Community that he has accepted the plausible substitutes. . . . We answer the mobilization of false community with a mobilization of true Community. . . . The Christian answer can only be given in terms of the Church.

Arguing that the church cannot be rebuilt by members who do not have a proper understanding of it, Miller, like Pauck, called for a new ecclesiology that acknowledged the church's dual divine and historical nature as well as its redemptive mission. If believers would accept this understanding, a worldwide community transcending "blood, class, and nation" would be created and the church could exercise its salvific yet critical vocation in the international arena. Looking for the church to become "the soul of the political and economic world society," Miller thought it would provide "human society as a whole with its '*raison d'etre*'" and supply "the principle of cohesion without which inter-national cooperation is impossible." Here was the first unambiguous extension of the group's theology into the largest public sphere: a new ecclesiology could lay the foundation for a new international politics.

By emphasizing the transcendence and essential unity of the church, these theologians sounded more Catholic than Protestant. The only element missing was a discussion of authority. The historian Bainton had raised the matter at the previous retreat, but the rest sidestepped such a thorny problem by resorting to "revelation in Christ," which they assumed to be a clearly apprehensible locus of authority for determining right belief. Still, they combined Christocentricity with thought about the church to arrive at a theology comprehending the world's peril. Oldham came away from the retreat stimulated to write his paper for Oxford.

Two months later, in January 1937, the Theological Discussion Group made its next retreat a rehearsal for the Life and Work conference, then only five months away. The theme was on relations between the church and the different political forms of the state—the major issue to be addressed by the world conference.[51] Cavert opened the session with a review of church-state relations in modern America, supposedly the ideal. He drew the conclusion that until the church developed an adequate self-concept, it would have no ground to stand on in criticizing the state when it went out of bounds. The result would be what had happened in Germany. "If we allow our people to go on believing that the Church has no mission to give ethical guidance to the State," Cavert said, "we are opening the door wide to such an extreme assertion of the absoluteness of the State as is presented today in Nazi Germany." At bottom it was the failure to instill in Christians the right conceptions of both state and church. More urgent now that the superstate was a reality, Cavert thought,

> is our need for a true view of the Church. One of the reasons why the State has become a creature of arrogant pretensions . . . is because the Church has failed to gain an adequate conception of its essential nature as a world community. . . . So long as the Church exists only in sectarian fragments, so long as it breathes the air of nationalism . . . so long will it lack the spiritual authority that will enable it to stand against an arbitrary nationalist State.

Thus he underscored the political as well as the theological need for an ecclesiology freed from sectarian and nationalist moorings, one giving a Christian internationalist perspective instead. It held promise for making the churches a real force in international affairs.

Tillich, the group's specialist on communism, now proposed what the church's response to that international competitor should be. To be more effective at countering its appeal, the churches had to understand the philosophical and historical bases of the communist ideology, rather than continue the hopelessly mistaken attempts to squelch the idea. By knowing the communist ideology, the church could make an accurate critique of its competing historicist view of the world. The churches were capable of this "especially" because they could "interpret Communism from the ultimate point of view." Tillich recommended seeing communism as a secularized form of the "prophetic" strain of social justice–seeking Christianity. The church should treat communism as another form of modern mass movement that attracted adherents at a time of social disintegration. In practical terms he said the churches should strike a balance between fighting the evils that made communism popular and the evils communism itself propagated. This meant the church had to expose communism as a modern heresy of an "immanentist" type (one that substituted "class struggle" for God as the moving force in history) while maintaining a sense of its own limits.

Cornelius Krusé, a professor at Wesleyan University in Connecticut, analyzed the allure of fascism to Christians. Like Christianity it extolled self-sacrifice, rejected a materialist interpretation of life, and enjoined obedience to law and order. He posed the question of whether churches should enter the political arena to oppose fascism directly. His answer was yes if the objective was to use politics to build a "Christian world-community" that would advance the cause of justice.

Georgia Harkness addressed the relation between the church and democracy. Her axial question was whether democracy could embody the Christian ethical ideal more effectively than other political arrangements. She thought so: Jesus' respect for "personality" was a common ground between Christianity and democracy, and though Jesus did not seek to establish a democratic state, he promulgated a moral principle necessary to democracies: the superiority of obligations over rights, especially the obligation to secure the rights of everyone. Because of this kinship between Christianity and democracy, the church had the obligation to free democracy from the social barriers it erected. The church also had to say a firm no to those who subordinated the Christian conscience to the demands of the state as in Nazi Germany. Harkness concluded, much as her peers had, by arguing that for the church to carry out its mission it would first have to understand the relationship of the divine and human elements within itself.

The group did not go beyond ecclesiological conceptualizing to recommend specific policies, ecclesiastical or political, for international engagement. That was for the upcoming Oxford conference to do. Now only months away, it would, they expected, give concrete expression to what they conceived were the realities of the church's essential unity.

In fact, the Theological Discussion Group's ability to influence the ecumenical movement was a result of Van Dusen's and Cavert's association with Oldham. In December 1936, several weeks after Oldham attended his first retreat with them, he met at Princeton with Archbishop William Temple of York and the American representatives to the five international Christian organizations with ecumenical interests—Life and Work, Faith and Order, the International Missionary Council, the World Alliance for Friendship through the Churches, and the World's Student Christian Federation. Temple opened by reporting about a recent series of meetings at York that had brought into existence an unofficial association of leaders from these organizations. They realized they had overlapping memberships and a common interest in Christian unity. Temple himself suggested the time had come to turn them into an interdenominational council for carrying out their common objectives. The first step was then taken: their ad hoc York meetings were given the status of a consultative committee.[52] Next, because Faith and Order had also scheduled its international conference for 1937, it seemed reasonable for both to meet in the same country on successive dates for the convenience of those who were delegates to both. Once that was decided, it seemed sensible to have a leadership committee meet beforehand to consider a joint future. That committee, to number thirty-five, would naturally include him, Oldham, and Cavert (for the Federal Council of Churches).[53] The Americans fell in with the plan. Cavert was now positioned to push the creation of an international council of churches as a way of embodying the Theological Discussion Group's ideas about the church and Christian internationalism.

After the meeting, Oldham went to New York to meet with a small group that included Van Dusen and Henry Sloane Coffin, the president of Union Theological Seminary. Oldham insisted they constitute themselves as an advisory council to determine the scope, method, and participants for the American preparatory study for the Life and Work conference, paralleling what was done in England by an analogous group he had commissioned a few months earlier. Van Dusen took charge, recruiting an inner steering committee that issued the invitations in January. By mid-February there were thirty acceptances, among them Harry Emerson Fosdick, the most popular preacher in America; Coffin, widely known in elite New York society; Methodist Bishop James Baker; John Foster Dulles; Professor James Weldon Johnson of Fisk University; Secretary of Agriculture Henry A. Wallace; Charles P. Taft; and Mary D. Wooley, president of Mount Holyoke College.[54] Meanwhile, Van Dusen arranged for members of his Theological Discussion Group to write explanatory material about the movement and the conference for the churchgoing public. Edwin Aubrey, a professor at the University of Chicago Divinity School, was to produce a series of pamphlets "translating" the highbrow theologians. He engaged three other Chicago theologians to help him: Charles Whitney Gilkey, Charles Clayton Morrison (editor of the *Christian Century*), and Wilhelm Pauck.[55] Van Dusen's friend John Bennett agreed to direct the American study program.

Van Dusen's position required him to mediate between Oldham and William Adams Brown, the ranking figure in the American Life and Work organization. Their relations, always strained, had deteriorated in the summer of 1936. Writing to John R. Mott, America's senior international churchman, Oldham commented "in the strictest confidence" that Brown had been "exceptionally difficult" at the last Life and Work executive meeting and had "succeeded in irritating almost everyone." He attributed it to two factors. As Brown aged he was "losing grip" but was determined to convince himself otherwise by trying "to take the initiative on every occasion," and he resented that Van Dusen had been put in charge of the study program instead of him. Oldham thought this symptomatic of Brown's "pathological" reluctance to pass leadership to the younger generation.[56] Van Dusen interceded, urging Oldham to soften his attitude and to work with Brown for two practical reasons: Brown was about to succeed the recently deceased S. Parkes Cadman, Life and Work chairman in America, and besides, Van Dusen thought Brown was in fact exceptionally capable. He "increasingly impressed" Van Dusen with his "invaluable contributions" to "almost every aspect of the church's enterprise" in America. Van Dusen conceded that Brown was "not always an easy man to work with," but, he reminded Oldham, overcoming personal differences was a chief task of the movement.[57]

The influence Van Dusen wielded over the organizers of the Life and Work conference was evident in November of that year when the American Section, having yet to nominate the "co-opted" delegates (as opposed to those appointed by the denominations), was induced by Van Dusen to cede him that responsibility via the steering committee he had handpicked from his advisory council. "The filling of these 28 places by exactly the right people is such a terribly vital matter," he wrote Henry Smith Leiper, "they cannot adequately be made by a referendum but only by a small group of those who know all the situations involved."[58] Van Dusen got his way.[59] But now he worried that the Theological Discussion Group was becoming too conspicuously dominant in the conference lineup. Writing to Oldham about the latter's recommendations for American speakers at the conference, Van Dusen remarked that three out of the four belonged to both the Theological Discussion Group and the faculty of Union Theological Seminary. This would "stir criticism," particularly "among the older leadership."[60] John Bennett thought so too.[61] Poised for a leadership coup,

Van Dusen and his peers felt somewhat awkward in their newly gained preeminence.

Yet because of them, the ecumenical movement, too, had gained prominence in America. Van Dusen and his associates had enlisted in the movement leaders from various sectors of the country's establishment—Wall Street, higher education, and church hierarchies. Though the New Haven–New York–Princeton axis still defined the Protestant elite geographically, its membership was changing with the meetings of these realist scholars and public figures who were directly involved in promoting an antifascist Christian international. Because of their work, interdenominational cooperation aiming at this Christian international was filling the void left by the moribund extradenominational associations. Subtly, their effort was reshaping and reinvigorating American Protestantism. They gave it an agenda of ecclesiastical internationalism for engagement in international causes.

Proclamation and Organization
1937–1939

ON THE EVE OF THE Life and Work and Faith and Order world conferences in July 1937, thirty-five men from twelve countries representing the
five Christian international organizations met at Westfield College in
northwest London to plan the future of the ecumenical movement.[1] Their
expectations were modest. At most it was thought they would devise a
plan for cooperation. Because they did not think anything momentous
would happen, they did not appoint a secretary to record their discussion.[2]
Oldham, however, had in mind the creation of a World Christian Counsel that yoked Life and Work with Faith and Order in study projects leading
to church unity. He had privately approached W. A. Visser 't Hooft,
secretary-general of the World's Student Christian Federation, to consider serving as the executive officer of such a body.[3] That was as far as it
got.

But at the meeting it became clear that others were thinking along
similar lines. The proposal came up matter-of-factly. First the chairman,
Archbishop Temple of York, remarked that in the quest for Christian
unity, Life and Work and Faith and Order complemented each other.
Yngve Brilioth of Sweden picked up the idea, recalling Archbishop
Söderblom's 1919 proposal for a council of churches. Temple quickly recognized they had a consensus, and he appointed a drafting subcommittee. The text it produced was a blueprint for a new international organization based on national and denominational representation combining
the Life and Work and Faith and Order organizations. Authority would

be vested in a general assembly of two hundred delegates convening every five years, with one-third of it being laity. To execute its decisions would be a "central council" of sixty, meeting annually, with a "first-class" staff to implement its directives. It was recommended that the upcoming world conferences empower a joint interim committee to work out the other necessary arrangements. The thirty-five representatives accepted the draft unanimously.[4]

One detail remained—a name for the new body. It seemed likely there would be a long, cumbersome title to reflect the interests of the tributary movements. But Cavert suggested a succinct alternative, "Why not World Council of Churches?" Silence followed, then Archbishop Temple broke in, "Why not? That's what we really want, isn't it?" The thirty-five agreed by acclamation and finished with a service of thanksgiving and dedication.[5] It was one thing for them to agree so suddenly on such a union; it was another to make their organizations accept it.

The Oxford Conference on Church, Community, and State

Three days later, on 12 July, four hundred Life and Work delegates and their alternates assembled at Oxford for the two-week-long world conference. They mingled as they gathered for the plenary sessions in the university's ornate baroque hall, the Sheldonian Theatre, seventy-five yards from the spot where three Reformation clerics were burned at the stake in 1555. Delegates from China and India greeted black-robed Orthodox priests from Greece and Yugoslavia. Leaders of Protestant Europe's church establishment mixed with "sectarian" Methodists, Baptists, and Reformed. Not all Christendom was represented. Roman Catholics and American fundamentalists had declined to participate. Nor were the Germans represented, Berlin having withdrawn its delegation's visas at the eleventh hour.[6] Radio broadcasts as well as newspaper coverage kept the world informed from the scene.[7]

The Oxford conference provided the occasion for the realist theologians to step to the helm of the movement and become a force in American Protestantism. Their ideas became the core of the conference's final pronouncements. Their leadership of its committees showed they had the political abilities to implement the international agenda that their convictions had led them to. As their speeches and comments commanded the Europeans' attention, this new fact got coverage in America's newspapers and radio, giving the Protestant view of international affairs a prominence it had not enjoyed for decades.

The Americans speeches in the plenary sessions made bold démarches challenging the Europeans to rethink the theological ground and structure of the ecumenical movement they had heretofore dominated. John Foster Dulles captured attention by declaring the realist thesis that the root of international discord was national (read: European) pride as well as individual pride, and the church alone had the capacity to mitigate it.[8] In every nation, he said, there were many individuals who derive self-satisfaction from feeling that the group they belong to is superior to others, and the logical outcome is the "desire to see such advantages consolidated and enlarged" in national aggrandizement. Sounding like the Theological Discussion Group, he said that surmounting this problem was fundamentally a religious matter, and Christianity held most of the answers because it stood opposed to the sins of "pride" and "selfishness." "Reason can chart the course," Dulles declared, but hope lay in a united Christian front, as well international arrangements for free trade and renegotiable treaties (read: never again a Versailles arrangement).

Reinhold Niebuhr made an electrifying speech, hammering out his analysis of the world crisis in terms of sin.[9] He asserted that the humanistic belief pervading contemporary life in a variety of forms was none other than the religion of self-glorification described in the first chapter of Paul's Epistle to the Romans. In recent times it had taken on new life as self-glorification of race and nation. The antidote was to preach the gospel of the cross because history is the place where salvation occurs. The church's role was to make this known. Echoing the Theological Discussion Group on the church and *The Church Against the World*, Niebuhr argued that the church must be an agent in establishing peace and justice yet had to have a contrite recognition of its own historic sinfulness. Complicating the task, secular dictatorships made national self-glorification palatable to the religiously inclined by lacing it with hollow statements about social justice. The church had to understand these dynamics and take a tough stand for justice but do it in a spirit of humility.

American leadership in the working groups commanded comparable attention. Before the conference, organizers had assigned delegates to one of the five sections charged with formulating position papers on aspects of the main theme.[10] The five sections addressed the tensions between church and community; those between church and state; and the relations of church, community, and state to the economy, education, and international affairs.[11] Each group had a core, a drafting committee of two to fifteen people, with the chairman as the consensus builder and principal editor, the chief influence over whom was the secretary. Two sections were chaired by Americans. Henry Sloane Coffin led the one on education with John Bennett as his secretary. John Mackay of Princeton Theological Seminary chaired the one on the church and international relations, sitting with Dulles, Mott, Van Dusen, Brown, Harkness, and Charles P. Taft.[12] Americans held several other key positions. Mott chaired the business committee, which controlled procedure and debate. Cavert was on it too, and on a special committee on war.

The Americans heavily influenced the sections' deliberations. Reinhold Niebuhr and Paul Tillich contributed two central concepts: Tillich, the definition of "demonic"; Niebuhr, the similarity of justice and natural law in the regulation of society.[13] There was a striking congruence of themes between the conference reports and the American contributions to the preparatory essays—particularly those by Theological Discussion Group members Edwin Aubrey, John Bennett, Robert Calhoun, Walter Horton, Niebuhr, and Tillich, and the Federal Council's sociologist H. Paul Douglass.[14]

Three themes ran through all of the reports. First, social disintegration was a worldwide phenomenon. Reiterating ideas from the two Theological Discussion Group retreats immediately before Oxford, the Americans argued that social decay afflicted communities worldwide and that the disintegration bred non-Christian solutions for reintegration, "dictatorial forms of government," as Tillich put it. Douglass identified the church and the state as the two natural contenders for integrating human life, the state increasingly taking over that role. Similarly, two of the section reports asserted that the growth of industrialization, urbanization, world trade, and unresolved problems from the Great War had eroded the morality, customs, and spiritual bonds holding society together. Fascism in Italy and Germany and communism in the Soviet Union were attempts at reintegration that made the nation or class the highest good. "Generally speaking," one of the reports said, "one can describe the situation as a mixture of far-reaching disintegration and attempts at totalitarian reintegration. . . . Men are following the many social and political symbols and banners with religious fervor because they promise them a unifying center for life and a new fellowship."[15]

The second "American" theme was the pervasiveness of sin as the root of social turmoil. The Americans criticized liberal Christianity for failing to take this seriously. Reinhold Niebuhr put it bluntly: "The real dimension of the problem of faith and the common life is obscured in secular and in liberal Christian morality because there is no appreciation of the fact of sin."[16] The notion was written into the report of the section on church and community: "The orders of family, community, people, nation are part of the God-given basis and structure of human life . . . yet man's sin—his pride, greed, fear, idolatry—has infected them all."[17] Christians were encouraged to be alert to sin in the church as well as the world. Simply by being aware of it they would be less prone to erect such false idols as nation or race.

The third theme was proclamation of the church as the antidote for the world's social ills. The Americans saw the church as both an historical and a supratemporal entity, the sole adequate social agent for salvation in history.[18] "Christian faith," wrote Niebuhr, "must provide the foundations for the edifice of a social ethic and the minarets for its superstructure." Appearing in the section reports and the concluding conference statement, the "Message," this theme trumpeted the church as the Christian corporate alternative to nationalism and communism, "that fellowship which binds men together in their common dependence on God and overleaps all barriers of social status, race, or nationality."[19] It was also a vocational matter with a corporate dimension. Because God calls the church to the ministry of reconciliation, Christians could not leave the task of peacemaking to secular agencies alone. Describing the church's role as "peacemaker," the conference asserted:

[W]hile giving discriminating support to work for peace and justice . . . through the League of Nations and kindred organizations, the church cannot leave the duty of peacemaking to political agencies. . . . The church should be able by the leading of the Spirit to discover characteristically Christian ways of intervening as a healing and reconciling influence in a world of conflict.[20]

The section on church and state had the most sensitive topic: of opposing the church to legitimate though totalitarian regimes. It took the position that to preach the good news of salvation, the church had to speak freely in proclaiming it, even if political authorities were disobeyed and criticized in the process. Mindful of their embattled colleagues in the German Confessing Church but unwilling to deal with the implications of it for traditional ecclesiology, the group's consensus was to stay on a theoretical plane, saying that the church is the community that does not view the state as the ultimate social order, and in which freedom in God is a reality.[21] This high-altitude evasion worked to achieve an entente of European neo-orthodoxy and American Christian realism. Transcendence was their common ground: emphasis on the church's transcendence accompanied emphasis on God's transcendence.

Though the delegates had diverse opinions about what political action to take, they held a consensus about the centrality of the church, supplanting the earlier one on the centrality of the person of Christ. They envisioned a world in which political thought and action stemmed from theological reflection stimulated by the church. "The more it is realized that the church is the great sustaining reality of life," the section report read, "the more will individual Christians and groups reach accord in their endeavors to bring political life under the sovereignty of Christ."[22] Calling the church the "leaven" through which Christ transforms society, it appealed for cooperation between the theologically and sociopolitically minded people at local and international levels. This would both propel the Christian unity movement and multiply the benefits it offered.[23]

To give concrete expression to these ideas, Archbishop William Temple presented the plan for the World Council of Churches that had been drawn up at the Westfield College meeting two weeks earlier. It was approved "in principle" pending a positive decision by the Faith and Order conference at Edinburgh. The leaders arranged to have seven of their number nominated to the interim joint committee of fourteen and authorized them to make any necessary modifications to the plan arising from their consultations. Of the seven the Americans were Brown and Mott; Cavert and the layman Charles P. Taft were chosen as alternates.[24]

The Life and Work conference was an experience that itself deepened the participants' commitment to church unity. Twice daily, they gathered for prayer in historic St. Mary the Virgin Church. Lasting twenty to thirty minutes, these were periods of guided meditation on the issues of that day; they engendered a unity of feeling that often precipitated or confirmed the rightness of insights left over from the day's meetings. The Orthodox and Anglo-Catholic clergy, however, had the opposite experience, feeling uncomfortable with the Protestant character of these services, but even that served to remind them of the church's brokenness and the need to seek unity.[25]

Though the organizers did not plan joint services of Holy Communion, they happened anyway.[26] On the first Sunday there were three separate eucharistic services: at St. Mary's according to the Anglican rite, at Hertford College's chapel according to the Byzantine rite, and at Mansfield College's chapel according to the Reformed rite. On the second Sunday the Church of England clergy took the extraordinary step of inviting all baptized and communicant delegates to join its Eucharist. To accommodate them all, there were two simultaneous services, at St. Mary's with the archbishop of Canterbury as celebrant (assisted by Bishop Azariah of India) and at St. Aldate's with Bishop Bell of Chichester as celebrant.

By the end of the conference, the experience of common worship and consensus in the sections made it seem feasible to intertwine public action with religious discernment. Among those so persuaded was the forty-nine-year-old John Foster Dulles. The son of a small-town Presbyterian minister in upstate New York, Dulles grew up among ministers and missionaries on his father's side and diplomats on his mother's. His grandfather was President Harrison's secretary of state, John W. Foster; his uncle, President Wilson's secretary of state, Robert Lansing.[27] His father was a theological liberal who followed contemporary trends in religious thought and believed it a scandal that Christians were so divided. All of this had shaped Dulles into a man of Christian principle, but now the experience of the Oxford conference opened his eyes to its potential for resolving international discord. A few days before the conference he had attended a League of Nations meeting at Paris, and the contrast with Oxford struck him. He "obtained great enlightenment" watching the church representatives calmly and productively deliberate problems he had just seen generate heated and fruitless wrangling among the diplomats.[28] "From then on I began to work closely with religious groups," he later wrote, "for I had come to believe . . . they could make the greatest contribution to world order."[29]

Still, Oxford was only a step, a gathering orchestrated by like-minded churchmen already "professionally" involved in international activities. They avoided friction by not probing the theological ground for a definition of the church but simply asserting their belief in its essential unity. The church and community section went furthest when it distinguished the church from other public institutions. Because of the church's origin in Christ and its mission of world salvation, the section declared, the church is more than a "form of human gregariousness and association."[30] This report refrained from any remark about the church's historical unity and disunity; such a thorny matter would have wrecked the organizers' hope of marrying Life and Work and Faith and Order and issuing a united statement against fascism. The theology of the Theological Discussion Group was not pressed into giving a more rigorous definition of the relations between reason, revelation, authority, and the church in proclaiming the truth against perverse regimes. This left unaddressed the issue the group had also left unresolved from three of its preconference retreats.

Nevertheless, the group's analysis of the world situation received a wide hearing at and after Oxford, and it became the movement's accepted assessment of the international situation. Oxford had been a pulpit for conveying the Theological Discussion Group's Christian internationalist vision, and now the mooted World Council of Churches promised an institutional vehicle to convey the group's message widely, even into circles of political power. Delegates left Oxford with unity of purpose and a plan for achieving it. Henry Smith Leiper observed that the participants went to the conference thinking about the churches but returned home talking about the church.[31]

Faith and Order at Edinburgh

On 3 August the Faith and Order world conference convened at Edinburgh in St. Giles Cathedral, where John Knox had preached the Reformation to the Scots. There were four hundred delegates and their alternates. As at Oxford, the mood was one of concern for the state of the world. Archbishop Temple, addressing this in his opening sermon, rhetorically asked how the church could bridge the divisions plaguing societies if it stayed burdened with its own.[32]

Among the Americans there were Mott, Cavert, Brown, American secretary Floyd W. Tomkins, Jr., Dean Willard Sperry of Harvard Divinity School, and J. Ross Stevenson of Princeton.[33] Other than Cavert no members of the Theological Discussion Group were present. They had not been involved with Faith and Order, preferring Life and Work for its orientation to social ethics and its opening to the political establishment.

American involvement in preparations for the Faith and Order conference had been under way since 1934.[34] After the 1927 international gathering, theologians were divided into three commissions to address subjects that had arisen from it: one on relations between the church and the Word, another on the ministry and sacraments, and the third on the church's unity in life and worship. Originally, the third commission was established as a concession to American churchmen who insisted the conference should deal with "living issues" in the contemporary church.[35] Entirely American, it included H. Paul Douglass, sociologist of the Federal Council of Churches; Angus Dun, professor of theology at Episcopal Theological Seminary; Floyd Tomkins, Jr., American secretary for Faith and Order; Willard Sperry, dean of Harvard Divinity School, its chairman; and several other prominent academic churchmen. For liaison with the other preparatory groups, it also had William Adams Brown, a member of Faith and Order's Continuation Committee as well as a senior participant in Life and Work. The commission's mandate was to link the churches' contemporary concerns with theology.[36]

By 1935, however, the theme had spawned so many related subjects that the commission mushroomed into five subcommittees, dealing with such topics as the meanings of unity and the communion of saints.[37] Its chairman, Willard Sperry, proposed expanding the commission's membership along with the scope, thinking it desirable to involve Europeans in a comprehensive look at the progress that had been made in the past

ten years and to define the unity being sought.[38] Until then participants
had assumed there was a common aspiration toward a certain *kind* of unity.
Now it was clear there was not. The Continuation Committee agreed to
Sperry's recommendation. Both the request and the response were indica-
tive of the extent to which theology on both sides of the ocean was becoming bound up with the unity movement.

The Americans who went to Edinburgh were overconfident of their
ability to supply answers to the questions faced by Faith and Order. Having focused on the sociological sources of Christian disunity and having
had the experience of church federation in the Federal Council, they took
it for granted that other Faith and Order delegates shared their conviction that this was the kind of unity that ought to be sought, particularly
because of the multiple social and cultural differences among the churches.
They were disappointed when their report on "the Church's unity in life
and worship" was read aloud and few in the hall paid attention. Sperry
was made to understand that their recommendations were regarded as
"trivial and avoidable options."[39] He attributed this indifference to lack
of concern over the class and racial divisions that the Americans had
thought vitally important.

At Edinburgh the proceedings were dominated by the continental
Europeans, who deemed theological differences of paramount importance.
Questions about the churches' relations to each other took precedence
over consideration of the churches' role in international relations. Theological differences were to be faced squarely, not glossed over in a rush to
reach superficial consensus. Indeed, acknowledgment of those differences
was considered the first necessary step in trying to find genuine common
ground. The section meetings did find such commonalities in teachings
about grace, Scripture as the Word of God, and the communion of saints—
though with reservations on each point. Consensus was also reached on
the requisites for unity: similarity of creedal confession, sacramental doctrine and practice, ministerial orders, and church polity. The section on
ministry and sacraments found that the churches' divisions sprang from
disagreements about the nature of ministry—opinions about the validity
of the sacraments correlated with beliefs about the validity of the clergy
celebrating them, and were based on differing interpretations of apostolic
succession. Though it was agreed all churches treasured that doctrine in
some way, questions arose over the meaning and efficacy of the "laying-
on of hands" in ordination, which at bottom meant differences over the
church's nature.[40] Further consideration of the matter was deferred, but
the discussion had resulted in clarifying areas of disagreement that had
persisted for centuries. The section recommended continued study of these

issues through regular contact between churches on local, national, and international levels.[41]

This recommendation seemed to imply support for establishment of a world council of churches. But when the actual proposal came to the floor, heated debate broke out. The organizers had known that some influential delegates were opposed.[42] Bishop A. C. Headlam of Gloucester, the leading dissenter, said he feared such a council would spend its time on resolutions about political issues, obscuring the theological work of Faith and Order, making it a weak cousin of Life and Work. The same objection was held by Floyd Tomkins, Jr., the American secretary for Faith and Order, an Episcopal priest, who also worried that Life and Work would supplant Faith and Order. (Besides, Tomkins was hostile to any idea connected with the Federal Council of Churches; he could not forget that Episcopal Bishop Charles Brent, whom he greatly admired, was never elected its president.)[43]

The opponents had four specific objections to the merger.[44] First, Life and Work admitted the Unitarian Church, while Faith and Order did not, its criterion for membership being belief in the Trinity. In particular, the consubstantiality of God the Father with God the Son ran contrary to the Unitarian confession. Second, up to a quarter of the delegates to the Life and Work conference had been "co-opted members," chosen without denominational mandate. The objection here was that only a body completely representative of the member churches could promote Christian unity. Third, with Life and Work dominating in the Federal Council of Churches in America, the opponents thought it would be the Federal Council that would pick the American nominees for the new organization, with prejudice against Episcopalians and Lutherans whose denominations did not belong as members. Fourth, they suspected the Americans associated with Life and Work (chiefly Cavert and Van Dusen) were engineering the merger and intended to control the new body, too. They doubted the World Council would truly represent all of non-Roman Christendom, including the Orthodox, Old Catholics, and Anglicans.

It took much persuading by Archbishop Temple and William Adams Brown to make the opponents go along.[45] Temple pointed out that the plan had stipulations protecting Faith and Order: no merger would take effect without being approved by its own Continuation Committee; and not the Federal Council but the churches would select the American delegates. On the positive side, the blueprint promised more than a pan-Protestant venture. Brown, the senior American ecumenist whom the opposition trusted, argued that it was the one proposal to come out of both conferences that could generate enthusiasm for church unity among the rank-and-file churchgoers. In the end, the opposition got Temple's safeguards in writing, drafted into five points to be added to the plan. Most important, Trinitarian confession was the "basis" for membership. Another was church-appointed representation. With that the opposition were satisfied no co-opted academics or "activists" would drive the organization down liberal roads where many churches had no desire to go.[46]

More debate followed. Close to midnight, the presiding chairman made a motion to adjourn to the next day. It was defeated. Then a motion to establish the World Council passed with only one dissent, Headlam's.[47] In the nominations that followed for the joint Committee of Fourteen the Americans chosen were J. Ross Stevenson, Episcopal Bishop George Craig Stewart, and Professor A. R. Wentz as an alternate—none of them associated with the Theological Discussion Group.

The closing plenary session adopted an affirmation of unity, a consensus statement demarcating what substantively existed among them: the *desire* for unity on the basis of Christocentricity, qualified by concern over matters of ecclesiology. It said their desire for unity had its origin in God's gracious acts through Christ and the Holy Spirit, not human initiative. Ultimate allegiance to Christ drew the churches together, *but* the divisions among Christians arose from serious differences in beliefs about the nature of the church. In effect, this was as far as the Theological Discussion Group had gone at its first retreat on the church before Oxford, and for the same reason. Emphasizing Christocentric commonality in order not to create further dissension at the very moment they were trying to come together, the Edinburgh Faith and Order Conference avoided addressing the cultural sources of disagreements about the locus of authority for determining right belief. "We are one in faith in our Lord Jesus Christ . . . ," its statement ran:

> We are one in allegiance to Him as Head of the Church, and as King of kings and Lord of lords. We are one in acknowledging that this allegiance takes precedence of any other allegiance that may make claims upon us.
> . . . We are divided in the outward forms of our life in Christ because we understand differently His will for His Church. We believe, however, that a deeper understanding will lead us towards a united apprehension of the truth as it is in Jesus.[48]

The conference ended with a prayer for unity in the face of worldwide social turmoil and threat of war. This "affirmation of unity" was read out by the archbishop of York at the concluding thanksgiving service in St. Giles Cathedral. The moment was "solemn and impressive."[49]

This was the turning point. Faith and Order had consolidated the decades-long drive for Christian unity from an extradenominational movement into a church-based organization. The notion that serious differences over the nature of the church lay at the root of the churches' divisions made ecclesiology the avenue for future progress. Ironically, of the two bodies coming together, it was the one preoccupied with doctrine, Faith and Order, that had determined the polity of the World Council, not through theological persuasion but by simply insisting.

Immediately after Edinburgh the joint Committee of Fourteen met in London to work out the details of constituting the World Council and to make interim arrangements for the continuation of ecumenical programs.[50] (In practice it would be a "committee of twenty-eight" because the alternates attended all meetings.) It decided to secure support from the churches by holding a special conference for the framing of the World Council constitution. The committee set the date and the place (9–12 May 1938, Utrecht), and issued an invitation under the signatures of Faith and Order chairman Archbishop Temple and Life and Work chairman William Adams Brown. Before adjourning it formed an "Ad Interim" Steering Committee: Brown, Temple, Cavert, Oldham, Marc Boegner of France, Greek Archbishop Germanos, J. Ross Stevenson, and Leonard Hodgson, with W. A. Visser 't Hooft as executive secretary. With Cavert, Oldham, Hodgson, and Visser 't Hooft on the committee, the "younger generation" was once again at the center.

An Organization for the Message

Back in the United States, where many churchgoing Americans were still hopelessly unemployed in the Great Depression, the ecumenical movement got a wider hearing for its public agenda. The NBC radio network had carried broadcasts from the Oxford conference. Features on ecumenical activity—international and local—started appearing regularly in church publications. To advance their project further, Van Dusen and Cavert set their hand to build institutions that would link the ecumenical movement directly to the denominations and thus give it permanence. By doing this, they realized, they made themselves vulnerable to being displaced from the center of power they had just reached. Nevertheless, convinced of their ultimate goal, they pressed forward. For them it was a personal imperative to put their theology into public life.

Already the word "ecumenical" had entered the American lexicon. As editor of the *Federal Council Bulletin*, Cavert had done much to popularize it, using the word interchangeably with "the international interdenominational bodies," meaning Life and Work and Faith and Order.[51] Over time he expanded its meaning along the lines discussed at the Theological Discussion Group retreats on the church. Associating "ecumenical" with "catholic" and "universal," he explained that the word "catholic" in the Apostles' Creed meant the church was "the whole Body of Christ throughout the world" in more than a geographical sense. It referred to the movement that combined Life and Work and Faith and Order, and the belief that they were on the way to realizing an ideal that offered a solution to the most pressing international problems of the day.[52]

Cavert's Federal Council staff turned "the ecumenical movement" into a nationwide educational campaign. Delegates returning from Oxford and Edinburgh were deluged with invitations to tell about their experiences.[53] They spoke to state conferences, youth gatherings, city clubs, women's meetings, and community forums. By January 1938 the *Federal Council Bulletin* reported that the delegates had given 1,725 addresses, led 288 discussion groups, and addressed 189 synods, dioceses, or other ecclesiastical bodies.[54] The churches of Evanston, Illinois, sponsored a citywide Conference on Christian Faith and Life to which congregations sent delegates for discussion of the Oxford and Edinburgh themes.[55] New York City ministers held an "Oxford" for the metropolitan area. Individual congregations sponsored their own "little Oxfords." Some used the Oxford conference report as the primary text for adult education programs on the role of the church in contemporary society. For others there was a small album of twenty photographs from the conference picked by Henry Smith Leiper, with his captions giving a much-simplified version of what happened.[56] Fund-raisers found it easy to talk about Oxford because those they approached thought the World Council would be a viable response to "the ever-increasing world-wide interest in Christian Unity . . . pertaining to the church and world affairs."[57]

Meanwhile the American ecumenical leaders met to plan for the Utrecht event and for future ecumenical activity in North America.[58] They had to select delegates and coordinate the American programs of Life and Work and Faith and Order to build popular support for the merger. It was decided to have the churches elect the delegates openly at an electoral conference in Washington, D.C. For interim coordination a steering group was set up, a Joint Executive Committee paralleling the international Committee of Fourteen, with seven representatives from the American branches of the two organizations. A joint educational program was envisaged to teach the churchgoing public systematically about the significance of the movement as a whole.[59]

The electoral conference went off more smoothly than expected, in a single day, at the Washington Cathedral College of Preachers. It took only two hours instead of the several anticipated days to reach an agreement about the method of election. Delegates were to be put forward by each of eleven "denominational families"—Northern Baptists, Southern Baptists, Presbyterian and Reformed churches, Disciples of Christ and the Congregationalists, the Lutheran churches, Southern Methodists, the Methodist Episcopal Church and Methodist Protestant Church, the Negro churches, the Friends and other "small" denominations, the Episcopal Church, and the Canadian churches. The delegates chose representatives from each.[60]

But to Van Dusen it did not seem such a glowing success. He was troubled to see the movement falling under denominational control. None of the usual personnel "co-opted" by Life and Work were picked to go to Utrecht. Van Dusen began to suspect that people like himself were being shut out. Anxious, he confided to Cavert, "I wish I could fully share your confidence that, in the new World Council, the leadership which was represented by the coopted delegates at Oxford can be fully conserved."[61] At stake was the quality of the future council's leadership: "It is the great issue of whether the free, prophetic elements within Christian leadership which are never comfortably domesticated within the ecclesiastical machinery and are seldom recognized or trusted by it are to have any vital part . . . in the administration of the Council." The implication was disturbing. Would it really be a Council of Christendom or yet another church bureaucracy staffed by mediocrities? At the very moment Van Dusen and his Theological Discussion Group had produced a theology appropriate to the times and were in positions to implement it, they seemed on the verge of being shunted aside. Van Dusen, his ego pricked, feared that without them there would be a dulling of the ecumenical movement's theological and ethical cutting edge. With denominational officials in charge, the council's actions would be so intertwined with the churches' institutional interests that they would lose the flexibility they needed for shaping the council's message and mobilizing public opinion around it.

The fate of the "co-opted" was settled when the constitutional conference convened at Utrecht. There were four items on the agenda.[62] First, the World Council's authority in relation to the churches was resolved without dissent: the council was not to be a superchurch and would not legislate for the churches; rather, the churches would decide independently whether to endorse the council's statements and actions. Second was the requirement for membership—the most contested issue. Debate turned on the appropriateness of Faith and Order's criterion—"confession of faith in our Lord Jesus Christ as God and Saviour." Some urged going beyond that anti-Unitarian formula by adding an explicit affirmation of Jesus' humanity as well as his divinity. Archbishop Temple, as chair, pointedly remarked that regardless of what confession of faith it chose, the council could not act as an ecclesiastical court passing judgment on churches' adherence to it; each church would have to determine that for itself. By a large majority a statement was adopted keeping the Faith and Order formula: "The World Council of Churches is a fellowship of Churches which accept our Lord Jesus Christ as God and Saviour." Ever the synthesizer and conciliator, Temple wrapped up the discussion by promising the council would pursue cooperation with churches that could not accept it.

The third issue was the organizational structure. The initial proposal from the Committee of Thirty-Five that the council have two representative commissions corresponding to Life and Work and Faith and Order was accepted. A general assembly of 450 church-appointed members, the highest authority, would meet once every five years, and a central committee of 90 from the assembly would meet annually to review and direct the executive's work.[63] Debate arose about how to allocate representation among the churches. Some preferred a scheme based on denominational groupings, such as Anglican, Lutheran, Reformed, or Orthodox. Others argued that the geographical identity of churches was as important, so, for example, German Lutherans should be represented separately from American Lutherans. Finding validity in both arguments, the conferees devised a territorially based plan supplemented by confessional representation ensuring that the Orthodox and smaller Protestant churches would not be underrepresented. They upheld the Westfield College recommendation that one-third of the assembly and central committee be from the laity, explicitly stating that "lay" meant "men *and* women." In recognition of Faith and Order's sensitivities about non-church-appointed participants, the two commissions were authorized to co-opt members for study projects but not for administration. This meant Van Dusen's intellectuals would not be excluded after all, but neither would they be at the helm.[64]

Last, the conference set up a Provisional Committee to direct work and oversee financial arrangements until the first general assembly, to be held at Washington, D.C., in 1941. The membership of this committee would be the Committee of Fourteen plus six others from Life and Work and Faith and Order. Its full name, the Provisional Committee of the World Council of Churches in the Process of Formation, was chosen to make it clear that the World Council would come into existence only at the first assembly.[65] First, the constitution agreed on at Utrecht was to be submitted to the churches for their approval.

The next day, 13 May, the Provisional Committee took its first steps.[66] Electing officers—in effect appointing themselves—Temple became chairman, and the three chosen as vice chairmen were supposedly representing the diversity of the movement—John R. Mott, Archbishop Germanos, and Marc Boegner. Visser 't Hooft was made general secretary, just as Oldham had suggested to him on the eve of the Westfield College meeting. To please the Americans, the Federal Council of Churches, and maintain close ties with the International Missionary Council (IMC), Henry Smith Leiper was made associate general secretary, as was William Paton, a close associate of Oldham's in the IMC. Before adjourning they found a way to keep Van Dusen in the leadership core. A smaller Administrative Committee of Temple, Cavert, Mott, Brown, and a few others thought that for the assembly to make any progress toward church unity a directed study like the ones carried out for Oxford and Edinburgh would be necessary. They immediately made Van Dusen its head and stipulated that he would attend Provisional Committee meetings but not have a vote.[67] Van Dusen felt uneasy about this, confiding to Cavert, "It is bad policy for the chairman of the Study Committee not to be a member of the Provisional Committee."[68] But he kept the post.

One of Van Dusen's first decisions was to put Bennett in charge of the American study. Bennett, who had just accepted a faculty position at the Pacific School of Theology in California, feared that separation from the movement's New York hub would leave him out of touch with the rest of the leadership. Cavert assured him he would be kept "closely geared into the developing plans."[69] Thus, the leadership core provided a way for the formerly "co-opted" theologians of the Theological Discussion Group to continue exercising influence a while longer.

The ecumenical quarterly *Christendom* also extended the group's influence, putting the journal under their tutelage. Charles C. Morrison, the editor, persuaded the publishers that *Christendom* could better promote the ecumenical merger if it were in the hands of the people running the American branches of Life and Work and Faith and Order.[70] It was turned over to the Joint Executive Committee led by Cavert and his friends. Dr. H. Paul Douglass was made editor in chief, and in short order a third of the Theological Discussion Group were put on the editorial board.[71]

Even Faith and Order let them into the kitchen. When the Continuation Committee met at Clarens, Switzerland, on 29 August to 1 September 1938, after reviewing the proposed World Council constitution, a long discussion occurred about having a study commission on the church and liturgical issues, a proposal made by Canon Leonard Hodgson, Faith and Order's general secretary. Bishop Headlam of Gloucester suggested creating two committees, one on the church and one on worship and the sacraments. Dr. R. Newton Flew of Cambridge University presented his ideas for the church study, recommending that it examine the nature of the church in terms of Scripture, historical traditions, and the confessions' different doctrines. Learning about the traditions would help them address the roots of their similarities and differences following the approach taken at Edinburgh. Flew had confidence that such a process, a dialectical testing, would produce a constructive synthesis. So did the others, up to a point. They decided to divide the study, endorsing the church study for now and deferring the liturgical study for later. Flew was put in charge and immediately requested the American branch to form a "theological committee." Fifteen theologians were invited, among them two members of the Theological Discussion Group, Van Dusen and Walter M. Horton.[72]

Over the next year the preparations for the World Council assembly were pressed forward while the nations readied for war. Some still hoped that war would be averted and that somehow God meant to use their project to that end; and at least if war did come, their efforts would have made bonds between Christians to keep the world from flying completely apart and succumbing to despair. The next Faith and Order Continuation Committee meeting, 21–23 August 1939, again at Clarens, coincided with Germany's diplomatic ultimatum against Poland.[73] Boegner, chairing, opened by remarking that the "clouds seemed to be darkening." While the committee was meeting in a beautiful, tranquil setting it was impossible not to think of the rest of the world "in its anguish and trial." All he could do was remind the members that because the church had Christ as its master, it possessed "the only solution." Two days were spent discussing the preparatory educational work for the first assembly. The committee heard an update on the church study and entertained other reports of work in progress. It was beginning to review proposals about the liturgy study when news came that war was imminent. The committee hurriedly adjourned to allow members to start for home before borders closed and sea voyage became dangerous. Boegner grimly quipped that instead of dancing on a volcano, they were praying on one.

A week later, the eruption came. The German blitzkrieg was launched against Poland. The ecumenical leadership took the news calmly, knowing the foundations of the World Council were laid. They had set the machinery in motion for it to come into existence, if not now, then after the war. Theirs was a vision of Christian unity, of the church transcendent, and of an international ecclesial organization leading the way into a new world order. That organization was their "witness to Christ," a model means of reconciling in truth those who had been at odds for centuries, allowing for differences and autonomy.

But first the civilized world had to deal with Nazi Germany. To the Americans of the Theological Discussion Group the war came as no surprise. It confirmed what they had been forecasting at their retreats for years: the shunting aside of Christianity and the erosion of civilization at the hands of a competing ideology. They now turned to sound the tune of politics, to giving their ideas to the national leadership as a way of ensuring that the mistakes made by the victors after World War I would not be repeated and the emerging international society would be saved from barbarities.

SIX

Making a New International Order
in the War Years
1939–1945

WHEN GERMANY CONQUERED POLAND in September 1939, the consensus of prominent Americans was that the event should not alter U.S. neutrality. Liberals and conservatives alike preached this position. Liberals worried the war would divert attention and money from domestic problems; conservatives feared the repetition of higher taxes and government expansion of the Great War. Pacifists advocating mediation made strange bedfellows with the America First Committee, arguing that there was no danger of invasion if Germany won in Europe. Behind this public rationale was a fundamental pride, a right of America to avoid entanglement in another "Old World war."[1] The attitude vexed the European ecumenical leaders. Visser 't Hooft wrote to Cavert, "[T]here is very great disappointment among all those who are working in international movements" because "America is giving so little response to the demands for help."[2]

World Council headquarters in Geneva, like the city itself, became the hub of a maze of wartime dealings. Diplomats, resistance movement agents, influential refugees, and church leaders from many nations congregated at the office, so information about Europe at war was available there as nowhere else.[3] The World Council staff had a German, Hans Schönfeld, and a Swede, Nils Ehrenström, whose contacts in the German diplomatic corps supplied news from the German-occupied countries and inside the reich itself. Visser 't Hooft had connections with the Dutch Resistance, receiving reports on microfilm smuggled out in fountain pens and toothbrushes. From Geneva the World Council's offices in London and New

York disseminated stories about the experiences of "fellow Christians in all parts of the world." Information went back, too, passed among church leaders and clandestine networks of Christians in occupied Europe. Just hearing it related brought some encouragement to those living under the Germans; to those Americans who heard it, there was something to say concretely about the evil of the Nazi regime.

Van Dusen and his group, meanwhile, seized the moment to sound the political themes arising from their ecumenical score. They used their political connections in Washington and New York to get done what their theology dictated in the way of laying the foundations for international engagement. In doing so, they simultaneously reinvigorated American Protestant thought and yoked it to national-level goals, perceptibly internationalizing Americans' moral outlook on the war.

Reaction to Isolationism

Even before the invasion of Poland, the American ecumenists tried to alert churchgoers to Nazi violence against the German Jews. Henry Smith Leiper, American secretary for Life and Work, returning from a meeting in Switzerland in August 1936 where he heard about the anti-Semitic "excesses," reported to Cavert. The two joined forces to make publicity for pressuring the U.S. government into addressing the plight of this people who shared a religious heritage with Christianity.[4] The *Federal Council Bulletin* regularly featured articles detailing anti-Semitic incidents in Germany and advertised lectures by Germans coming to America with information about them.[5]

After the Germany-wide *Kristallnacht* pogrom in November 1938, Leiper and Cavert urged the churches "to combat every manifestation of anti-Semitism" in the United States and "to give support to the movement to aid refugees from Germany." The Federal Council endorsed the Wagner-Rogers Bill to admit twenty thousand Jewish refugee children above the annual immigrant quota for Germans. To generate support for the measure, the council sponsored a nationwide radio broadcast of a dramatization of the pitiful life of German Jewish children, read by Katharine Hepburn and Burgess Meredith.[6] No other organization was doing this kind of advocacy, and this before war broke out.

While the overwhelming majority of American churchgoers clung to neutrality, several of the Theological Discussion Group came out against it, arguing it was both a morally indefensible and politically perilous policy for America to hold when the Germans blitzed through Belgium and pinned the British army in France against the Channel late in the spring of 1940. Francis Miller led off, tapping the influential friends he had made while working for the pro-British Council on Foreign Relations and the National Policy Committee, an association opposing special interest groups in government.[7] Over the first weekend in June, Miller and his wife, Helen, hosted a small party of such men to come up with ways to change Americans' isolationist attitude. They soon discovered they all felt the same way: the United States should immediately declare war on Germany. But to get the public emotionally prepared and to precipitate a reorientation in the national consensus, they saw the necessity of provoking citizen response by issuing an unequivocal appeal signed by notable people. Whitney Shepardson, a longtime member of the Council on Foreign Relations, wrote the text alone in Miller's study while the others brainstormed to compile a list of people who might endorse it. Among those who did were Episcopal Bishop Henry W. Hobson of Cincinnati, astronomer Edwin P. Hubble, essayist Lewis Mumford, and Admiral William H. Stanley, retired chief of naval operations. Miller had the statement to the newspapers by Sunday, hoping to get it on the front pages following the usual weekend news lull.

"A Summons to Speak Out" appeared in the nation's leading newspapers on Monday, asserting Nazi Germany posed a mortal threat to American democratic ideals, institutions, and way of life. It called Americans to put aside their isolationism: "The frontier of our national interest is now on the Somme."[8] The statement did not command the headlines, however, because Italy had entered the war over the weekend by attacking France. Nevertheless, the *Detroit Free Press*, *Louisville Courier-Journal*, and *Richmond Times-Dispatch* carried the appeal on the front page; the *Washington Post* and the *New York Times* ran it as a story on the inside pages.

Miller, oddly, had not solicited Van Dusen's signature. Van Dusen, upset, called him wanting to know about plans for follow-up action. After several conversations they decided on a bipartisan dinner party of prominent interventionists, hosted by a wealthy businessman.[9] Van Dusen arranged it. The host he enlisted was Lewis Douglas, president of the Mutual Life Insurance Company. Henry Sloane Coffin, president of Union Theological Seminary, and magazine publisher Henry R. Luce were among the guests. The dinner, at the exclusive Century Club in New York, produced the idea of what would come to be known as "lend-lease" (or destroyers-for-bases). With Britain having nothing to export to pay for desperately needed war materiel, and the German submarine blockade restricting supply lines across the Atlantic, it was suggested to "lend" Britain some of the Navy's vintage destroyers in "payment" for leasing bases on British possessions in the Caribbean and the Atlantic. Members of the

Century Group (named for the club where the dinner was held) took it upon themselves to promote the scheme, persuading Britain's ambassador Lord Lothian to recommend it to Whitehall and Washington. They also placed newspaper articles and sponsored radio endorsements by General John J. Pershing and others with name recognition.[10] Republican presidential candidate Wendell Wilkie was pressured to give an assurance that he would not make lend-lease a campaign issue. On September 3 President Franklin D. Roosevelt formally announced the program.

Meanwhile, Reinhold Niebuhr approached Miller and Van Dusen about launching a journal of opinion in opposition to the *Christian Century*, the mouthpiece of liberal Protestantism, which held out for neutrality.[11] With the sway it held over the churches, this editorial line bothered Niebuhr enormously. "It isn't merely that its doctrine is politically dangerous," he wrote John Bennett, "but morally very bad." He thought an element of ignorance underlay such opinions: "Americans simply don't know what kind of slavery the Nazis will impose upon the world. Last night I read the laws for the occupied territories of Poland and Czechoslovakia. They give one the creeps."[12] The horrors he and his peers had predicted were coming true. A board of sponsors was recruited with big names from the ecumenical movement, among them Mott, Brown, Coffin, Bishop Henry Hobson, and Charles P. Taft. But the chiefs of the editorial board, of course, were Niebuhr, Van Dusen, and Miller.

They called their journal *Christianity and Crisis*. Three themes dominated: what the crisis was, remedial arrangements for the postwar world, and promoting ecumenism. Miller's lead editorial in the first issue (10 February 1941) explained that "crisis" was not restricted to any particular segment of social life but afflicted "the whole social order." A second editorial, "Holy Wars," declared the commitment to finding realistic answers that avoided the extremes of self-righteous fanaticism and idealistic inaction. Reinhold Niebuhr, in his inaugural statement, revealed the journal's polemical purpose: it aimed to combat "false interpretations" of Christianity and "false analyses" of the world situation. A third editorial, "The World After the War," laid down that an acceptable plan for the postwar world had to deal with five "great problems," chief among them countries' surrender of absolute sovereignty to bring about genuinely international political arrangements. Underscoring the journal's ecumenical orientation, another article called attention to a recent series of interdenominational meetings in Britain on how to establish "a just and durable peace." A regular feature reported the struggles of Christians in occupied Europe. The editors promised to visit this entire agenda regularly.[13]

Van Dusen remarked to Bennett that there was a direct relation between the journal's commitment to the ecumenical movement and its opposition to isolationism. In contrast to the pacifist *Christian Century*, the founders of *Christianity and Crisis* "knew more about international realities firsthand" from their involvement with the World Council. They not only advocated intervention but were setting plans in motion for the postwar world.[14]

The journal was an immediate success, with subscriptions soon exceeding seven thousand.[15] Among those who signed up were Supreme Court Justices William O. Douglas and Felix Frankfurter. Van Dusen and his colleagues could proceed confident that the Protestant establishment no longer relied so heavily on the *Christian Century*, seeking guidance from them instead. They also believed such thoughtful Americans were ready to be receptive to their arguments for entering the European war. Drawing together their theological rationale for church unity and ideas about secular international organization, they began emphasizing the practical, political implications of their views and pushing for their implementation. In a short time *Christianity and Crisis* went from pioneering the recommendations of a handful to articulating the unspoken thoughts of many Americans.

Given the enormity of their overall project, these theologians knew that publication of *Christianity and Crisis* was not enough. With Europe at war, they set their sights on changing American opinion by using every channel available, chief among them the Federal Council of Churches. The Federal Council had been giving lip service to the idea of having the churches play a role in determining the suitable bases for a just and lasting peace, but this rested on the assumption that the churches could advocate their findings more credibly if they remained neutral. Hiding behind this cloak of "neutrality," the council made morally satisfying pronouncements while maintaining the isolationist attitude of its member churches. Van Dusen's circle aimed to change this. They did not want an unhappy repetition of the Versailles debacle. If they had not been able to prevent a second world war, they would prevent a third one by politicking for a saner settlement. By swaying the council they could turn the American churches into Christian-internationalist agents like themselves and overcome Americans' resistance to the establishment of a new international system that would include an organization akin to the League of Nations. Cavert, Federal Council general secretary, gave them the opening. At his suggestion, Walter Van Kirk, the council's director of the Department of International Justice and Goodwill, engaged members of the Theological Discussion Group in commissioned studies on the future peace.

They saw to it that John Foster Dulles was part of this, too. Dulles was picking up on these theologians' strategy and becoming an active agent for it inside the New York–Washington elite. Because of his experience at the Oxford conference in 1937, he was convinced the churches should and could have a decisive role in creating the educated transnational community necessary for a lasting peace.[16] He himself wanted to develop the churches' potential for bringing this about, to make them the agents within the public arena for restoring a sense of mutual responsibility through renewed faith in a transcendent God, worship of whom would preclude any repetition of the Nazi-type deification of the state. Dulles put these ideas across in the keynote address to a Federal Council conference at Philadelphia on 27–29 February 1940, speaking to nearly three hundred representatives from the churches and Christian agencies.[17] His notion of their mission dominated in the conference proceedings and its closing statement: against nations' claims to absolute sovereignty stood God's sovereignty; and the churches were to prepare their membership for a new international political system after the war, one that introduced cooperation on currency and free trade arrangements. The churches were also to encourage their membership to study the forthcoming World Council publications about the church's role in international affairs. By casting the problem in terms of the future, where Allied victory was assumed, Dulles enlarged the scope of the vision and shifted the focus away from the immediate contest over neutrality and intervention to a seemingly more remote situation, subtly nudging the representatives to "think globally." Endorsing this, the Federal Council disseminated these ideas in a study guide issued after the conference as follow-up material for the churches.[18]

The Theological Discussion Group core soon joined Dulles in pressing their common internationalist agenda in this roundabout way. Federal Council directors, persuaded by a speech Dulles delivered at their Biennial Meeting in December 1940, authorized the formation of a committee "to cooperate with the World Council in preparing for the postwar world." As was to be expected, among its personae were Cavert, Van Dusen, Niebuhr, and several others of the Theological Discussion Group. They dubbed it the "Commission to Study the Bases of a Just and Durable Peace" (known less formally as the Commission on a Just and Durable Peace). Using language that again made the American churches think globally by referring to a remote future, they gave themselves four tasks: elaboration of the moral, political, and economic foundations of lasting peace; preparation of American Christians for the change of perspective it would require (read: must be made willing to support it); coordination with the World Council; and promotion of the idea of assembling Christian leaders after the war to generate public support for a peace consistent with Christianity.[19]

Dulles was asked to be the chairman, but he initially declined, not wanting to be a figurehead for yet another study project. He wanted instead to direct something that would really influence national policy by educating the public about international issues and their spiritual dimension.[20] After a month of persuasion from various quarters he was brought around to see that the new commission was what he had in mind. Dulles, the Federal Council, and the theologians had arrived at an arrangement to their mutual benefit: he got the vehicle he sought for achieving his goals, and they got a world-renowned chairman with entrée to the highest circles of American politics.

The public campaign began with the commission's publication of a "handbook" on Christianity and international relations, put together by Dulles and polished by, among others, Van Dusen, Bennett, Georgia Harkness, and Edwin E. Aubrey.[21] The commission met on 21 March 1941 to review the draft. Dulles's preface defined their mission as "to arouse Christians generally to their responsibility and opportunity." The point was to prevent America from rejecting international cooperation again. To deal with the tension between advocates of neutrality and intervention, Dulles urged commission members themselves to set an example of cooperation: "If we can preserve unity and the effectiveness it gives," he urged them, "and have faith in God working through us, then we can accomplish far more than now seems possible."

Six days later the Federal Council issued the handbook, "A Just and Durable Peace," in 450,000 copies. To promote its use the council inaugurated Worldwide Communion Sunday. All Christians in the United States and abroad would receive the sacrament on the same day, the first Sunday in October 1940.[22] It was hoped that a symbolic experience of Christian unity would make communicants conscious of their "spiritual oneness" with Christians around the world. The council distributed a prayer of intercession that called worshipers to be mindful of their fellow believers' sufferings and the unity they shared because of Christ's having suffered for all. Testimonies of profoundly moving moments came back from congregations. The next year there would be more still as the deteriorating diplomatic situation vis-à-vis Japan made it increasingly unlikely the United States would be staying out of the war. With the first of the many thousands of American men drafted came chaplains' testimonies of World Communion Sunday observed to great effect at training centers, bases, and even on ships at sea.

As the war entered its crisis in Russia and North Africa in late 1941, the Federal Council decided to send Cavert to Europe to gain firsthand knowledge of wartime conditions, demonstrate American concern, and assess what assistance World Council agencies needed for ministering to prisoners of war and refugees.[23] The planned tour was brought to President Roosevelt's attention, and on his endorsement the State Department expedited visas and secured a seat for Cavert on a transatlantic flight to depart on 9 December. With the bombing of Pearl Harbor on the 7th, Cavert postponed his trip.[24]

Strategy for a New International Order

Intervention no longer needed promoting, but now the issue of national sovereignty in the postwar international order had to be faced. The Federal Council gave its support to the war on the grounds of national defense and called the churches to take the lead in preparing the public for a "just and durable peace."[25] To get church leaders on board, Dulles's Commission on a Just and Durable Peace held a study conference on "the winning of the peace" in March 1942, at Ohio Wesleyan University in Delaware, Ohio.[26] The conference drew 377 participants, including representatives of many interdenominational state and city councils of churches. Sitting in four sections, respectively, on the political, economic, social, and ecclesiastical aspects, the conferees were led to endorse a set of "Guiding Principles" prepared in advance by Dulles's commission. The principles declared that the churches' work was based on the ecumenical premise that "it is the purpose of God to create a world-wide community in Jesus Christ, transcending nation, race and class." Moreover, the gospel's universality gave the churches a unique part to play in nurturing an international ethos. The "Guiding Principles" were well received in the churches. In seven months over ninety thousand copies were ordered.[27]

This did not satisfy the intellectuals who thought the conference did not probe deeply enough. Van Dusen, reviewing the conference for *Christendom*, saw three specific issues that should have been faced squarely but were not: "Who is to be responsible for the determination and maintenance of the peace? What principles should be intrinsic to the peace we seek? . . . How can they be translated from the realm of ideals into the decisions of statesmen and the policies of nations?"[28] The weakness in the conference agenda was the silence on the question of what kind of war America was entering. Dulles wanted to avoid making it an issue.[29] "Thus the conference was compelled to fly in the face of the most fundamental axiom," Van Dusen went on, "that the war and the peace to follow are organically related." Which country or countries won the war would determine the nature of the peace settlement. William Adams Brown, reviewing the conference in *Christendom*, pointed out that it had subjected a political issue to ethical testing, which was good, but it failed to show what the nature of the church had to do with winning the peace.[30] Van Dusen and Brown both had identified the heart of the matter, which had not been faced since the World Council project began: Whose would be the authoritative voice for a worldwide community in Jesus Christ? Dulles and his associates did not presume "the church transcendent" would be the *source* of truth at the center of the postwar order. They spoke instead of the churches being *instrumental* in building it. They had enough grasp of reality to limit themselves to saying what basic postwar arrangements would accord with a "Christian" order.

This was just what Secretary of State Cordell Hull was looking for. He had been cut out of the policy making for the wartime alliance and was devoting his time and staff at the State Department to projecting schemes for a postwar international order. From these study committees a small cadre of officials formed who, at the beginning of 1943, were prepared to respond to the British and Soviet London Forum proposing an internationally operated food and resources organization. By May they had worked out the governing principles of a Relief and Rehabilitation Administration. These were to be submitted for approval by the "United Nations" (the twenty-seven countries of the alliance), but first they were explained to congressional leaders by President Roosevelt and then—when that went off without trouble—released for public discussion.

At this juncture Dulles had his Commission on a Just and Durable Peace reissue the "Guiding Principles" in a popularized form to crystallize public support for America's entering a body like the League of Nations. He thought it would have to be sold as something essentially different from the failed League, something that American Christians had participated in building. Dulles reduced the "Guiding Principles" to what he called the "Six Pillars of Peace." They were six, one-sentence statements that outlined a program for the maintenance of peaceful international relations: continued collaboration of the Allied powers, international agreements for free trade, adaptable treaty structures, autonomy of subject peoples and decolonization, suppression of militarism, and preservation of human rights.

He went public with the text on 18 March at a luncheon in New York held for the occasion, and promotion of it went on the rest of the year.[31] A copy of the "Six Pillars" went to every Protestant chaplain in the armed forces. *Christianity and Crisis* featured a series of commentaries by prominent personalities.[32] The Federal Council issued an eighty-five-page study guide with background essays, charts, and typical discussion questions for Sunday school classes and church groups. Advance orders totaled eighteen thousand. Articles were placed in over a hundred newspapers across America. The London *Times* featured the text on its front page.[33] The easy acceptance of the "Six Pillars" was due in part to Dulles's language, subtly conciliating those who wanted radical, comprehensive organization of the peace from the start and those who preferred a gradual supplanting of national prerogatives by international arrangements.[34] With neither camp sniping at it, the average pastor or churchgoer found nothing alarming in the document.

To the contrary, the main Protestant denominations all had top-down campaigns under way in a matter of weeks to mobilize support for international organization among the membership. The Methodists, led by Bishop G. Bromley Oxnam, called it a "Crusade for a New World Order." For the first time since Prohibition the Methodists were spurred to one political task: to have every member write the president and Congress conveying his or her desire for international cooperation. Believing it necessary "to move from . . . public meetings to the local parish," the denomination's leaders enlisted their boards and agencies. The Board of Education revised its Sunday school curriculum for young people and adults; church publications of all kinds featured articles on the subject; and the Commission on Information had broadcasts over national radio networks. The Woman's Division and the Board of Lay Activities cooperated in a "two-by-two" home visitation program to present the case for international organization to each household, leaving behind a leaflet, *Your Part*, with instructions for writing letters to Washington. Some two million copies were distributed. Its slogan was: "The Peace May Be Won with a Three-Cent Stamp."[35]

Dulles's own Presbyterian Church (USA) was less methodical. A year earlier the church had adopted a pro forma statement at its General Assembly endorsing the Ohio Wesleyan principles of international organization, but nothing more had been done. When Dulles's "Six Pillars" came out, the denomination's Department of Social Education and Action had its subsidiaries at the presbytery and synod levels focus on the benefits of international organization and urge the membership to take political action. The General Assembly called for individuals to study and act on the "Six Pillars." The journal *Social Progress* ran features about congregations and presbyteries that had their members write or send telegrams to their senators in Washington.[36]

The Congregationalists and the Northern Baptists sponsored drives, too. On a designated Sunday, Congregational ministers presented a World

Order Compact modeled on the Mayflower Compact, by which their congregations pledged to work for "a just and cooperative world order" that would include an international organization to facilitate the "interdependent life of nations."[37] The Northern Baptist Convention simply recommended that its members write Washington supporting a "world organization in which every nation is invited to participate."

In the fall of 1943 the Federal Council boosted these efforts with a traveling preaching campaign billed as the Christian Mission on World Order.[38] It was run like a revival, featuring noted preachers engaged for the "evangelical" goal of reviving the faith necessary to undergird peace. It began on 28 October with an opening worship service at the Cathedral of St. John the Divine in New York, with five thousand attending. Dulles spoke, as did Senator Joseph Ball, who applauded the churches for spearheading the drive. *Life* magazine featured a photo essay about it. In three weeks nearly a hundred cities were visited, and over ninety clergy and lay speakers were involved.

The combined result was dramatic. An unprecedented volume of mail swamped Congress. Unlike all other such campaigns, there were few form letters; the vast majority were handwritten notes and postcards with simple, heartfelt declarations. Most said isolationism was unchristian and a policy of international cooperation was needed.

The "Six Pillars" came up for discussion in the presence of foreign churchmen in July 1943 at an International Roundtable of Christian Leaders sponsored jointly by the Commission on a Just and Durable Peace and the United Church of Canada and held at Princeton.[39] Besides the churchmen of North America there were five Chinese, a Russian, and several German and Japanese exiles. Two Australians came on a bomber provided by General Douglas MacArthur. The roundtable endorsed the "Six Pillars" and went beyond them, adding some specifics required for progress toward world order. But the "Six Pillars" was still the consensus document of the American churches. Dulles and his associates wanted the churches to regard it as a yardstick for measuring governments' projects for the postwar era.[40]

Meanwhile, Secretary of State Cordell Hull had been pushing a plan for a postwar United Nations Organization empowered to use force if necessary to preserve international peace, a "Town Meeting of the World" where the smaller countries would be admitted on an equal footing with the powerful. Roosevelt was taken with the notion. So was Senator Arthur Vandenberg, ranking Republican minority member of the Foreign Relations Committee, only recently a die-hard isolationist. With his backing, the Senate undoubtedly would go along. The hurdle was to get the Russians aboard. When Roosevelt broached the project at Tehran in November, Soviet leader Joseph Stalin's opinion was that if Russia, Britain, and the United States wanted to keep the world at peace they had the power to do so and had no need for others' permission. The principled Roosevelt would not contemplate this. Nor could Senator Vandenberg's support have been counted on with any such desertion of the internationalist principle for which he now was on record. It was agreed to negotiate an arrangement at the foreign-ministry level before the leaders next met.

Convened at the Dumbarton Oaks estate in Washington in August 1944, the Prevention of War Conference did manage to settle all but the one article of the United Nations Charter that would let the organization act against any one of the powers that belonged as a Permanent Member of the Security Council. The Soviet negotiator rejected the U.S. draft principle that a permanent member involved in a dispute must abstain from voting on measures to resolve it. The issue was left for an endgame settlement, but when informal soundings of the Soviet position on compromise proposals came back with unsatisfactory results, the negotiators became absorbed by the point and spent the balance of the six-week meeting fruitlessly. Hull's last card was to inform the Soviets he would have no choice but to tell the American people the conference failed, and that could cost Roosevelt reelection that fall. The Soviets called the bluff. The closing communiqué was self-congratulatory, and Roosevelt's public statement said the results of the conference gave him a feeling of full satisfaction, even amazement, that on such a difficult problem so much had been accomplished in so little time. But could more have been? Dulles and his ecumenist associates were not satisfied.

Afterward the State Department received many messages from civic and religious organizations conveying their assessment and advice regarding the Dumbarton Oaks proposals. As expected, the Dunbarton Oaks agreement drew commentary from the Commission on a Just and Durable Peace. The State Department surveyed the messages, then arranged a series of meetings with the leading groups responsible as part of the education campaign to swing public opinion behind Dumbarton Oaks.[41] The first was on 16 October 1944, led by Under Secretary Edward R. Stettinius. Among the groups represented were the Rotary Club, the League of Women Voters, the National Association for the Advancement of Colored People, and the American Bar Association. Walter Van Kirk attended for the Commission on a Just and Durable Peace. Stettinius assured these representatives that the State Department would "welcome every constructive suggestion" for the unresolved points of the Dumbarton Oaks draft agreement.

The Commission on a Just and Durable Peace took up the invitation, reviewing the draft at a conference in Cleveland on 16–19 January 1945.[42] The usual organizing went on beforehand, with two study commissions drawn up: one under Harvard professor W. E. Hocking, examining the Bretton Woods and Dumbarton Oaks agreements in light of the "Six Pillars of Peace"; the other, chaired by Oberlin professor and Theological Discussion Group member Walter M. Horton, going further in identifying the problems of peace the churches would face in the coming years and the churches' continuing role in generating public support for the postwar international arrangements. When the conference convened, five hundred strong, the discussion emerging from the Hocking and Horton reports found that the Dumbarton Oaks draft did not measure up to the "Six Pillars" but was "good enough to support as a first step" toward world order.[43] Nine proposed amendments were adopted, which included the following steps: an explicit statement of intent to develop and codify international law, and create an agency for hastening decolonization; provisions for prompt disarmament, the protection of smaller nations against subjection to the mighty, and for membership eventually to be universal; establishment of a Commission on Human Rights and Fundamental Freedoms in addition to the proposed Economic and Social Council to uphold the sacred worth of the individual and protect the free exercise of religion; and above all, a declaration in the preamble that the purpose of the international body was to promote human welfare and worldwide justice. These details brought the Dumbarton Oaks draft in line with the "Six Pillars." It remained to get them confirmed by having the amendments accepted in the final diplomatic round.

At the Yalta Conference in February between the Allied leaders, the Soviets conceded on the issue of voting in the United Nations, accepting that a permanent member would abstain when party to a dispute before the Security Council. The deadlock broken, it was agreed to finish the United Nations Charter at a conference to convene in San Francisco on 25 April. The United States delegation would include the bipartisan leadership of the Senate Foreign Relations Committee, Vandenberg, the ranking Republican, and Tom Connally, the Democratic chairman. Among the few delegation advisers enlisted was John Foster Dulles as assistant to Senator Vandenberg. Accepting the position, Dulles resigned from the Federal Council to avoid the appearance of conflicting interest.[44]

The delegation had to decide whether to have an advisory committee of representatives from sympathetic civic and religious groups to secure public support for the United Nations.[45] There were objections, but Roosevelt himself thought such a committee would be expedient. The

State Department identified forty-two individuals, "a fair cross-section of citizen groups," among them Van Kirk, Methodist Bishop James C. Baker, and Dr. O. Frederick Nolde, dean of the Graduate School at the Lutheran Theological Seminary in Philadelphia. Hope ran high for San Francisco, suffusing even the Senate. When Vandenberg finished his closing remarks before setting out, the members rose to their feet on both sides of the aisle, applauding (in violation of Senate rules), and surged forward to shake his hand and embrace him and Connally.[46]

The San Francisco conference of the United Nations opened with a minute of silence for solemn meditation.[47] Amendments to the Dumbarton Oaks draft charter were considered by the appropriate "technical" committees assigned to deal with the respective sections of the charter. Proposals had come from many sources, but those from the American religious organizations were particularly successful. Four of the nine submitted by the Commission on a Just and Durable Peace entered the final document: a preambulatory statement of the moral aims of the United Nations Organization; a commitment to develop a body of customary international law; a Trusteeship Council to move colonial peoples toward self-government; and a declaration of fundamental human rights over which there was much haggling to accommodate Soviet and South African objections.[48] When the conference ended three months later, President Harry Truman personally carried the United Nations Charter from San Francisco to Washington and presented it to the Senate for ratification. The political and public groundwork having been laid, it met with speedy passage.

While it is impossible to say that public opinion shifted toward international organization because more Americans now considered it a religious matter, it was certainly sold as such, coming through the churches' educational programs and campaigns, ultimately informed by the theology proposed in the Theological Discussion Group. These theologians' realist analysis of the causes of the world crisis, particularly their ideas about corporate sinfulness and their rejection of the inevitability of progress, translated directly into advocacy for political measures to check governments that would violate basic human rights and the sovereignty of weaker countries. The United Nations Charter did not satisfy all of their requirements in this respect, but it did establish a structure for thwarting sinful aggression through collective international action. This, plus the welfare apparatus of the United Nations Organization, made it acceptable to Protestant Americans as the beginning of a Christian means for fighting evil on an international scale. That acceptance resonated from the theologians to the churches at a time when the country was being lectured by the secular establishment to regard the United Nations as a triumph of reason and the hope of humankind. The churches' endorsement was likely to have reinforced that message in many a Protestant's mind, if not elevating it for a brief while to crusade status.

Voicing a Shared Theology

Though for momentarily expedient reasons discussion about the church had disappeared from the theologians' work on behalf of the United Nations, the theologians did not neglect it in the more "purely" theological projects they undertook at the same time. While they devoted much of their wartime effort to the Commission on a Just and Durable Peace, they also engaged in an inquiry stemming from the Oxford and Edinburgh conferences and tried to answer the specifically theological questions raised by the war.

The subject of the church had first claim on their attention. While the war precluded working with their counterparts in Europe, the American Committee of Faith and Order—which included Theological Discussion Group members Van Dusen, Walter M. Horton, and Harvie Branscomb—made an initial survey of the American denominations' beliefs and practices regarding intercommunion and open communion.[49] To stimulate the Europeans to do the same kind of survey when the situation there would permit, secretary Leonard Hodgson arranged for the American material to be translated into German and French. The American Committee issued a report delineating "principle areas of agreement" and "divergent conceptions" about the nature of the church. Unlike previous studies and ones that followed, it did not avoid presenting disagreements over the sensitive matter of the standards of authority for determining doctrine and church polity. It also laid out the vicissitudes of unity and diversity in Christian history and described the contemporary spectrum of thought about the social function of the organized church. But the report did not produce anything new. It papered over the sharp disagreements about the legitimacy of each communion's clergy and the validity of their sacraments, and it did not propose lines of inquiry for uncovering the origin of these differences.[50]

Similar productions came out of Life and Work. The Provisional Committee of the World Council, which had taken over the executive functions of Life and Work, commissioned its Study Department to explore "The Living Church in Modern Society," focusing on "the ethical reality and function of the church."[51] The terms of reference for the project restricted it to two safe questions: What influence should the church expect to have on the character of civilization and the ethical decisions of its members? And what should the church's strategy be to influence institutions and the spiritual climate of the world? This narrowed the scope to investigating the social-instrumental nature of the church, preventing discussion of the sensitive matter of the church's essence and the legitimate ways for its truth to find expression.

What prompted the project was an essay from Visser 't Hooft in Geneva about the ecumenists' hope for a "new Christendom." He maintained that it was wrong to work for the goal of a Christian civilization, a *Corpus Christianum*, whether in the medieval form or a post-Reformation Christian state. Such attempts in the past were based on self-deception, not on strong biblical and theological grounds. The right alternative was the Body of Christ, the *Corpus Christi*, which was the authentic New Testament concept of the church. Such a church, he said, claims responsibility for its members' actions in the world but only indirectly uplifts civilization. Though Visser 't Hooft thought it vital that the church build up the world, it had to be independent of the world to succeed in doing so. This ran contrary to the direction American theology was taking as it became apologetic, trying to be appealing in persuading Americans to accept international organization in both the secular and religious realms. John Bennett got the Visser 't Hooft essay first, found it provocative, and sent it along to Van Dusen, who had it circulated to the American participants in the World Council preparatory study.

One copy went to Edwin Aubrey's newly formed Chicago Discussion Group, the second offshoot of the New Haven mother group (Bennett's Pacific Coast Theological Discussion Group being the first).[52] Everybody in Aubrey's group regarded Visser 't Hooft as unduly pessimistic, and felt he went too far in his extremely sharp separation of the church and the world. Viewing the essay as a challenge begging a reply, they drafted one for a World Council study conference at Toronto in June 1941. The Chicago group's statement called for optimism and asserted that the church could and should seek to build a new Christendom, though without the naïve illusions of the past, which had produced the false claims that one's civilization was Christian. Such folly would be precluded if Christians lived by the same ethical principles in the world as they did in the church, though at times this would put them at odds with the prevailing mores of society, if not the state regime. For Visser 't Hooft such dissidence was the point, the church's exit route from the world—understandable for a man whose country was under German occupation but not helpful for all that because it was stated in sweeping generalities.

Meanwhile, the Theological Discussion Group proceeded with its examination of Christian doctrine. As individuals and collectively, they were working at a systematic theology, not just responding to the current events in Europe but having in mind that those events were symptomatic of a deeper problem which they believed could be addressed only theologically. Following the 1937 international conferences there were retreats on the Holy Spirit, the relation between grace and nature, eschatology, and Christian ethics. New members were drafted as the topic required: Angus Dun, a theologian and dean of the Episcopal Theological Seminary in Cambridge, Massachusetts; Theodore M. Greene, a professor of philosophy at Princeton University; Harvie Branscomb, a professor of New Testament at Duke; and John Knox, a professor of New Testament at Chicago. Their discussions and that of the satellite groups all tended to the same conclusions now. This prompted Van Dusen to remark to Bennett: "Interesting, isn't it that the differences between Yale, Union, Princeton, Chicago and San Francisco are diminishing so that they may shortly appear indistinguishable?"[53]

To articulate their growing awareness of this consensus, Van Dusen induced the Theological Discussion Group to put together a book. In the introduction he wrote for it, he made their common perception explicit: the members of the group "have sensed a movement of conviction among them toward a consensus, none the less real because difficult to define."[54] It seemed part of a worldwide phenomenon, a convergence among leading Christian thinkers everywhere, though one that had "not yet achieved definition." It was by now typical of Van Dusen and his associates to set themselves the task of giving it definition. Initially, the book was to have four chapters, each assigned to the four university centers where the members were clustered—New York, Princeton, New Haven, and Chicago.[55]

Plans changed in the spring of 1943 when several group members were engaged to do a study for the Federal Council defining the church's role in wartime. Forming an interdenominational commission, their mandate was to produce a theory about the appropriate role without specifying policy that would constrain the member denominations.[56] Of the twenty-five participants, eighteen were members of the Theological Discussion Group, including the chairman, Robert L. Calhoun.[57] Cavert, the Federal Council general secretary, was ex officio director.[58]

The methodology for both the book and the Federal Council study was as important as the findings. The content of Christian faith was expounded by analyzing the most urgent questions the churches were facing, each issue being sharpened and deepened until the essence of the problem was reached and appropriate answers could "unavoidably" be discerned in Christian revelation. This method was akin to Tillich's evolving "method of correlation," proceeding on the assumption that existential and theological questions were interdependent and begged theological answers. The group organized the book, "correlating" the contents of each chapter with an underlying question:

1. Alternative Diagnoses of, and Remedies for, the Present Situation
   (Why Take Christianity Seriously?)
2. Bases of Christian Belief
   (Is Christian Belief Intellectually Honest?)
3. The Content of the Christian Gospel
   (What Has Christianity to Offer?)
4. Christianity in Action
   (What Does Christianity Propose, and How Can It Become Effective?)[59]

They expected the theology that they would develop in answer would "be related very clearly to the questions that are urgent in the existing situation."[60] Work on the book and the Federal Council study ran simultaneously, treated in consecutive meetings at their usual weekend retreats.[61]

The group finished the Federal Council project first and released it in November 1944. "The Relation of the Church to the War in the Light of the Christian Faith" emphasized that to make sense of the war, Christians must interpret the phenomena Christocentrically, in light of the Trinity. The document declared: *The primary ground for a distinctive Christian understanding of any situation is the revelation of God in Jesus Christ* (emphasis in original).[62] God's specific relation to the war was described in Trinitarian terms as "Creator," "Redeemer," and "Life-Giver." Addressing the "Creator" aspect first, the authors asked rhetorically whether war is a natural fact, a punitive act of God, or, as they saw it, the result of humankind's sinful choices. As for "Redeemer," they explored how the concepts of judgment and forgiveness fit in war. "Is war itself a Golgotha," they asked, "and suffering humanity a new embodiment of the crucified Redeemer?" The answer was both yes and no. Yes, because good soldiers die so others may have more life, war is crucifixion; but no, for unlike Jesus' death, fatalities in war are not of a piece with the ultimate source of salvation in him. In addressing God's role as "Life-Giver," they said that in wartime God nurtures believers' faith so they become more devoted and better people. "This is the Spirit's work of sanctification," the authors asserted, "springing from God's redemptive love, and issuing in human life transformed, redirected, with new dimensions in which to grow."

In the closing theological argument they asked, Is war a recurring inevitability? The answer was unequivocally no. The church had work to do to prevent future wars. Institutional change must accompany individuals' regeneration and subsequent reeducation; the church, as God's instrument, was the agent of that change. As an ecumenical institution it was to show the world that all people have a transcendent kinship with each other despite the diversity of nationality, race, class, and sex. The importance of the ecumenical movement in advancing the church's reconciliatory work was underscored by the title of the conclusion, "The Church as the Nucleus for World Community." By ending this way, promoting the church's role in the new internationalism, the theologians emphasized the sociopolitical nature of the church. The price, however, was a loosening of their conceptions of it from its theological moorings. This emphasis on "function of the church" became institutionalized as World War II brought on new practical tasks, obscuring and narrowing discussion about the nature of the church.

When the report appeared in November, several journals of religion reprinted portions of it; the Congregationalists' *Social Action* published it in its entirety.[63] *Christianity and Crisis*, unabashedly praising its own editors' handiwork, ventured that the report would "be an important landmark in the development of an ecumenical theology in America"—this despite the authors having repeatedly called for critical distance to prevent error stemming from overconfidence in one's own judgment. Consensus was on their side. The handful of journals that gave the study extensive coverage were already sympathetic and did not carry dissenting reviews.[64]

The Theological Discussion Group finished its collaborative book shortly thereafter, calling it *The Christian Answer*.[65] It distilled their common theological position, the consummation of what Van Dusen had anticipated eleven years before when he convened them for the first time. The subthemes were by now familiar: "the character of the crisis which grips contemporary culture," "the necessity of Christianity for its resolution," and "the essential answer of Christian faith to this crisis."[66] The book reiterated much of what the group wrote for the Federal Council study. Methodologically descended from what members had done since their student days, the group's "method of collaboration" corresponded to their substantive goals: their collegiality was expressly a model of the process they hoped nations would adopt in implementing international organization in the United Nations.

Ecumenical Strategy for a New International Order

Consistent with their commitment to advance the new internationalism along ecclesial as well as secular lines, the American theologians worked for the institutional development of the World Council during the war. They believed it would be a key agency in building a new Europe. Even the limited contacts Geneva had with the ecumenical leaders in German-occupied Europe somewhat blessedly relieved their isolation and prepared them to join in the "rehabilitation" as soon as Allied forces arrived. Contacts resumed between the American and British church communities first. When William Temple was elected archbishop of Canterbury in the spring of 1942, four Americans attended his enthronement, among them Henry Smith Leiper, representing the World Council Provisional Committee.[67] While in Britain Leiper met with Faith and Order secretary Leonard Hodgson to discuss their similar duties as World Council secretaries. He spent an afternoon at Lambeth Palace talking with Temple, Visser 't Hooft, and William Paton about how to resurrect the disrupted plans for launching the World Council.[68]

Leiper also prepared the way for Dulles and Van Kirk to meet the British counterpart of their Commission on a Just and Durable Peace. The meeting took place at Balliol College, Oxford, later that summer.[69] On the British side were Archbishop Temple, Bishop Bell, and Professor Arnold Toynbee. The Americans and British found they were in agreement about the postwar world order needing a spiritual foundation, but there were individual differences of opinion about how the United States and Britain should dominate in the international community. Dulles also used the trip to make personal contacts, meeting in London with Foreign Secretary Anthony Eden and Deputy Prime Minister Clement Atlee.

In September 1942, just before the Germans occupied Vichy France, Cavert made the European trip he had planned before Pearl Harbor. He went via Lisbon to Geneva to discuss relief and reconstruction with the World Council staff and to attend the meeting of the Provisional Committee.[70] Both the American and European sides wanted to be in a position to begin work immediately when the war was over. Cavert proposed that a central agency be formed to coordinate the churches' efforts. The World Council staff seemed the natural vehicle: it was already in contact with the churches in occupied Europe, even the Orthodox in the Balkans, and could tap into the post–World War I relief network that had been inherited by Life and Work.[71] Cavert and Visser 't Hooft drew up the blueprint for an ecumenical relief organization, operating through national agencies, in which "all churches which could help would help all churches which needed help."[72] It would aim at more than physical restoration of buildings and congregations; the goal was to prepare churches for their vanguard role in the new world order. But the implementation of these plans would have to wait two and a half years, until the Allied armies liberated Europe.

Even before the fighting ended in the spring of 1945, the World Council arranged the first return visit to North America by European members of the Provisional Committee. Arriving in New York three days after Germany surrendered in May, Visser 't Hooft, Marc Boegner, and Bishop Bell of Chichester came to stir interest in the World Council, raise money, and recruit for the Geneva staff.[73] They also wanted to make Americans aware of how it was to live in a devastated society and how spiritually changed their countries were because of the war.[74]

While in New York Visser 't Hooft met with John D. Rockefeller, Jr. Leiper arranged for them to be introduced at a dinner hosted by Wall Street financier Thomas Lamont, an Episcopalian.[75] Rockefeller invited Visser 't Hooft to his office the next day, where they discussed the World Council's future. Rockefeller, keenly interested in the idea of establishing an educational ecumenical institute, asked Visser 't Hooft for a memorandum laying out the project. Visser 't Hooft penned one on the spot, but, being used to operating on a shoestring during the war, he projected a budget Rockefeller thought far too modest. Rockefeller gave him a million dollars—half for the World Council institute and half for the reconstruction of European church life.

At an interview with the Federal Council Executive Committee the Europeans requested that Cavert be loaned to them for six months to help the Geneva staff expand its operations.[76] Hearing reluctance from the committee, Bishop Bell remarked it would be a sign of genuine American commitment to the World Council, and, as Cavert was so well respected in Britain, his appointment would stir hope and enthusiasm in a people exhausted by war. That was persuasive. Cavert was granted leave at full pay.

He reached Geneva in mid-September and a month later went to Stuttgart with the World Council delegation attending the first meeting of the newly formed Council of the Evangelical Church of Germany.[77] They went hoping to restore fellowship with the Germans, but they were in a quandary about how to do it. "On the one hand," Visser 't Hooft recalled, "we could not make confession of guilt the condition for a restoration of fellowship, for such a confession could only have value as a spontaneous gesture; on the other hand, the obstacles of fellowship could only be removed if a clear word were spoken." The solution was proposed by the French clergyman Pierre Maury, who suggested they say to the Germans, "We have come to ask you to help us to help you." The evening they arrived they attended a special worship service. Martin Niemöller, a leader in the persecuted Confessing Church, preached on Jeremiah 14:7–11: "Though our iniquities testify against us, act, O Lord, for Thy name's sake. . . ." He and Bishop Otto Dibelius tactfully invited reconciliation by both acknowledging their own country's wrong, each confessing the failure of their church as a whole to resist.[78] This "Stuttgart Declaration" allayed the anxiety of the World Council observers and made it possible for them to recommend the Germans resume participation in the ecumenical movement. This freed the World Council to proceed in aiding the reconstruction of the German churches. It also marked the first instance of German society returning to the international community on an equal footing with the victors. The act was fully in the spirit of the ecumenical movement, and, paralleling the establishment of the United Nations a few months earlier, appeared to the ecumenical theologians to be a crucial step toward their sought-after international order.

The American theologians had played the main supporting role by putting that order on the public agenda in their country. Based on their ideas about sin, its nationalist manifestations, and the Christian imperative for peace, they derived a moral equation that required institutionalized international cooperation as its solution. Halting governments' aggression, preserving human rights, and providing large-scale relief operations could be accomplished in this way. These leaders had harmonized their theology and politics with American realities both in their scholarly work and in public action, setting forth the theological foundations of international engagement. They had successfully pushed American church life and high political circles in the direction they thought necessary, and had begun to do the same for European Protestantism. As a result, they had proved themselves a force in shaping American attitudes. They had moved a churchgoing nation to demand peacetime international cooperation, and in so doing revived the authority of Protestantism to define a mission for America.

SEVEN

From the Center to the Margins
1945–1948

THE REALIST THEOLOGIANS HAD successfully drawn together politics, ecumenism, and theology into a plan of action, but one task remained: to attend to the birth of the World Council of Churches. After the war, however, their influence on the ecumenical movement was blunted as the churches and World Council staff prepared to take over in accord with the World Council constitution drawn up at Utrecht in 1938. The American theologians knew their centrality in the council would be temporary, but nonetheless they gave themselves to the task of bringing it into existence, in the belief that it would be the vehicle to bring the churches' spiritual power and political influence to bear on the new international order. They set the agenda for the first World Council assembly with this in mind, and then submitted to the transfer of control to the church bureaucracies despite having misgivings about the character of leadership that would result. New voices—especially women's voices—were calling for a share of the leadership and the intellectual authority to set the movement's course. Still, the generation who kept together in the Theological Discussion Group had the satisfaction of seeing their intellectual brainchild come to fruition: they had built a consensus that was holding, one broad enough to encompass a diversity of communions yet with a distinct enough mission to give it cohesion. Amid the postwar disorder and chaos in Europe and Asia, they exited as they had entered the scene a quarter of a century earlier, seeking to fulfill what they believed was God's design: "that they all may be one."

Preparations for the First Assembly

By the end of the war the World Council assembly was technically four years overdue. This was the business before the Provisional Committee meeting at Geneva on 21–23 February 1946. There, long-parted colleagues greeted each other with sober joy.[1] Their reunion made them feel acute loss over those absent: Temple, Brown, and others had died of natural causes; Bonhoeffer had been hanged for his involvement in the failed June 1944 assassination attempt on Hitler. Some had survived years in prison. Martin Niemöller and Norwegian bishop Eivind Berggrav were deeply moved seeing each other alive and well after their release. When Niemöller met Temple's successor, Geoffrey Fisher, they grinned and all but embraced, then began chatting about the situation of the church in Germany.[2]

This first convocation began with a thanksgiving service in the Cathedral of St. Pierre. Spectators thronged in to see the procession of delegates extending the length of the nave.[3] The colors of their vestments reflected the variety of religious traditions represented. Archbishop Geoffrey Fisher and Swiss pastor Dr. Alphons Koechlin offered the prayers of intercession in English, the hymns were sung in French, and Archbishop Germanos read the New Testament in Greek. There were short sermons, by Chester Miao of China, Berggrav, and Niemöller. All three spoke of the life and work of the church that could not be thwarted by the war, and of the penitence, humility, and renewal that were now reuniting Christians. Berggrav confessed the trepidation he had felt about their reunion. "I wondered," he said,

> what it would be like to meet Christians from all over the world. My surprise was that it is no surprise . . . because in these last years we have lived more intimately with each other. . . . We prayed together more, we listened together more to the Word of God, our hearts were together more. This is only the manifestation of what we knew already, that today God has not a weak World Church, but one founded on Himself. The time is past when the world-wide fellowship of Christians was only an experiment. . . . During the war Christ has said to us, "My Christians, you are one."[4]

The Provisional Committee convened for business the next day, Boegner presiding. Three proposals expanding the council's operation were quickly approved: refugee relief operations, a church organization devoted to international politics, and World Council membership.[5] The committee approved a continuation of financial support for displaced persons, adequate relief provisions for them, the advocacy of asylum claims for those swept up in population transfers, and unequivocal protest against persistent anti-Semitism. It also decided to create an agency to monitor nations' foreign policies and promote the council's interests, the Churches Commission on International Affairs (CCIA). Its first task was to coordinate the American Commission on a Just and Durable Peace with counterpart groups elsewhere, starting with an organizing conference that summer. On membership, the number of acceptances received had grown to ninety-two but with few of the Orthodox churches replying. Visser 't Hooft, pointing out from his experience that personal contact worked wonders, suggested sending a delegation to encourage them.[6]

The meeting then passed to the main item on the agenda, the assembly. The date, place, and theme had to be set and responsibilities assigned for the preparations.[7] The committee had difficulty with the date because its first choice, 1948, conflicted with other planned church gatherings, chiefly the Anglicans' Lambeth Conference. Moreover, because the war had badly depleted the European churches' resources, committee members feared many would be unable to afford sending delegates to more than one. But the desire to take advantage of the worldwide hope in ecumenical internationalism outweighed the financial considerations, and 1948 was chosen. The location posed more of a problem. Before the war, the Provisional Committee had planned to hold the assembly in Washington, D.C., but now the Europeans felt a European site would spare them the expense of transatlantic fares for their delegations. Others wanted the site not to be in an English-speaking country because the movement was turning out to be dominated by English speakers. The Americans pressed for staying with the original plan, arguing that appreciable public support (and funds) would be generated only if the assembly were held in the States. The debate was not amicable. Cavert moved to defer the decision until the next meeting and to hold that meeting in the United States. His motion carried.[8]

Adopting the theme for the assembly was easier. "Man's Disorder and God's Design" expressed the common conviction that the church's task was to place "*world reconstruction in a totally different perspective by announcing . . . that God Himself is at work rebuilding His own order amid the disorder of man*" (emphasis in original).[9] Four subthemes were elaborated to reflect the different agendas encompassed by the World Council: "The Universal Church in God's Design" (Faith and Order's interest in the theology of the church); "The Church's Witness to God's Design" (the International Missionary Council's evangelistic work); "The Church and the Disorder of Society" (Life and Work's social preoccupation); and the "Church and International Disorder" (the concern of the soon-to-be-established CCIA). This focus on the church as the point at which public life meets God's intention for public life had been a central theme of the Theological Discussion Group during the war. The committee charged the World Council Study Department, still headed by Van Dusen, to conduct a preparatory study on this theme, "at least equalling" the ones for Oxford and Edinburgh, so delegates could "grasp afresh God's design."

The meeting then passed to the nomination of a new president to fill the vacancy caused by the death of Archbishop Temple. This raised the question of leadership, which Van Dusen had identified several years earlier as the determining issue for the council's future. There had already been much discussion of it before the meeting. The Geneva staff and Cavert favored Temple's successor, Archbishop Geoffrey Fisher, because he could secure Anglican participation worldwide and be an intermediary to the Orthodox. But the British delegation preferred Van Dusen! As there was no consensus, it was decided to have a five-man collegial presidency, making the office more symbolic, its powers reduced to that of a parliamentary chairmanship. The five selected were Boegner, Mott, Archbishop Germanos, Archbishop Fisher, and Archbishop Eidem of Uppsala.[10] Cavert would head the Arrangements Committee, the real power that would set the procedure for the assembly and assign delegates to study groups and commissions.[11] Van Dusen had already been made chairman of the preparatory study. With the power of the presidency no longer vested in one person, the helm was in the hands of General Secretary Visser 't Hooft and the committee chairmen, particularly Cavert and Van Dusen. But now that William Adams Brown was dead, there was no one of his stature to bridge the interests of Faith and Order and Life and Work, so the impact of America's theological heavyweights was going to be diminished once these bodies came together. Moreover, their appointments were only temporary, to last through the assembly.

The meeting ended on an ambivalent note of anticipation. Boegner led in prayer, giving thanks to God for what the Provisional Committee had accomplished, asking for steadfastness in faith as the members parted, and petitioning for help in their work. One member recalled that as Boegner spoke they all felt the poignancy of the occasion and looked forward with hope and fear to what lay ahead.[12]

Under Van Dusen the Study Department aimed to prepare the delegates for the assembly with four volumes of essays, one on each of the subthemes approved by the Provisional Committee. Van Dusen and the staff believed the assembly's success would depend on the quality of the work, as Oxford and Edinburgh had. They replicated what had been done for Oxford, setting up national study groups and engaging hundreds of scholars around the world. Because participants were scattered across the globe and could not meet, much of the essay review was done through the mail. Van Dusen gave the reviewers four critical questions to be used as standards: "(a) does the paper give a first-rate contribution to the particular subject . . . ? (b) are there important elements . . . which the paper fails to deal with? (c) on what major points does the paper give a false, inadequate, or obscure, or misleading exposition . . . ? (d) what helpful suggestions have you . . . [regarding] presentation and style?" Above all, in the spirit of Christian collegiality, he urged them to "speak the truth with love."[13]

Naturally, Van Dusen enlisted his associates in the Theological Discussion Group to write some of the essays: John Bennett, Reinhold and H. Richard Niebuhr, Wilhelm Pauck, Paul Tillich, Edwin Aubrey, Georgia Harkness, and Walter Horton.[14] They reviewed each other's papers and wrote additional essays on themes the assembly would discuss but were not specifically assigned to any of them. Oldham consulted the group about his paper, like he did before Oxford—this time his subject was "Technics and Civilization" for the volume on the church and the disorder of society.[15]

Meanwhile, a separate commission worked on the Faith and Order volume. The authors were instructed to focus on "The Authority and Significance of the Social and Political Message of the Bible Today," the American Section having laid the groundwork in a wartime study on the standard of authority for ecclesiology—a sensitive assignment in view of the problem with authority avoided since Oxford and Edinburgh.[16] The commission sponsored a conference in the summer of 1947 at the newly established Ecumenical Institute in Bossey, Switzerland, obtained with Rockefeller's gift to W. A. Visser 't Hooft. The meeting brought Reformed and Lutheran scholars together to discuss the assembly theme. As Van Dusen had discerned three years earlier, a rapprochement was under way among the Europeans akin to the consensus that had formed among his American peers. It surfaced in an exchange between the Swiss Reformed theologian Karl Barth and the Swedish Lutheran Anders Nygren over the nature of revelation and its political message. At one point Barth declared, "'If that is Lutheran, then I am Lutheran,' and Nygren responded, 'If that is Reformed, then I am Reformed.'" The people in the room were stunned. An American present thought it meant that the differences between European and American theologians would also diminish as they moved toward a common perspective in which appeal to Scripture was the primary authority in dealing with the churches' variant confessional statements.[17] This was a narrowing of the issue, but no one seemed to mind. Focusing the assembly on scriptural authority rather than the authorities interpreting Scripture would have the same salubrious effect as the "Christocentric" focus did at the prewar ecumenical conferences, allowing the process to go forward and not bog down over the authoritative status of the churches.

The rapprochement, however, did not carry over to the politics of the organization. The conflict over leadership reemerged. There was mutual respect and cooperation among those participating in the study, but not between the chairman, Van Dusen, and the study staff working from the Geneva headquarters. As early as 1939, Van Dusen had disagreed with Nils Ehrenström, the staff director, over what "equal representation" meant in sponsoring studies. To Van Dusen it meant parity of Continental, British, and American participation, the same number of theologians engaged from each of the three geographical areas. Ehrenström interpreted it to mean parity representation of the various European schools of thought, which would have given the Europeans far greater weight.[18]

During the war the issue faded from view until it was scarcely noticed, but it was never taken off the agenda, a latent flash point for a transatlantic leadership struggle. It resurfaced in subtle ways during 1946. Van Dusen considered resigning, complaining he was not as near the center of ecumenical "theology" (i.e., policy) as he had been recently.[19] Two years later, frustrated at being frozen out of the World Council provisional administrative structure, he wrote to alarm Visser 't Hooft. The bureaucrat was becoming the leadership type for the council's future, "ecclesiastical wheelhorses," who would take the positions as a career step instead of "the ablest," people like himself who had given the movement its sharp theological and political edge.[20] He had reason to be concerned. The Geneva office had issued statements filled with vacuous platitudes. J. H. Oldham remarked to Bennett: "What I object to, and what many of the best of the younger generation react against, is the facile formulation of pious aspirations . . . to which ecclesiastical bodies are prone."[21] Language style was part and parcel of the contest for power between the administrators and those theologians they had marginalized since the Utrecht conference. Stifling his fears, Van Dusen continued to head the study program. He even turned down an offer to be president of Smith College in order to devote himself to it.

The Role of Women

Though most of the preparatory study simply picked up where the Oxford and Edinburgh programs left off, a new area began to be explored, the life and work of women in the church. Advocacy of women's views, particularly their role in the churches' leadership and their special theological concerns, implied that something was amiss with the dominance of the Americans who had seemed to encompass so adequately a broad range of theological and social outlooks in their theology. Not only was the Theological Discussion Group core being marginalized in the World Council, it was now getting its first dose of the intellectual challenge that would push the group in the 1960s and '70s to make Christian internationalism inclusive of causes striving for recognition, women's first of all.

The project started as the brainchild of Twila Lytton Cavert. A graduate of Ohio Wesleyan, she had served as a missionary, taught and administered college, and married Samuel McCrea Cavert. As a member of the National Board of the YWCA she learned that the YWCA had carried out extensive surveys of women's involvement in the church. She urged Visser 't Hooft to use the data in planning the program of the World Council assembly. He responded by inviting her to design and circulate her own questionnaire on the subject crafted for World Council purposes.[22]

Women's advance in American and European society during the war made such a survey timely. The mass induction of men into the military had opened lines of work previously closed to women. They entered the professions and headed numerous voluntary associations, including religious bodies. Some now feared that with the men returning the women would be relegated to their prewar roles.[23] Their suspicions of the war's horrors lent urgency to their thinking about the kind of world they wanted for their children. These factors and their implications for the church unity movement stimulated Twila Cavert's curiosity and made her resolve to carry out the project.

Van Dusen and the Study Department did not throw up obstacles, and Cavert got help from many sides: the offices of the national interdenominational agencies, executives of Protestant and Orthodox communions, councils of churches, and councils of church women. Churches in fifty-eight countries participated. Based on the questionnaire she drafted, Cavert collected the first comprehensive set of data about women's involvement in local churches, their leadership in denominational life, and their positions in church hierarchies. It brought to light their new roles and increased effectiveness in traditional ones, the rules and practices conditioning their participation, and the growing number of women who served on local and national councils of churches.

A preliminary report was released at an ecumenical "all-women's" conference in March 1948.[24] Twila Cavert presented it, pointing out that many personal stories, letters, and diaries had accompanied the returned questionnaires, and that from these it was learned many women felt extremely dissatisfied with their status in the church, or rather, their lack of it. They wanted to be judged for their abilities, experience, and education, not automatically assigned to "ladies aid" slots. Many expressed frustration over the lack of vocational opportunity and the nonrecognition of their talents. Few churches ordained women. Volunteers wanted formal acknowledgment of their services. Professional women felt they had lower status in the church than they did in society. But, all told, women would not have the men assume that their church roles would be the same as their domestic ones. The data suggested they viewed the church as a kind of community that differed essentially from secular society.

The "all-women's" conference endorsed a statement directed to the World Council. It called for women to be given more responsibilities in the new body, for the appointment of more women to the council's study commissions and major committees, and for the council to take initiatives in fostering the exchange of ideas among church women and establishing a worldwide women's fellowship. The French delegation proposed that a committee at the assembly be established to take up women's issues.[25] Hewing to the assembly theme of the church and God's intention for society, the women raised the question of authority in regard to themselves: whether the church was a community to which men and women belonged equally, and, if so, whether women were to carry out *all* aspects of its ministry. This would make it hard for the core of American theologians and the World Council leaders to continue to avoid the contentious issue of ecclesial authority, especially the validity of the different communions' ordination (because some ordained women) and the apparent contradiction between the inclusive claims of the church and its gender-exclusive actions. Acknowledging the seriousness of the "woman question," the World Council staff accepted the French women's recommendation for a subcommittee on "The Life and Work of Women in the Church."[26]

The Provisional Committee held its last meeting in April 1947 at Buck Hill Falls, a resort in Pennsylvania. The main item on the agenda was to settle on a site for the assembly. This time it found ready resolution. Since the previous meeting at Geneva, church leaders of the Netherlands had approached Cavert's Arrangements Committee with an invitation to hold the assembly at Amsterdam. The Americans, having come around to agree that a European city would be better, endorsed the proposal and the full committee accepted the offer.[27] Before adjourning, the committee issued the formal announcement of the assembly, with a "Call" asking all Christians to pray that it might serve as an occasion for commitment to unity in proclaiming the gospel and for a revival in the churches. It recommended that the "Call" be read from all pulpits and that a Sunday in May be set aside as a Day of Prayer for the Assembly.[28]

As the time approached, in January 1948 the committees with the main responsibility for the program met in Geneva to iron out the remaining details. The press conference that followed marked the beginning of a concerted publicity campaign. It lasted two hours, and though a snowstorm blew outside, the sixty-eight correspondents stayed until Visser 't Hooft adjourned it.[29] A few months later *Life* magazine featured a story on the American delegation, with pictures from the public briefings held in New York and St. Louis.[30] The Federal Council designated Pentecost Sunday, traditionally the "birthday" of the church, as the day of prayer for the assembly, and distributed a unity prayer nationwide for use on that day.[31]

Amsterdam and After

Arriving in Amsterdam in the third week of August, the delegates beheld the city decked out for the golden jubilee of Queen Wilhelmina and the crowning of her daughter, Princess Juliana, to succeed her. The only vestige of the war was the food-rationing coupon books each delegate received when registering. A state reception for the delegates was held at the renovated Rijksmuseum amid an exhibit of the paintings of Rembrandt, the Holbeins, and other masters recently recovered from wartime hiding places. The city gave a second reception in the Royal Palace and a nighttime boat ride through the canals and harbors lit up with orange lights for the royal celebration.[32]

The assembly opened with worship on the evening of 22 August in the thirteenth-century Nieuwe Kerk Cathedral. Nearly three thousand attended. The delegates wore the garments of their respective traditions, some in academic gown, others in business suit and tie, and still others in Reformation-style starched bands and ruffles. The last in the procession were the five copresidents of the World Council, followed by one of the speakers, Dr. D. T. Niles of Ceylon, and finally Dr. Koenrad Gravemeyer, chief delegate of the Netherlands Reformed Church and a concentration camp survivor. The service opened with the hymn "All People That on Earth Do Dwell" sung simultaneously in French, German, and English, the languages of the assembly. An American delegate remarked that the multilingual singing "in itself was a unifying influence." The archbishop of Canterbury led the congregation in the Apostles' Creed. Leaders from other communions offered the prayers and read the scripture. The eighty-

three-year-old Mott gave the first address, recalling the steps the movement had taken to reach this point, from the formation of the World's
Student Christian Federation to the 1910 International Missionary
Conference in Edinburgh, to the Oxford and Edinburgh conferences of
1937, and through the war up to the present hour.[33]

The next morning delegates gathered in the Concertgebouw Hall,
Archbishop Fisher presiding.[34] In a stately voice Marc Boegner read the
resolution of the Provisional Committee: "that the formation of the World
Council be declared to be and is hereby completed." The motion to adopt
passed unanimously, and long applause followed. The archbishop inter-
rupted and asked the assembly to stand in silence. He then offered a prayer
of thanksgiving. When he finished, a great many looked at their watches
to mark the hour. It was 10:30 A.M.

Midway through the assembly there was a celebration of Holy Communion according to the rite of the Netherlands Reformed Church. All
baptized Christians were invited to participate. A long table was draped
in white linen, with one hundred chairs around it. The celebrants at the
central places faced the congregation. Different ministers presided over
each seating, speaking in their native tongues. In English, French, German, Dutch, and Japanese the communicants were called forward, and
the bread and wine were blessed. The celebrants passed the elements to
the people on either side, and they in turn served the person next to them.
When everybody had received, one of the celebrants dismissed them with
a quotation from John 17, the chapter that told of Jesus' prayer, "That
they all may be one." Nearly eleven hundred were served.[35] Newspapers
and radio around the world carried the story.[36]

Predictably, the American theologians did not have as prominent a
role at the assembly as they had in the preparatory study. Only three
members of the Theological Discussion Group served as chairman or secretary of a working group—Bennett, Angus Dun, and John Mackay. Of
the fifty speakers at the plenary sessions, only two—Reinhold Niebuhr
and Samuel McCrea Cavert—were from the old group.[37]

Dulles was the American who attracted attention. He made a speech
attacking the ethics of communism and the Soviet regime, drawing a
heated reply from Professor Joseph Hromadka, a communist sympathizer
from Czechoslovakia. But the disturbance was brief. The matter was not
seriously debated in the section on the Church and the International
Disorder; instead a bland balancing statement in its report ("the Christian churches should reject the ideologies of both Communism and laissez-
faire capitalism . . .") was all that marked the episode in the proceedings.[38]
But the American press picked it up, and back in the United States it was

widely misunderstood to mean the World Council somehow favored communism. This was devastating, coming on the heels of the 1 April Soviet blockade of Berlin. Support for the council immediately began to cool, particularly among the businessmen who were its financial backers.[39] This forced the American ecumenical leaders to enter into explanations at the very moment they wanted to be pressing ahead with interchurch dialogue. Moreover, the offending statement was not easily explained away.

When the assembly ended on 4 September the leadership that emerged as the Central Committee and World Council staff was noticeably different from the one than went in as the Provisional Committee. Of the Americans, not one had been a member of the Theological Discussion Group. Reporting on the assembly in *Christianity and Crisis*, Van Dusen remarked: "Many faces disappear, including some who have carried major responsibilities and whose experience and judgment may be sorely missed." Trying to put it charitably, he went on: "Many new persons without extensive previous knowledge of the Council's life insure the infusion of fresh blood."[40] As he had foreseen, denominational administrators, "wheelhorses," who had less appreciation of the theological foundation that supported the institution they now served, had pushed him and his kind out from the center.

Fixtures at the Margin

The theologians were now limited to participating in the ecumenical movement as consultants engaged for specific projects. Though many of them were ordained ministers, their churches did not regard them as stalwarts of the denomination but as mavericks operating in another sphere, habitually independent of denominational politics. Ironically, their success in bringing the churches together stemmed from this habit of avoiding encumbrance in denominational politics, of jumping over them and using the extraecclesiastical channels they had developed from their days in the Student Volunteer Movement and YMCA. But this protean insider-outsider behavior status, which had empowered them, quickly became a liability once the World Council was handed over to the churches.

Though no longer at the center of the World Council, the American theologians did not fade away. They found that from peripheral, mainly academic, posts they enjoyed a vantage from which to press their case for a realist approach to Christian internationalism. They went on voicing their realist opinions on the issues of the day, advocating Christian engagement in American foreign policy. Several remained active in ecumenical affairs, hoping to cultivate ecumenics in theology. To their last days they remained wedded to the theology they set forth before the war.

Van Dusen, president of Union Theological Seminary in New York from 1945 to 1963, built up the ecumenical component of the curriculum, securing endowments from the Luce and Rockefeller Foundations to establish two chairs for visiting scholars, the Luce Professor of World Christianity and the Fosdick Visiting Professorship.[41] Among those who held these positions were men he had come to know during the formation of the World Council: Paul Devanandan and D. T. Niles from India, Hendrik Kraemer from the Netherlands, and John Baillie from Scotland. Van Dusen also oversaw the building of an ecumenics archive, the William Adams Brown Ecumenical Library, set aside as a special section within the main library system. He was instrumental in setting up the Program of Advanced Religious Studies in 1955, a widely publicized course of study that brought twenty-five promising young leaders from churches around the world to Union, where they were to study as a group a curriculum covering the world's moral and spiritual travails, non-Christian religions and secularism, and the role of the church in the world. Van Dusen loved to teach, and throughout his tenure as president he offered his favorite course, "Ecumenical Christianity." He occasionally undertook special assignments for the World Council, such as organizing the second assembly in Evanston, Illinois, in 1954, and coauthoring with Niebuhr, Brunner, Baillie, and others the manifesto of that ssembly, "The Hope of the World." *Time* magazine put him on the cover of the Easter Week issue.

John Bennett, who also taught at Union, followed Van Dusen as president and expanded the ecumenical emphasis. He founded cooperative programs with Catholic and Jewish seminaries and dared bring Catholic and Jewish scholars onto the faculty. In the mid-1960s Bennett increasingly worked against American involvement in Vietnam and became an antiwar activist.[42]

Cavert served as the American secretary for Faith and Order from 1954 until his retirement in 1958, all the while heading the Federal Council of Churches, and then in 1950 becoming the first general secretary of the National Council of Churches (formed in 1950 from the Federal Council and several associated bodies).

Other members of the Theological Discussion Group—which continued to meet until old age and death took their toll—pursued the political implications of their theology. Reinhold Niebuhr was the leading voice on the American Left denouncing communism. Expressing his opinions both as an officer in the Liberal Party and in numerous essays for journals of opinion ranging from the *Christian Century* to *Commonweal*, he shaped the thinking of many a public figure in the American political establishment, among them Paul Nitze, Arthur Schlesinger, Jr., George F. Kennan, Jr., and McGeorge Bundy.[43]

Francis Miller ran for office twice in Virginia as a liberal Democrat challenging the entrenched "Dixiecrat" Byrd machine. In 1949 he sought the gubernatorial nomination and did so well in early polls that the Byrd machine got thousands of Republicans to vote against him in the primary; even so, Miller came within twenty-four thousand votes of winning. Three years later he pitted himself against Senator Harry Byrd, Sr., in the senatorial primary.

With the onset of the cold war the crucial problem for the ecumenical community became how to persevere toward unity and work for a just peace while the rest of the world was insisting on taking sides for or against communism. The World Council set about to defuse the East-West conflict by positioning itself to allow the communist-controlled churches in the Soviet Union and Eastern Europe to participate. It also put "peace" and "colonialism" on the agenda. Increasing attention was paid to the condition of Europe's colonies, ultimately in the 1960s extending the council's commitment to "justice" to mean supporting liberation movements in Africa, Latin America, and Asia, so much so that the name World Council of Churches became associated with the Left in the popular American mind. The same process turned the National Council of Churches, successor to the Federal Council, into a target for the Right. So by the late 1960s ecumenical Protestantism's consistent opposition to racism and war ironically made it a contributor to the dissolution of the national consensus that it had helped hold together for many years. For the new "sixties-generation" theologians these same two issues, war and racism, had a polarizing effect, forcing Christians to choose sides over American involvement in Vietnam and the civil rights movement. The Christian realism of their elders, once a unifying platform over the chaos of a worldwide upheaval, came to be seen as outdated. A few years on, in the successive waves of liberation theologies, it was passed over as the theology of a bygone era. The realists' reassertion of God's transcendence and its implications for America's international engagement gave way to a renewed emphasis on God's immanence. Now God was seen to be working out his will in the struggles of liberation movements.

Conclusion

IN THE FINAL ANALYSIS, Henry P. Van Dusen and his peers succeeded in laying out a Protestant theology for international engagement and greatly helped in moving the United States toward accepting the moral responsibilities of a world power. From their college years and through World War II, the Christian realists were motivated by an urgency to bring about a new international order, and they believed that Christians could and should take the lead in its creation. Remarkably, they made no mention of a pre- or postmillennial mandate as earlier generations of Protestant leaders had. The group focused on the "here and now." Their theology made nothing of Christ's Second Coming or America's exceptional destiny; it was a "realist" theology, essentially a strategy for the "time between." Not trying to achieve absolute renewal of the world, their goal was to mitigate international hostility. Their mode was not a crusade to hasten the Second Coming but thoughtful Christian engagement in politics and interchurch relations.

The realists' internationalist design, first coming into focus in their involvement with the YMCA and the Student Volunteer Movement, began as a Christocentric vision of the world united in Jesus' transcendent embrace of those who confessed him as Lord and Savior. But in the wake of World War I, they considered this naïve, utopian. Yet experience of the YMCA and SVM successes implanted in them the twin convictions that the nations of the world were interlinked and that theology held the sovereign remedy for international discord.

The theologians' thought along these lines turned more concrete from the mid-1930s into the 1940s when they moved on to ecclesiology through involvement with the ecumenical movement. As the Theological Discussion Group they led American Protestantism in thinking through the state of international relations, particularly in regard to Germany and Japan. The realists did not shrink from factoring in ideological fervor and the brute reality of power relations among nations. They concluded that Christianity was the one ideology that could rival fascism and that the church, were it united, could check the decline of secular politics that would plunge the world into violent barbarism.

First a new ecclesiology was needed, one that the Theological Discussion Group believed it could devise. The group's point of departure was the church transcendent, not that they took it to mean the church was the source of truth, for like its founder the church had its human as well as its divine aspects. From this vantage they pointed to a self-critical ecclesiology that would foster a self-critical internationalism. At its heart was the Christocentricity of their youth, but with a realist turn: in Christ's light all people were shown to be sinful and in need of salvation. Holding such a view would perpetually challenge the pride of nations and international alliances. The group also saw a universality in sin and grace, which disregarded borders and denominational boundaries. Armed with this vision, the realist theologians aimed to strike a balance between self-critical humility and determined moral action. To this end they spoke of the church being instrumental first in pronouncing which international arrangements accorded with Christian order and then in establishing them through institutions, the United Nations in the secular form and the World Council of Churches in the religious. In the upshot of these campaigns they were diverted from fully articulating their theology of the church, however; instead they spent their time and energy responding to current events, trying to stretch their theology over the twin threats of atomic war and the spread of communism.

When all they did was toted up, it can be said that the members of Theological Discussion Group had a hand in prying America from its traditional aversion to foreign entanglement to sustained institutional involvement in international affairs. Challenging the views of the 1930s, wherein the prevailing idea of American internationalism was amoral engagement in free trade, these theologians argued to the contrary that for America to uphold its responsibilities it had to become permanently involved in international institutions, the United Nations and its agencies, and—because they were equally preoccupied with the spiritual health of the world—the World Council of Churches. The theologians' conspicuous leadership in this twin project was out of proportion to the manifest support they had from the churchgoing population, but the very misperception that they had public stature actually strengthened their hand at crucial junctures such as the 1944 campaign to promote UN membership.

Their success testifies to the reality that in America a religious movement of significance draws strength by gaining support from a variety of social leaderships at the same time. The internationalist message of the Christian realists resonated with the wartime expansionism of the Washington establishment and the visionary business elite of New York. To the churches it gave a vision of the church and its role in the changed world for the rest of the century. To the academic elite it spoke a cosmopolitan gospel.

The way the Christian realists combined their theology with politics set a precedent for later movements in American Protestantism, the civil rights movement in the 1950s and '60s, and the Religious Right in the 1970s and '80s. Familiar religious terms were deployed in a critical, "prophetic" way to connect with what many Americans knew in their hearts to be true ("sin" was the root of war, racism, social degeneracy). Remedies that many Americans were initially unwilling to accept were prescribed (intervention, UN membership, racial integration, pro-life activism). The message reached the public not primarily through the secular mass media but through publications launched by these leaders themselves or by existing religious media (*Christianity and Crisis*, denominational monthlies, CBN). Finally, a church-related but not church-controlled organization with an ideological leadership at the core planted an agenda in sympathetic social soil (the ecumenical movement in the 1930s, the Southern Christian Leadership Conference in the 1950s, the Moral Majority and then the Christian Coalition from the 1970s to the present).

Thus the story of the Christian realists illustrates what Protestant religious power meant in mid–twentieth century America: their easy ascendancy showed how open the country's elites were to a successful yoking of religion to their agenda. Their story also opens the way to understanding how issues of international engagement became a characteristic of mainline Protestantism up to our own day.

Notes

INTRODUCTION

1. William R. Hutchison, ed., *Between the Times: The Travail of the Protestant Establishment in America, 1900–1960* (Cambridge: Cambridge University Press, 1989), x, 4.

2. Later writers labeled it either neo-orthodoxy or neoliberalism. See Gabriel Fackré, "Theology: Ephemeral, Conjunctural, and Perennial," in *Altered Landscapes: Christianity in America, 1935–1985*, ed. David W. Lotz with Donald W. Shriver, Jr., and John F. Wilson (Grand Rapids, Mich.: William B. Eerdmans, 1989), 248–249; Dennis Voskuil, "Neo-Orthodoxy," in *Encyclopedia of the American Religious Experience: Studies of Traditions and Movements*, vol. 2, ed. Charles H. Lippy and Peter W. Williams (New York: Scribner, 1988), 1147–1157; Kenneth Cauthen, *The Impact of American Religious Liberalism* (New York: Harper and Row, 1962), 228–255; William Hutchison, *The Modernist Impulse in American Protestantism* (Cambridge, Mass.: Harvard University Press, 1976), 288–311. Such writers have identified as neo-orthodox the Niebuhrs, Miller, and Walter M. Horton, and as neoliberal Van Dusen, Bennett, and Harkness. The notable exception to this categorization is Martin E. Marty, who discussed the movement as Christian Realism in *The Noise of Conflict, 1919–1941* (Chicago: University of Chicago Press, 1991), volume 2 of his four-volume work *Modern American Religion*; see especially chapter 8, "The Age of Realism."

3. Paul A. Carter, *The Decline and Revival of the Social Gospel: Social and Political Liberalism in American Protestant Churches, 1920–1940* (Ithaca, New York: Cornell University Press, 1954; reprint Hamden, Conn.: Archon Books, 1971); Donald Meyer, *The Protestant Search for Political Realism, 1919–1941*, 2d ed. (Berkeley: University of California Press, 1960, 2d ed., reprint, Middletown,

Conn.: Wesleyan University Press, 1988); Richard H. Pells, *Radical Visions and American Dreams: Culture and Social Thought in the Depression Years* (New York: Harper and Row, 1973); Richard Wightman Fox, "The Niebuhr Brothers and the Liberal Protestant Heritage," in *Religion and Twentieth-Century American Intellectual Life*, ed. Michael J. Lacey (Cambridge: Woodrow Wilson International Center for Scholars and Cambridge University Press, 1989), 94–115.

4. Ruth Rouse and Stephen Neill, eds., *A History of the Ecumenical Movement, 1517–1948* (Philadelphia: Westminster Press, 1968); Samuel McCrea Cavert, *The American Churches in the Ecumenical Movement, 1900–1968* (New York: Association Press, 1968); William Richey Hogg, *Ecumenical Foundations: A History of the International Missionary Council and Its Nineteenth-Century Background* (New York: Harper and Brothers, 1952); H. George Anderson, "Ecumenical Movements," in *Altered Landscapes: Christianity in America, 1935–1985*, ed. David W. Lotz with Donald W. Shriver, Jr., and John F. Wilson (Grand Rapids, Mich.: William B. Eerdmans, 1989), 97.

5. For example, William J. Schmidt, *Architect of Unity: A Biography of Samuel McCrea Cavert* (New York: Friendship Press, 1975); and Charles Howard Hopkins, *John R. Mott, 1865–1955: A Biography* (Grand Rapids, Mich.: William B. Eerdmans, 1979); Eberhard Busch, *Karl Barth: His Life from Letters and Autobiographical Texts*, trans. John Bowden (London: SCM Press, 1976); and Eberhard Bethge, *Dietrich Bonhoeffer: Man of Vision, Man of Courage*, trans. Eric Mosbacher, et al. (New York: Harper and Row, 1970; reprint, 1977).

6. See William Hutchison and Robert Schneider's call for such study in the preface and "Voice of Many Waters: Church Federation in the Twentieth Century," in *Between the Times: The Travail of the Protestant Establishment in America, 1900–1960*, ed. William R. Hutchison (Cambridge: Cambridge University Press, 1989), vii–xv, 95–121.

ONE / HIGH TIDE OF AMERICAN PROTESTANTISM

1. Alan Trachtenberg, *The Incorporation of America: Culture and Society in the Gilded Age* (New York: Hill and Wang, 1982), 70–100; Henry F. May, *The End of American Innocence: A Study of the First Years of Our Own Time, 1912–1917* (New York: Knopf, 1959); Robert H. Wiebe, *The Search for Order, 1877–1920* (New York: Hill and Wang, 1967).

2. Charles Howard Hopkins, *The Rise of the Social Gospel in American Protestantism, 1865–1915* (New Haven, Conn.: Yale University Press, 1940).

3. Grant Wacker, "The Holy Spirit and the Spirit of the Age in American Protestantism, 1880–1910," *Journal of American History*, 72, no. 1 (June 1985), 45–62.

4. Daniel T. Rodgers, "In Search of Progressivism," *Reviews in American History*, 10, no. 4 (December 1982), 113–132.

5. William Hutchison, *The Modernist Impulse in American Protestantism* (Cambridge: Harvard University Press, 1976).

6. E. C. Smyth et al., "Christianity and Its Modern Competitors," *Progressive Orthodoxy: A Contribution to the Christian Interpretation of Christian Doctrines* (Boston: Houghton Mifflin, 1885), 402; cited in ibid., 102.

7. For example, see Theodore T. Munger, *The Freedom of Faith* (Boston: Houghton, Mifflin, 1883), 22.

8. William Adams Brown, *The Essence of Christianity* (New York: Scribner, 1906), 256.

9. Hopkins, *The Rise of the Social Gospel*; Robert T. Handy, ed. *The Social Gospel in America, 1870–1920: Gladden, Ely, Rauschenbusch* (New York: Oxford University Press, 1966); Hutchison, *The Modernist Impulse*; and Robert T. Handy, *Undermined Establishment: Church-State Relations in America, 1880–1920* (Princeton, N.J.: Princeton University Press, 1991).

10. David Healy, *U.S. Expansionism: The Imperialist Urge in the 1890s* (Madison: University of Wisconsin Press, 1970); Richard W. Van Alstyne, *The Rising American Empire* (New York: Oxford University Press, 1960); Akira Iriye, *From Nationalism to Internationalism: U.S. Foreign Policy to 1914* (London: Routledge and Kegan Paul, 1977); and William E. Leuchtenberg, "Progressivism and Imperialism: The Progressive Movement and American Foreign Policy, 1898–1916," *Mississippi Valley Historical Review*, 39 (December 1952), 483–504.

11. Charles S. Olcott, *The Life of William McKinley* (Boston: Houghton Mifflin, 1916), vol. 2, 110–111; also cited in Winthrop S. Hudson and John Corrigan, *Religion in America: An Historical Account of the Development of American Religious Life*, 5th ed. (New York: Macmillan, 1992), 306.

12. Kenneth Scott Latourette, *A History of the Expansion of Christianity*, 7 vols. (New York: Harper, 1937–1945); John King Fairbank, ed., *The Missionary Enterprise in China and America* (Cambridge, Mass.: Harvard University Press, 1974); William R. Hutchison, *Errand to the World: American Protestant Thought and Foreign Missions* (Chicago: University of Chicago Press, 1987); Paul Varg, *Missionaries, Chinese and Diplomats: The American Protestant Missionary Movement in China, 1890–1952* (Princeton, N.J.: Princeton University Press, 1958).

13. Robert L. Beisner, *From the Old Diplomacy to the New, 1865–1900*, 2d ed. (New York: Thomas Y. Crowell, 1975), cited in Handy, *Undermined Establishment*, 94; Hutchison, *The Modernist Impulse*, 133–134.

14. David O. Levine, *The American College and the Culture of Aspiration, 1915–1940* (Ithaca, N.Y.: Cornell University Press, 1986); Charles Howard Hopkins, *History of the Y.M.C.A. in North America* (New York: Association Press, 1951), 271–273, 276–279, 292–293.

15. Hopkins, *History of the Y.M.C.A.*, 283–286.

16. Ibid., 295–298; Charles Howard Hopkins, *John R. Mott, 1865–1955: A Biography* (Grand Rapids, Mich.: William B. Eerdmans, 1979), 24–27; Martha Lund Smalley, "Historical Sketch of the Student Volunteer Movement for Foreign Missions," in "Archives and Manuscript Register, Manuscript Group Number 42, Archives of the Student Volunteer Movement for Foreign Missions" (New Haven, Conn.: Yale Divinity School, 1980).

17. Hopkins, *History of the Y.M.C.A.*, 304.

18. Smalley, "Historical Sketch of the Student Volunteer Movement for Foreign Missions," 17.

19. Ruth Rouse, *The World's Student Christian Federation: A History of the First Thirty Years* (London: SCM Press, 1948), 25; Hopkins, *John R. Mott*, 123–131.

20. John R. Mott, *The W.S.C.F. Origins, Achievements, Forecast* (1920), 5–7, in Rouse, *The World's Student Christian Federation*, 62.

21. Report letter from John R. Mott, Constantinople, 4 October 1895, cited in Rouse, *The World's Student Christian Federation*, 64.

22. Hopkins, *John R. Mott*, 208; Hopkins, *History of the Y.M.C.A.*, 634.

23. Herbert Reece Coston, Jr., "The World's Student Christian Federation as an Ecumenical Training Ground" (Ph.D. diss., Northwestern University, 1963).

24. William Richey Hogg, *Ecumenical Foundations: A History of the International Missionary Council and Its Nineteenth-Century Background* (New York: Harper and Brothers, 1952); Kenneth Scott Latourette, "Ecumenical Bearings of the Missionary Movement and the International Missionary Council," in *A History of the Ecumenical Movement, 1517–1948*, ed. Ruth Rouse and Stephen Neill (Philadelphia: Westminster Press, 1968), 353–403.

25. Tissington Tatlow, "The World Conference on Faith and Order," in *A History of the Ecumenical Movement, 1517–1948*, ed. Ruth Rouse and Stephen Neill (Philadelphia: Westminster Press, 1968), 405–444.

26. *Joint Commission Appointed to Arrange for a World Conference on Faith and Order* (Boston: D. B. Updike, 1910; reprint, March 10, 1913), pamphlet no. 1, series I, 1, 4. All sources noted this way belong to the World Council of Churches' microfilm archive of *The Commission on Faith and Order: Official Numbered Publications, 1910–1948* (Geneva, 1970).

27. Charles S. Macfarland, *The Churches of Christ in Time of War* (New York: Missionary Education Movement, 1917), 129–137; John A. Hutchison, *We Are Not Divided: A Critical and Historical Study of the Federal Council of Churches of Christ in America* (New York: Round Table Press, 1941); John Braeman, Robert Hamlett Bremner, and David Brody, *Change and Continuity in Twentieth-Century America: The 1920s* (Columbus: Ohio State University Press, 1968).

28. C. Roland Marchand, *The American Peace Movement and Social Reform: 1898–1918* (Princeton, N.J.: Princeton University Press, 1972).

29. John F. Piper, *The American Churches in World War I* (Athens, Ohio: Ohio University Press, 1985).

30. Nils Karlström, "Movements for International Friendship and Life and Work, 1910–1925," in *A History of the Ecumenical Movement, 1517–1948*, ed. Ruth Rouse and Stephen Neill (Philadelphia: Westminster Press, 1968), 509–544; Samuel McCrea Cavert, *The American Churches in the Ecumenical Movement, 1900–1968* (New York: Association Press, 1968), 116–119.

31. Smalley, "Historical Sketch of the Student Volunteer Movement for Foreign Missions," 18.

TWO / THE FOUND GENERATION

1. Ernest Hemingway, *A Moveable Feast* (New York: Scribner's, 1964; reprint, New York: MacMillan, 1987), 29; Malcolm Cowley, *Exile's Return: A Literary Odyssey of the 1920s* (New York: Norton, 1934; reprint, New York: Penguin, 1986), 3.

2. Richard Wightman Fox, *Reinhold Niebuhr: A Biography* (New York: Pantheon, 1985; reprint, San Francisco: Harper and Row, 1987), 7.

3. Francis Pickens Miller, *Man from the Valley: Memoirs of a Twentieth-Century Virginian* (Chapel Hill: University of North Carolina Press, 1971), 9.

4. Henry P. Van Dusen, outline attached to "Application for Fellowship from the National Council of Religion in Higher Education," 15 February 1930, Henry P. Van Dusen Papers, "Personal," Special Collections, the Burke Library, Union Theological Seminary (hereafter, Van Dusen Papers).

5. Fox, *Reinhold Niebuhr*, 7.

6. Rosemary Skinner Keller, *Georgia Harkness: For Such a Time as This* (Nashville: Abingdon Press, 1992), 50–51.

7. Stephen A. Schmidt, *Architect of Unity: A Biography of Samuel McCrea Cavert* (New York: Friendship Press, 1975), 5–6.

8. Cowley, *Exile's Return*, 28, 30.

9. Samuel McCrea Cavert, "The Early Years" (1970), 10 ff., a handwritten manuscript in Schmidt's files, cited in Schmidt, *Architect of Unity*, 16.

10. Van Dusen, "Application for Fellowship," 2–3.

11. Georgia Harkness, "Days of My Years," 16–17, an unpublished autobiography Harkness wrote for the Pacific Coast Theological Group during the 1950s, Georgia Harkness Collection, Garrett-Evangelical Theological Seminary, Evanston, Illinois, quoted in Keller, *Georgia Harkness*, 90.

12. Miller, *Man from the Valley*, 18–27.

13. Ibid., 32.

14. Karl Mannheim, *Essays on the Sociology of Knowledge*, ed. Paul Kecskemeti (New York: Oxford University Press, 1952).

15. Paula S. Fass, *The Damned and the Beautiful: American Youth in the 1920s* (New York: Oxford University Press, 1977), 292–326.

16. Ronald Schaffer, "The War Department's Defense of ROTC, 1920–1940," *Wisconsin Magazine of History*, 53, no. 2 (winter 1969–1970), 108.

17. Kenneth Scott Latourette, "Are Our Campuses a Menace to Peace?" *Intercollegian*, 42, no. 1 (October 1924), 4. Latourette later became well known as the historian of Christian expansion and overseas missions.

18. David D. Roop, "Collegiate Cavalry at the University of Arizona, 1921–1941," *Arizona and the West*, 27 (1985), 55–72; "Military Training," *Intercollegian*, 46, no. 6 (March 1929), 189.

19. Schaffer, "The War Department's Defense of ROTC," 110.

20. Frank Olmstead, "The Christian Student and the R.O.T.C.," *Intercollegian*, 42, no. 1 (October 1924), 13.

21. Bolton C. Waller, "The Federation and International Brotherhood," *Intercollegian*, 37, no. 7 (April 1920), 7.

22. Robert P. Wilder, "A Retrospective—Five-Year Report by the General Secretary to the Executive Committee [of the Student Volunteer Movement for Foreign Missions]," 27 September 1924, Archives of the Student Volunteer Movement for Foreign Missions, Manuscript Group no. 42, Special Collections, Yale Divinity School Library (hereafter SVM Archives).

23. These attitudes so troubled the older generation that educators undertook systematic inquiry into their causes. Though most of the studies did not appear until the second half of the decade, they relied on data collected in the early 1920s. See Stanley High, *The Revolt of Youth* (New York: Abingdon Press, 1923); George A. Coe, *What Ails Our Youth?* (New York: Scribner, 1924); R. H. Edwards, J. M. Artman, and Galen M. Fisher, *Undergraduates: A Study of Morale in Twenty-Three American Colleges and Universities* (Garden City, N.Y.: Doubleday, Doran, 1928); Daniel Katz and Floyd Henry Allport, *Student Activities: A Report of the Syracuse Reaction Study* (Syracuse, N.Y.: Craftsman Press, 1931).

24. "In Brief," *Intercollegian*, 37, no. 5 (February 1920), 4; Earl H. Kelsey, "The Convention in the College Press," *Intercollegian*, 37, no. 7 (April 1920), 10.

25. George A. Coe, "New Social Horizons," *Intercollegian*, 37, no. 5 (February 1920), 3.

26. "Ground Plan of Exhibit, Auditorium, Des Moines, Iowa," SVM Archives.

27. David R. Porter, "The Des Moines Convention," *Student World*, 13, no. 2 (April 1920), 67.

28. Nathan D. Showalter, "The End of a Crusade: The Student Volunteer Movement for Foreign Missions and the Great War" (Th.D. diss., Harvard University, 1990), 147.

29. "Student Volunteer Council Meets," *Intercollegian*, 37, no. 8 (May 1920), 9.

30. Robert A. Hume, "Missions in the New Day," *Religious Education*, 15, no. 6 (December 1920), 338; advertisement for John Leslie Lobingier's *World Friendship Through the Church School* (Chicago: University of Chicago Press, 1923) in *Religious Education*, 18, no. 3 (June 1923), and no. 4 (August 1923). See also review of Lobingier in "Book Notes," *Religious Education*, 18, no. 3 (June 1923), 215–217.

31. Milton T. Stauffer, "A Message to Student Volunteers," *Student Volunteer Movement Bulletin*, 3, no. 4 (October 1922), 156–158.

32. "Meeting of the Sub-Committee on Program," 22 March 1923, 1, SVM Archives.

33. "Report of the General Secretary to the Executive Committee, Student Volunteer Movement [for Foreign Missions]," 29 September 1923, 6; "Meeting of the Quadrennial Committee on Arrangements," 16 October 1923, 3; "Meeting of the Quadrennial Convention Committee on Arrangements," 27 October 1923, 3, 5, SVM Archives; Harrison Sacket Elliott, *The Why and How of Group Discussion* (New York: Association Press, 1923), 1, 3.

34. Kendig Brubaker Cully, "A Later Look at Harrison Sacket Elliott," in *Pioneers of Religious Education in the Twentieth Century: A Festschrift for Herman E. Wornom*, ed. Boardman W. Kathan, special issue, *Religious Education* (September–October 1978), 559–561; "Notes on Contributors," *Student World*, 15, no. 2 (April 1922), 84.

35. Elliott, *The Why and How of Group Discussion*, 7.

36. Ibid., 56.

37. "Coming to Grips with the Racial Problem," *Federal Council Bulletin*, 4, no. 5 (August–September 1921), 100; "Why Race Relations Sunday," *Federal Council Bulletin*, 6, no. 6 (November–December 1923), 12–13; John A. Hutchison, *We Are Not Divided: A Critical and Historical Study of the Federal Council of Churches of Christ in America* (New York: Round Table Press, 1941), 131–138; "Southern Women Against Lynching," *Federal Council Bulletin*, 6, no. 3 (April–May 1923), 7; John Patrick McDowell, *The Social Gospel in the South: The Woman's Home Mission Movement in the Methodist Episcopal Church, South, 1886–1939* (Baton Rouge: Louisiana State University Press, 1982), 87–98.

38. Sherwood Eddy, *Eighty Adventurous Years: An Autobiography* (New York: Harper and Brothers, 1955), 101, 103; Eddy, *A Pilgrimage of Ideas, or The Re-Education of Sherwood Eddy* (New York: Farrar and Rhinehart, 1934), 182.

39. Eddy, *Pilgrimage of Ideas*, 183; Eddy, *Eighty Adventurous Years*, 128.

40. Eddy, *Eighty Adventurous Years*, 129, 132–134.

41. Keller, *Georgia Harkness*, 138–139.

42. Schmidt, *Architect of Unity*, 63.

43. Fox, *Reinhold Niebuhr*, 75, 81–82, 85; C. Howard Hopkins, *History of the Y.M.C.A. In North America* (New York: Association Press, 1951), 643–645.

44. Francis P. Miller, *Man from the Valley*, 19.

45. Ibid., 58.

46. H. C. Rutgers, "The Meeting of the General Committee," *Student World*, 15, no. 3 (July 1922), 128; "Editorial," *Student World*, 15, no. 3 (July 1922), 85–86.

47. Francis P. Miller to Henri-Louis Henriod, 2 November 1921, Archives of the World's Student Christian Federation, Manuscript Group no. 46, Special Collections, Yale Divinity School Library (hereafter, WSCF-YDS).

48. Francis P. Miller to John R. Mott, 14 January 1922, WSCF-YDS.

49. Francis P. Miller, "The Task of Federation," *Student World*, 16, no. 1 (January 1923), 26.

50. "Minutes of the Subcommittee on Program for the Quadrennial Convention," 26 February 1923, revised copy; "Meeting of the Sub-Committee on Program," 22 March 1923, SVM Archives.

51. D. J. Fleming, "Embodying International Goodwill," *Intercollegian*, 40, no. 9 (June 1923), 9–10; "Race Questions and Indianapolis," *Intercollegian*, 41, no. 2 (November 1923), 2.

52. "Proposals on Race Problems" and "A Chance for the Black Race: An Address by F. Eugene Corbie," *Intercollegian*, 41, no. 5 (February 1924), 19–20.

53. Goodwin B. Watson, "How the Discussion Groups Worked Out," *Stu-*

dent Volunteer Movement Bulletin, 5, no. 2 (February 1924), 97–98; "Editorial," *Student Volunteer Movement Bulletin*, 5, no. 2 (February 1924), 117–118; D. J. Fleming, "The Convention's Significance to American Education," *Intercollegian*, 41, no. 5 (February 1924), 7–8; "High Peaks in Convention Discussion," *Intercollegian*, 41, no. 5 (February 1924), 19–20.

54. Robert E. Speer, "The Relation of the Foreign Missionary to the World Situation Today," *Intercollegian*, 41, no. 5 (February 1924), 13–18.

55. "Proposals on War" and "They Discussed War," *Intercollegian*, 41, no. 5 (February 1924), 20.

56. "Floor Plan of Exhibit" and "Plans for Exhibit, Quadrennial Convention, Indianapolis, Indiana, December 28 to January 1," SVM Archives.

57. This led some students to criticize the college fraternity system for inculcating an exclusivist frame of mind. See E. Fay Campbell, "Why I Returned My Pin," *Intercollegian*, 41, no. 7 (April 1924), 9–10; and Lyman Hoover, "Fraternities and a Fraternal World," *Intercollegian*, 42, no. 4 (January 1925), 115–116.

58. Henry P. Van Dusen, "The Spiritual Tone of Indianapolis," *Student Volunteer Movement Bulletin*, 5, no. 2 (February 1924), 104–107.

THREE / AGE OF NEGATIVISM

1. Henry Pitney Van Dusen, "What Are Christian Students Thinking About?" *Intercollegian*, 45, no. 3 (December 1927), 60.

2. Robert T. Handy, "The American Religious Depression," *Church History*, 29 (March 1960), 3–16.

3. Martin E. Marty, *The Noise of Conflict, 1919–1941*, vol. 2 of *Modern American Religion* (Chicago: University of Chicago Press, 1991), 155–214; Robert T. Handy, *Undermined Establishment: Church-State Relations in America, 1880–1920* (Princeton, N.J.: Princeton University Press, 1991), 3–6.

4. J. M. Artman and Ruth Shonle, "Biennial Report of Trends in Religious and Character Education," *Religious Education*, 22, no. 6 (June 1927), 661–684, 690–692.

5. Mark G. Toulouse, *The Transformation of John Foster Dulles: From Prophet of Realism to Priest of Nationalism* (Macon, Ga.: Mercer University Press, 1985), 18–25; Dean Keith Thompson, "Henry Pitney Van Dusen: Ecumenical Statesman" (Ph.D. diss., Union Theological Seminary, Richmond, Virginia, 1974), 46–49.

6. John C. Bennett, interview with Teresa Thompson, 20 June 1990.

7. "Evanston," *Intercollegian*, 43, no. 5 (February 1926), 148.

8. Ibid., 149.

9. "What Some Delegates Thought," *Intercollegian*, 43, no. 5 (February 1926), 151.

10. Roland Marchand, *Advertising the American Dream: Making Way for Modernity, 1920–1940* (Berkeley and Los Angeles: University of California Press, 1985); and William E. Leuchtenberg, *The Perils of Prosperity, 1914–1932* (Chicago: University of Chicago Press, 1958; reprint, 1973).

11. Robert P. Wilder, "A Retrospect—Five Year Report by the General Secretary to the Executive Committee," 27 September 1924, 10, SVM Archives.

12. R. Ambrose Reeves, "Milwaukee and the Church Universal," *Intercollegian*, 44, no. 5 (February 1927), 119; "Conference Statistics," *Intercollegian*, 44, no. 5 (February 1927), 131; Walter W. Van Kirk, "Students Face Christian Living in Modern World," *Federal Council Bulletin*, 10, no. 1 (January 1927), 13; Francis P. Miller, ed., *Religion on the Campus: Report of the Milwaukee National Student Conference* (New York: Association Press, 1927), 197.

13. Miller, *Religion on the Campus*, 188.

14. Ibid., ix, 186–187; Grace Loucks, "Whither Bound—Discussion Groups?" *Intercollegian*, 44, no. 7 (April 1927), 199.

15. W. O. Mendenhall, "Race Discrimination at Detroit," *Intercollegian*, 48, no. 5 (February 1931), 144–146.

16. "Evanston," 148.

17. "After Milwaukee—What?" *Intercollegian*, 44, no. 4 (January 1927), 98.

18. "Editorials," *Intercollegian*, 44, no. 5 (February 1927), 137. Van Dusen and Miller served on the Business Committee, the main organizing body of the conference. See Miller, *Religion on the Campus*, 197–198.

19. Ibid., 150.

20. "Memo" in "Commission of Ten on the Student Volunteer Movement, 1925" folder; "Meeting of the Executive Committee of the Student Volunteer Movement," 4 January 1926; and "Report of the Commission of Ten on the Student Volunteer Movement," SVM Archives.

21. Robert P. Wilder, "Annual Report for the Year 1925–1926, The Student Volunteer Movement," SVM Archives.

22. "Minutes of the General Council of the Student Volunteer Movement," 4–9 September 1926, 16, SVM Archives.

23. Robert P. Wilder to E. Fay Campbell, 27 November 1924; and E. Fay Campbell to Robert P. Wilder, 2 December 1925, SVM Archives. Also cited in Martha Lund Smalley, "Historical Sketch of the Student Volunteer Movement for Foreign Missions," in "Archives and Manuscript Register, Manuscript Group No. 42, Archives of the Student Volunteer Movement for Foreign Missions" (New Haven, Conn.: Yale Divinity School, 1980), 24, 27.

24. Robert P. Wilder, "Report of Robert P. Wilder," 9–10, in "General Council, 1927" folder, SVM Archives. The SVM eventually dissolved itself in 1966.

25. Clarence Prouty Shedd, *The Church Follows Its Students* (New Haven, Conn.: Yale University Press, 1938).

26. Kenneth Cauthen, *The Impact of American Religious Liberalism* (New York: Harper and Row, 1962), 3–40; William E. Hordern, *A Layman's Guide to Protestant Theology*, rev. ed. (New York: Macmillan, 1955; reprint, 1978), 73–110.

27. William Adams Brown, "The Homeless Liberal," *Religious Education*, 22, no. 1 (January 1927), 12.

28. Eberhard Busch, *Karl Barth: His Life from Letters and Autobiographical Texts*, trans. John Bowden (London: SCM Press, 1976), 98–100.

29. Ibid., 99.

30. John C. Bennett, interview with Teresa Thompson, 20 June 1990.

31. Francis P. Miller, ed., *The Church and the World* (New York: Association Press, 1926). Contributors included such widely respected missions leaders as J. H. Oldham, Kenneth Scott Latourette, and Robert Speer.

32. Henry P. Van Dusen, *In Quest of Life's Meaning: Hints Toward a Christian Philosophy of Life for Students* (New York: Association Press, 1926).

33. "Among the New Books," *Federal Council Bulletin*, 10, no. 4 (April 1927), 32–33; "News from the Field," *Intercollegian*, 43, no. 8 (May 1926), 255–256; Henry P. Van Dusen, "Apprehending Truth Is Conditional," *Intercollegian*, 44, no. 4 (January 1927), 91–92, an excerpt from *In Quest of Life's Meaning*.

34. Reinhold Niebuhr, *Does Civilization Need Religion?: A Study in the Social Resources of Religion in Modern Life* (New York: Macmillan, 1927; reprint, 1928); Richard Wightman Fox, *Reinhold Niebuhr: A Biography* (New York: Pantheon, 1985; reprint, San Francisco: Harper and Row, 1987), 100; Reinhold Niebuhr, "Christianity and Contemporary Politics," *Christian Century*, 17 April 1924, 498–501; "Is Protestantism Self-Deceived?" *Christian Century*, 25 December 1924, 1661–1662; "Shall We Proclaim Truth or Search for It?" *Christian Century*, 12 March 1925, 344–346.

35. "Some of the Best New Religious Books," *Federal Council Bulletin*, 11, no. 1 (January 1928), 32.

36. Samuel McCrea Cavert, *The American Churches in the Ecumenical Movement, 1900–1968* (New York: Association Press, 1968), 129, 163.

37. Henry S. Leiper, "Universal Life and Work Develops Permanent Organization," *Federal Council Bulletin*, 13, no. 10 (December 1930), 12–13.

38. Nils Ehrenström, "Movements for International Friendship and Life and Work, 1925–1948," in *A History of the Ecumenical Movement, 1517–1948*, ed. Ruth Rouse and Stephen Neill (Philadelphia: Westminister Press, 1968), 559.

39. Ibid., 555; "Church Leaders of Many Nations Assemble at Prague," *Federal Council Bulletin*, 11, no. 8 (October 1928), 19–21.

40. Ehrenström, "Movements for International Friendship and Life and Work," 557.

41. Worth M. Tippy, "'Life and Work' at Eisenach," *Federal Council Bulletin*, 12, no. 9 (November 1929), 18.

42. Henry S. Leiper, "Geneva Meeting Marks Advance in World Unity," *Federal Council Bulletin*, 15, no. 8 (October 1932), 19.

43. "New Secretary for International Church Relations," *Federal Council Bulletin*, 13, no. 6 (June 1930), 22.

44. "World Conference of Churches in 1935," *Federal Council Bulletin*, 15, no. 1 (January 1932), 19.

45. Frances Parkinson Keyes, "The Conference at Lausanne," reprinted from *Good Housekeeping*, December 1927 (Boston: The Secretariat, May 1928), Pamphlet no. 57, Series I; Rt. Rev. Charles H. Brent, "The Call to Unity," *Federal Council Bulletin*, 10, no. 8 (October 1927), 9–10; "The Meaning of Lausanne: A Symposium," *Federal Council Bulletin*, 10, no. 8 (October 1927), 25–26.

46. William Adams Brown to Helen Brown, 13 August 1927, William Adams Brown Papers, Special Collections, Burke Library, Union Theological Seminary, New York (hereafter, Brown Papers).

47. Tissington Tatlow, "The World Conference on Faith and Order," *A History of the Ecumenical Movement 1517–1948*, ed. Ruth Rouse and Stephen Neill (Philadelphia: Westminister Press, 1968), 422.

48. Ibid., 422–423; Cavert, *The American Churches in the Ecumenical Movement*, 131–132; *Reports of the World Conference on Faith and Order, Lausanne, Switzerland, August 3 to 21, 1927* (Boston: The Secretariat, January 1928), Pamphlet no. 55, Series I, 20; *Reports of the World Conference on Faith and Order, Lausanne, Switzerland, August 3 to 21, 1927* (Boston: The Secretariat, September 1927), Pamphlet no. 54, Series I, 8.

49. *Reports of the World Conference on Faith and Order, Lausanne, Switzerland, August 3 to 21, 1927* (Boston: The Secretariat, September 1927), Pamphlet no. 55, Series I, 8. Eight months later in Jerusalem, the IMC incorporated part of this report in its own message to the churches. *Records of the Continuation Committee on Faith and Order, Prague, Czecho-Slovakia, September 6–8, 1928* (Boston: The Secretariat), Pamphlet no. 58, Series I, 14; Tatlow, "The World Conference on Faith and Order," 424–425.

50. *Records of the Continuation Committee of the World Conference on Faith and Order, Maloja, Engadine, Sweden, August 27–30, 1929* (Boston: The Secretariat), Pamphlet no. 60, Series I, 3–4.

51. Tatlow, "The World Conference on Faith and Order," 428–429.

52. William Adams Brown, *Toward a United Church: Three Decades of Ecumenical Christianity* (New York: Scribner, 1946), 112.

53. Ibid., 12.

54. *Report of the Theological Committee, 19th August 1931, The Theology of Grace* (Boston: The Secretariat, November, 1931), Pamphlet no. 66, Series I.

55. *Records of the Continuation Committee of the World Conference on Faith and Order, High Leigh, Hoddesdon, England, August 18–21, 1931* (Boston: The Secretariat), Pamphlet no. 65, Series I, 15.

56. William Richey Hogg, *Ecumenical Foundations: A History of the International Missionary Council and Its Nineteenth-Century Background* (New York: Harper and Row, 1952), 239.

57. John R. Mott, "A Creative International Fellowship," *International Review of Missions*, 17, no. 67 (July 1928), 421–422.

58. Hogg, *Ecumenical Foundations*, 241.

59. Cavert, *The American Churches in the Ecumenical Movement*, 134.

60. "The Jerusalem Conference," *Federal Council Bulletin*, 11, no. 4 (April 1928), 3.

61. Hogg, *Ecumenical Foundations*, 246–248; Twila Lytton Cavert, "'From East and West They Came,'" *Intercollegian*, 46, no. 1 (October 1928), 18.

62. Hogg, *Ecumenical Foundations*, 248.

63. Ibid., 251–252; Cavert, *The American Churches in the Ecumenical Movement*, 134.

64. Hogg, *Ecumenical Foundations*, 260–261.

65. Karl Barth, "The Inward Man," *Student World*, 21, no. 3 (July 1928), 309–315.

66. H. Emil Brunner, *The Theology of Crisis* (New York: Scribner, 1930), ix–x.

67. John C. Bennett, interview with Teresa Thompson, 20 June 1990. From Brunner they also learned that "crisis theology" was hardly uniform, though its proponents shared distinct commonalities of thought. Sharp debate occurred between Barth, on the one side, and Brunner, Gogarten, and Bultmann, on the other, over the role of natural theology. "Negativism" struck crisis theology, too.

68. Jesse R. Wilson, "Reviews," *Far Horizons*, 11, no. 7 (April 1931), 31. *Far Horizons* was a new version of the *Student Volunteer Movement Bulletin*. See also J. H. Oldham in "Review of Books," *International Review of Missions*, 19, no. 74 (April 1930), 280.

69. Reinhold Niebuhr, "Our World's Denial of God," *Intercollegian*, 44, no. 5 (February 1927), 127–130; printed in English and in French in *Student World*, no. 2 (April 1927), 78–86.

70. Reinhold Niebuhr, *Moral Man and Immoral Society: A Study in Ethics and Politics* (New York: Scribner, 1932; reprint, 1960).

71. Norman Thomas, "Moral Man and Immoral Society," *World Tomorrow*, 14 December 1932, 565, 567; also cited in Fox, *Reinhold Niebuhr*, 142.

72. Theodore Hume, "Moral Man and Immoral Society," *Christian Century*, 4 January 1933, 18; also cited in Fox, *Reinhold Niebuhr*, 142.

73. Charles S. Macfarland, "Among the Best New Books," *Federal Council Bulletin*, 16, no. 4 (April 1933), 13.

74. Fox, *Reinhold Niebuhr*, 142–144.

75. H. Richard Niebuhr to Reinhold Niebuhr, n.d. [mid-January 1933], Reinhold Niebuhr Papers, Library of Congress, cited in Fox, *Reinhold Niebuhr*, 143.

76. W. A. Visser 't Hooft, "A Farewell to the Social Gospel," *Student World*, 26, no. 3 (July 1933), 275–276.

77. Henry P. Van Dusen, *The Plain Man Seeks for God* (New York: Scribner, 1933), 3–4.

78. *Federal Council Bulletin*, 16, no. 6 (June 1933), 14.

79. *Federal Council Bulletin*, 16, no. 8 (October 1933), 16.

80. W. A. Visser 't Hooft, "The God of Reason and the God of Faith," *Student World*, 26 no. 4 (October 1933), 371–372.

81. Francis P. Miller, in "The Bookshelf," *Intercollegian*, 50, no. 9 (June 1933), 257–260.

FOUR / EUROPEAN UPHEAVAL, THEOLOGICAL FERMENT

1. William Adams Brown to Thatcher M. Brown, 19 March 1933, Brown Papers.

2. William J. Schmidt, *Architect of Unity: A Biography of Samuel McCrea Cavert* (New York: Friendship Press, 1975), 101, 123 n. 6; Eberhard Bethge, *Dietrich Bonhoeffer: Man of Vision, Man of Courage*, trans. Eric Mosbacher et al. (New York: Harper and Row, 1970; reprint, 1977), 203–204; Robert P. Ericksen, *Theologians Under Hitler: Gerhard Kittel, Paul Althaus, and Emanuel Hirsch* (New Haven, Conn.: Yale University Press, 1985), 48–49.

3. Bethge, *Dietrich Bonhoeffer*, 237–238; Eberhard Busch, *Karl Barth: His Life from Letters and Autobiographical Texts*, trans. John Bowden (London: SCM Press, 1976), 229.

4. Busch, *Karl Barth*, 236–245; Bethge, *Dietrich Bonhoeffer*, 297.

5. *Junge Kirche*, 1934, 673, cited in Bethge, *Dietrich Bonhoeffer*, 299. The oath declared: "I . . . swear before God . . . that I . . . will be true and obedient to the Führer of the German people and State, Adolf Hitler, and I pledge myself to every sacrifice on behalf of the German people such as befits an Evangelical German . . ."

6. William Adams Brown to Thatcher M. Brown, 19 March 1933, Brown Papers.

7. Henry Smith Leiper, "Christians of the World Face German Situation," *Federal Council Bulletin*, 16, nos. 9 and 10 (November–December 1933), 8.

8. Minutes of the Meeting, Novi Sad, 2, 15, 37 ff., and *Die Eiche*, 1933, 368 ff., cited in Bethge, *Dietrich Bonhoeffer*, 242–243.

9. "Meeting the Crisis in Our Relations with German Protestantism," *Federal Council Bulletin*, 16, nos. 9 and 10 (November–December 1933), 5–6; and Bethge, *Dietrich Bonhoeffer*, 248–250.

10. Nils Ehrenström, "Movements for International Friendship and Life and Work, 1925–1948," in *A History of the Ecumenical Movement, 1517–1948*, ed. Ruth Rouse and Stephen Neill (Philadelphia: Westminister Press, 1968), 58.

11. W. A. Visser 't Hooft, "German Protestantism at the Crossroads," *Student World*, 26, no. 3 (July 1933), 256–259.

12. Bethge, *Dietrich Bonhoeffer*, 303–307.

13. "Minutes of the Meeting of the Council, Fanø," 37, cited in Bethge, *Dietrich Bonhoeffer*, 307.

14. Ehrenström, "Movements for International Friendship and Life and Work," 583–584.

15. Samuel McCrea Cavert, *The American Churches in the Ecumenical Movement, 1900–1968* (New York: Association Press, 1968), 164; "World Conference Announced for 1937," *Federal Council Bulletin*, 18, no. 4 (April 1935), 10–11; Henry Smith Leiper, "Christians of the World Plan United Front," *Federal Council Bulletin*, 18, no. 8 (October 1935), 6–7.

16. J. H. Oldham to Henry P. Van Dusen, 8 February 1935; Henry P. Van Dusen to J. H. Oldham, 9 March 1935; J. H. Oldham to Henry P. Van Dusen, 12 March 1935; "Outline of Proposed Volume on Church, Community, and State in Relation to Education"; J. H. Oldham to Henry P. Van Dusen, 15 June 1936, Archives of the World Council of Churches in Formation, "Life and Work," Special Collections, the Burke Library, Union Theological Seminary (hereafter,

WCC-LW); John C. Bennett to Henry P. Van Dusen, 25 July 1936, Archives of the World Council of Churches in Formation, "Correspondence of Henry P. Van Dusen," Special Collections, the Burke Library, Union Theological Seminary (hereafter, WCC-HPVD).

17. Ehrenström, "Movements for International Friendship and Life and Work," 585, 587; Cavert, *The American Churches in the Ecumenical Movement*, 165.

18. Ericksen, *Theologians Under Hitler*, 3–24.

19. John C. Bennett, "After Liberalism—What?" *Christian Century*, 8 November 1933, 1403–1406.

20. Gregory Vlastos to John C. Bennett, 27 November 1933, John C. Bennett Papers, "Correspondence," Special Collections, the Burke Library, Union Theological Seminary (hereafter, Bennett Papers).

21. Walter M. Horton to John C. Bennett, 11 November 1933, Bennett Papers. The outline was as follows:

Realistic Theology

I. The Decline of Liberalism and the Rise of Realism
II. A Realistic View of Our Human Predicament
III. A Realistic Faith in the Providence of God
IV. A Realistic Estimate of Christ and the Church
V. A Realistic Plan of Salvation

A year later he published it, reworked, as a monograph; see Walter M. Horton, *Realistic Theology* (New York: Harper and Brothers, 1934). Horton also credited a letter from Bennett to Van Dusen that summer as the source of his title.

22. Henry P. Van Dusen to Walter Horton, 10 August 1933, Bennett Papers. The "recruiters" were Francis Miller, Adelaide Case of Columbia University Teachers College, Leslie Blanchard, E. A. "Syme" Yarrow of the Hazen Foundation, and two young scholars, John M. Moore and Walter M. Horton.

23. Henry P. Van Dusen to John C. Bennett, 8 August 1933; Henry P. Van Dusen to John C. Bennett, 20 August 1933, Bennett Papers; Schmidt, *Architect of Unity*, 87–88; Richard Wightman Fox, *Reinhold Niebuhr: A Biography* (New York: Pantheon, 1985; reprint, San Francisco: Harper and Row, 1987), 142; Francis P. Miller, *Man from the Valley: Memoirs of a Twentieth-Century Virginian* (Chaptel Hill: University of North Carolina Press, 1971), 69; Henry P. Van Dusen to Walter Horton, 10 August 1933; Henry P. Van Dusen to John C. Bennett, 30 October 1933, Bennett Papers; "Proposed Conference-Retreats of Younger Christian Thinkers," "Theological Discussion Group" notebooks, Henry P. Van Dusen Papers, Special Collections, the Burke Library, Union Theological Seminary (hereafter, TDG-UTS).

24. Walter M. Horton to John C. Bennett, 11 November 1933, Bennett Papers.

25. Malcolm Cowley, *Exile's Return: A Literary Odyssey of the 1920s* (New York: Viking Press, 1956), 7.

26. Henry P. Van Dusen to the Members of the Retreat of February 2–4, 12

January 1934, Theological Discussion Group Papers, Manuscript Group no. 43, Special Collections, Yale Divinity School Library (hereafter, TDG-YDS); "Proposed Conference-Retreats of Younger Christian Thinkers," and subsequent agendas, TDG-UTS; "Young Theologians," *Federal Council Bulletin*, 13, no. 3 (March 1930), 28.

27. Henry P. Van Dusen to the Members of the Younger Christian Thinkers Group, 18 November 1933, TDG-YDS.

28. The papers ranged from six to twelve single-spaced pages. Sometimes the papers were a digest of members' works in progress.

29. Henry P. Van Dusen to the Members of the Theological Discussion Group, 12 June 1934, TDG-UTS; Henry P. Van Dusen to the Members of the Theological Discussion Group, 12 October 1934, TDG-YDS.

30. "Memorandum" from Henry P. Van Dusen to the Theological Discussion Group, October 1943, TDG-YDS; John C. Bennett, interview with Teresa Thompson, 20 June 1990.

31. In 1937 they faced the problem of filling vacancies for the first time. Van Dusen circulated a list of candidates; the members voted for two. This became their procedure. The first so elected were Benjamin Mays, dean of the School of Religion at Howard University, and Alexander Zabriskie, professor and later dean of the Virginia Theological Seminary in Alexandria. "Names Suggested for Future Membership in the Theological Discussion Group," February 1937; Henry P. Van Dusen to the Members of the Theological Discussion Group, 12 October 1937, TDG-YDS.

32. Henry P. Van Dusen to Samuel McCrea Cavert, 1 October 1935, WCC-HPVD.

33. Henry P. Van Dusen to J. H. Oldham, 9 March 1935, WCC-LW.

34. Henry P. Van Dusen to the Theological Discussion Group, 14 December 1935, TDG-UTS.

35. "Preparation for a World Conference on the Church, the State, and the Community," enclosed with Henry P. Van Dusen to the Theological Discussion Group, 14 December 1935, TDG-YDS.

36. R. L. Calhoun, "The Christian Doctrine of Man I. Aspects of the Church's Thought About Man: A Historical Outline"; Gregory Vlastos, "The Christian Doctrine of Man II. A Brief Analysis of Human Nature"; H. Richard Niebuhr, "Man the Sinner"; Wilhelm Pauck, "Man as Saved," TDG-YDS. Niebuhr subsequently published his paper as "Man the Sinner," *Journal of Religion*, 15, no. 3 (July 1935), 272–280.

37. J. H. Oldham to Henry P. Van Dusen, 20 May 1935, WCC-LW.

38. "Preparing for Ecumenical Conference, 1937," *Federal Council Bulletin*, 18, nos. 9 and 10 (November–December 1935), 15; "Dr. Oldham's Appeal to the Churches," *Federal Council Bulletin*, 18, nos. 9 and 10 (November–December 1935), 4.

39. Henry P. Van Dusen to the Theological Discussion Group, 5 March 1935; Henry P. Van Dusen to the Theological Discussion Group, 18 October 1935; Walter M. Horton, "Revelation"; Roland H. Bainton, "Authority and Religious

Knowledge"; John M. Moore, "Scientific Method and Religious Knowledge"; Douglas Van Steere, "The Role of Mystical Experience in Religion and Morality," TDG-YDS.

40. H. Richard Niebuhr, Wilhelm Pauck, Francis P. Miller, *The Church Against the World* (Chicago: Willett, Clark and Company, 1935).

41. Miller, *Man from the Valley*, 69.

42. H. Richard Niebuhr, "Introduction—The Question of the Church," in *The Church Against the World*, 1–13.

43. Wilhelm Pauck, "Part One—The Crisis of Religion," in *The Church Against the World*, 17–69.

44. Francis P. Miller, "Part Two—American Protestantism and the Christian Faith," in *The Church Against the World*, 73–119.

45. H. Richard Niebuhr, "Part Three—Toward the Independence of the Church," in *The Church Against the World*, 123–156.

46. Samuel McCrea Cavert, "Whither the Church," *Federal Council Bulletin*, 19, no. 2 (February 1936), 13.

47. Henry P. Van Dusen to the Members of the Theological Discussion Group, 11 December 1935; George F. Thomas, "Can We Believe in Progress?"; John Mackay, "Historical and Superhistorical Elements in Christianity"; H. Richard Niebuhr, "Reflections on the Christian Theory of History"; Paul Tillich, "The Marxist View of History," TDG-YDS.

48. J. H. Oldham to Henry P. Van Dusen, 26 March 1935, WCC-LW.

49. Henry P. Van Dusen to Dr. Howard C. Robbins, Dr. S. M. Cavert, and Professor A. C. Zabriskie, 8 October 1936, WCC-LW.

50. Henry P. Van Dusen to the Members of the Theological Discussion Group, 9 October 1935, TDG-YDS; Henry P. Van Dusen to J. H. Oldham, 15 October 1936, WCC-LW; Wilhelm Pauck, "The Church Idea in Christian History. Part II"; Daniel A. McGregor, "II. The Holy Catholic Church"; Francis P. Miller, "The Church as World Community"; Henry P. Van Dusen, "The Church, IV," TDG-YDS.

51. Henry P. Van Dusen to the Members of the Theological Discussion Group, 8 December 1936; Henry P. Van Dusen to the Members of the Theological Discussion Group, 18 January 1937; Samuel McCrea Cavert, "Distinctive Issues in Relation of the Church and State Arising from American History"; Paul Tillich, "What Strategy Should the Church Adopt with Reference to Communism?"; Cornelius Krusé, "What Strategy Should the Church Adopt with Reference to Fascism?"; Georgia Harkness, "What Strategy Should the Church Adopt with Reference to Democracy?" TDG-YDS.

52. "Archbishop Strengthens Ecumenical Outlook," *Federal Council Bulletin*, 19, no. 1 (January 1936), 9; William Adams Brown, *Toward a United Church: Three Decades of Ecumenical Christianity* (New York: Scribner, 1946), 137–138; Cavert, *The American Churches in the Ecumenical Movement, 1900–1968*, 161–162; W. A. Visser 't Hooft, "The Genesis of the World Council of Churches," in *A History of the Ecumenical Movement, 1517–1948*, ed. Ruth Rouse and Stephen Neill (Philadelphia: Westminster Press, 1968), 701.

53. Cavert, *The American Churches in the Ecumenical Movement*, 162.

54. J. H. Oldham to Henry Sloane Coffin, 5 November 1934, WCC-HPVD; "Meeting of the "Steering Committee" of the American Advisory Council 1935 Council on Church, Community, and State, January 5, 1936"; Unsigned statement about the Life and Work conference, 15 January 1936, WCC-LW; "American Advisory Council, Conference on Church, Community, and State (Proposed Membership)," 15 February 1936, WCC-LW.

55. Henry P. Van Dusen to Edwin E. Aubrey, 24 February 1936, WCC-LW; Edwin E. Aubrey to Henry P. Van Dusen, 5 March 1936, WCC-LW.

56. J. H. Oldham to John R. Mott, 1 September 1936, John R. Mott Papers, Manuscript Group no. 45, Special Collections, Yale Divinity School Library.

57. Henry P. Van Dusen to J. H. Oldham, 10 September 1936, WCC-LW. Nobody mentioned again the strained relationship between Oldham and Brown, but Brown, despite his obvious qualifications, was never invited to the inner circle of Oldham and the Theological Discussion Group.

58. Henry P. Van Dusen to Henry Smith Leiper, 14 November 1936, WCC-LW.

59. Henry P. Van Dusen to Georgia Harkness, 6 March 1937, WCC-LW.

60. Henry P. Van Dusen to J. H. Oldham, 3 March 1937, WCC-LW.

61. John C. Bennett to Henry P. Van Dusen, 20 March 1937, WCC-HPVD.

FIVE / PROCLAMATION AND ORGANIZATION

1. "Appendix B, Report of the Committee of Thirty-five Appointed in Pursuance of Resolutions Adopted by the Authoritative Bodies of the Life and Work and the Faith and Order Movement in August and September, 1936," in *The Oxford Conference (Official Report)* (Chicago: Willett, Clark and Company, 1937), 261.

2. Samuel McCrea Cavert, *The American Churches in the Ecumenical Movement, 1900–1968* (New York: Association Press, 1968), 162; William Adams Brown, *Toward a United Church: Three Decades of Ecumenical Christianity* (New York: Scribner, 1946), 140; W. A. Visser 't Hooft, *Memoirs* (London: SCM Press, 1973), 78.

3. Henry P. Van Dusen to John R. Mott, 3 July 1937, WCC-LW; Visser 't Hooft, *Memoirs*, 78.

4. Cavert, *The American Churches in the Ecumenical Movement*, 162; Visser 't Hooft, *Memoirs*, 78; William J. Schmidt, *Architect of Unity: A Biography of Samuel McCrea Cavert* (New York: Friendship Press, 1975), 104; "Appendix B, Report of the Committee of Thirty-five," 264–266.

5. Transcription no. 2 of a tape made by Samuel McCrea Cavert and Barbara Ann Griffis, librarian of the William Adams Brown Ecumenical Library, Union Theological Seminary, 6 May 1972, 5, cited in Schmidt, *Architect of Unity*, 104–105; Brown, *Toward a United Church*, 139; Visser 't Hooft, *Memoirs*, 79, 102; Cavert, *The American Churches in the Ecumenical Movement*, 163.

6. "A Message from the Oxford Conference to the Christian Churches," in *The Oxford Conference (Official Report)*, 45; "Oxford and Edinburgh Mark New World Unity," *Federal Council Bulletin*, 20, no. 7 (September 1937), 6; John R. Mott, "The Ecumenical Movement," *Christendom*, 2, no. 4 (autumn 1937), 533; Cavert, *The American Churches in the Ecumenical Movement*, 163; Nils Ehrenström, " Movements for International Friendship and Life and Work, 1925–1948," in *A History of the Ecumenical Movement, 1517–1948*, ed. Ruth Rouse and Stephen Neill (Philadelphia: Fortress Press, 1968), 587–588. One Roman Catholic was present as a co-opted delegate.

7. Henry Smith Leiper, "World Conference at Oxford Next Month," *Federal Council Bulletin*, 20, no. 5 (June 1937), 6; C. Howard Hopkins, *John R. Mott, 1865–1955: A Biography* (Grand Rapids, Mich.: William B. Eerdmans, 1979), 688; John Crosby Brown to Helen Brown, 27 July 1937, Brown Papers.

8. Mark G. Toulouse, *The Transformation of John Foster Dulles: From Prophet of Realism to Priest of Nationalism* (Macon, Ga.: Mercer University Press, 1985), 52–53; John Foster Dulles, "The Problem of Peace in a Dynamic World," in *The Universal Church and the World of Nations*, The Church, Community and State Series (London: George Allen and Unwin, 1937), 145–168.

9. J. H. Oldham, "Introduction," and "Appendix C, Program of the Conference," in *The Oxford Conference (Official Report)* (Chicago: Willett, Clark and Company, 1937), 25–27, 269; Richard Wightman Fox, *Reinhold Niebuhr: A Biography* (New York: Pantheon Books, 1985; reprint, San Francisco: Harper and Row, 1987), 180; Austen K. de Blois, "Ecumenical Fellowship: The World Conference at Oxford," *Watchman-Examiner*, 25, no. 38 (September 1937), 1060–1062.

10. J. H. Oldham, "Introduction," 14–18; William Adams Brown to John Crosby Brown, 21 July 1937, Brown Papers; Ehrenstrom, "Movements for International Friendship and Life and Work, 1925–1948," 590; "New Spirit Seen in Session at Oxford," *Living Church*, 17 August 1937, 202.

11. "Appendix C, Program of the Conference," 268–274.

12. Schmidt, *Architect of Unity*, 106.

13. "Additional Report of the Section on Church and Community," in *The Oxford Conference (Official Report)*, 180–181, 192–193.

14. Edwin E. Aubrey, "Church and Community," in *Church and Community*, in the Church, Community and State Series (London: George Allen and Unwin, 1937), 171–190; John C. Bennett, "The Causes of Social Evil," in *The Christian Faith and the Common Life*, in the Church, Community and State Series (London: George Allen and Unwin, 1937), 175–196; Robert L. Calhoun, "The Dilemma of Humanitarian Modernism," in *The Christian Understanding of Man*, in the Church, Community and State Series (London: George Allen and Unwin, 1937), 45–81; Walter M. Horton, "The Christian Understanding of Man," in *The Christian Understanding of Man*, in the Church, Community and State Series (London: George Allen and Unwin, 1937), 217–241; Reinhold Niebuhr, "The Christian Faith and the Common Life," in *Christian Faith and the Common Life*, in the

Church, Community and State Series (London: George Allen and Unwin, 1937), 69–97; Paul Tillich, "The Kingdom of God and History," in *The Kingdom of God and History*, in the Church, Community and State Series (London: George Allen and Unwin, 1937), 105–142; H. Paul Douglass, in "Church and Community in the United States," in the Church, Community and State Series *Church and Community* (London: George Allen and Unwin, 1937, 193–259.

John Foster Dulles also had an essay in the preparatory volumes. Though it did not make an immediate impact on ecumenical theology, it set forth recommendations later incorporated in American theologians' ideas about postwar peace as well as the UN Charter and the Marshall Plan. See Dulles, "The Problem of Peace in a Dynamic World," 145–168.

15. "Additional Report of the Section on Church and Community," 173–174; "Additional Report of the Section on Church and State," in *The Oxford Conference (Official Report)*, 224–227; "Report of the Section on Church and Community," in *The Oxford Conference (Official Report)*, 56.

16. Niebuhr, "The Christian Faith and the Common Life," 72.

17. "Report of the Section on Church and Community," 58–59; "Additional Report of the Section on the Church and Community," 182.

18. Aubrey, "Church and Community," 183; Douglass, "Church and Community in the United States," 197; Tillich, "The Kingdom of God and History," 111, 115, 121.

19. "A Message from the Oxford Conference to the Christian Churches," 47; "Report of the Section on Church and Community," 60.

20. "Report of the Section on the Universal Church and the World of Nations," in *The Oxford Conference (Official Report)*, 161.

21. "Additional Report of the Section on Church and State," 236, 248; "Report of the Section on Church and State," in *The Oxford Conference (Official Report)*, 71.

22. "Additional Report of the Section on Church and State," 236.

23. "Report of the Section on the Universal Church and the World of Nations," 167–171.

24. "Appendix B, Report of the Committee of Thirty-five," 267; "Appendix C, Program of the Conference," 236.

25. Oldham, "Introduction," 10–12; "Oxford and Edinburgh Mark New World Unity," *Federal Council Bulletin*, 20, no. 7 (September 1937), 7; Ehrenström, "Movements for International Friendship and Life and Work, 1925–1948," 589.

26. Ehrenström, "Movements for International Friendship and Life and Work, 1925–1948," 589.

27. Toulouse, *The Transformation of John Foster Dulles*, 4–12, 28.

28. John Foster Dulles, "The Churches and the World Order," address to the graduating class of Princeton Theological Seminary, 16 May 1944, published in *Theology Today*, October 1944, in Henry P. Van Dusen, ed., *The Spiritual Legacy of John Foster Dulles: Selections from His Articles and Addresses* (Philadelphia: Westminster Press, 1960), 25.

29. John Foster Dulles, "Faith of Our Fathers," address at the First Presbyterian Church, Watertown, New York, 28 August 1949, in Van Dusen, *The Spiritual Legacy of John Foster Dulles*, 7.

30. "Additional Report of the Section on Church and Community," 187–188.

31. Henry Smith Leiper, "Preface to the American Edition," in *The Oxford Conference (Official Report)*, viii.

32. Samuel McCrea Cavert, "The Issues at Edinburgh," *Federal Council Bulletin*, 20, no. 7 (September 1937), 7–8.

33. Tissington Tatlow, "The World Conference on Faith and Order," in *A History of the Ecumenical Movement, 1517–1948*, ed. Ruth Rouse and Stephen Neill (Philadelphia: Westminister Press, 1968), 431; Clifford P. Morehouse, "Advance Toward Unity," *Living Church*, 4 September 1937, 273–274; *Who's Who at Edinburgh 1937* (Winchester and New York: The Secretariat, August 1937), Pamphlet no. 89, Series I, 3–86; "Edinburgh Approves World Council Plan," *Living Church*, 28 August 1937, 257–258; Francis J. Bloodgood, "Report of the Edinburgh Conference Prepared," *Living Church*, 4 September 1937, 288, 293; Cavert, *The American Churches in the Ecumenical Movement*, 166.

34. *The 1934 Meeting of the Continuation Committee at Hertenstein, Switzerland, September 3–6* (Winchester, England and New York City: The Committee), Pamphlet no. 71, Series I.

35. Brown, *Toward a United Church*, 112.

36. *The 1935 Meeting of the Continuation Committee, Hindsgaul, Middelfart, Denmark, August 4–7* (New York: The Committee, 1935), Pamphlet no. 73, Series I; Tatlow, "The World Conference on Faith and Order," 430.

37. *The Meanings of Unity, Report No. 1 Prepared by the Commission on the Church's Unity in Life and Worship, Edinburgh, 1937* (New York: Harper and Row, 1937), Pamphlet no. 82, Series I, v; *The Communion of Saints, Report No. 2 Prepared by the Commission on the Church's Unity in Life and Worship, Edinburgh, 1937* (New York: Harper and Row, 1937); Brown, *Toward a United Church*, 113.

38. *The 1935 Meeting of the Continuation Committee*, 12–16.

39. *Report of the Second World Conference on Faith and Order, August 3–18, 1937* (Winchester and New York: the Secretariat, August 1937), Pamphlet no. 90, Series I, 58–59.

40. Ibid., 19–24.

41. Ibid., 36–44.

42. W. A. Visser 't Hooft, "The Genesis of the World Council of Churches," *A History of the Ecumenical Movement, 1517–1948*, ed. Ruth Rouse and Stephen Neill (Philadelphia: Westminister Press, 1968), 703–704; Bloodgood, "Report of the Edinburgh Conference Prepared," 288; Schmidt, *Architect of Unity*, 108.

43. Schmidt, *Architect of Unity*, 108.

44. Clifford P. Morehouse, "Edinburgh and the World Council Proposal," *Living Church*, 28 August 1937, 248.

45. Ibid.; Bloodgood, "Report of the Edinburgh Conference Prepared," 288.

46. *Report of the Second World Conference on Faith and Order, August 3–18,*

46–47; "Toward a World Council of Churches," *Federal Council Bulletin*, 20, no. 7 (September 1937), 9–10.

47. *Report of the Second World Conference on Faith and Order, August 3–18*, 50; Visser 't Hooft, "The Genesis of the World Council of Churches," 703; Tatlow, "The World Conference on Faith and Order," 434.

48. Cavert, *The American Churches in the Ecumenical Movement*, 166; Tatlow, "The World Conference on Faith and Order," 434; *Report of the Second World Conference on Faith and Order, August 3–18*, 51–52.

49. Morehouse, "Advance Toward Unity," 273; Tatlow, "The World Conference on Faith and Order," 435.

50. *Private and Confidential to Members of the Constituent Committee and Their Alternates*, 1–4, Archives of the World Council of Churches, Manuscript Group no. 500, Special Collections, Yale Divinity School Library (hereafter, WCC-YDS); "Toward a World Council of Churches," 9–10; Visser 't Hooft, "The Genesis of the World Council of Churches," 704; Cavert, *The American Churches in the Ecumenical Movement*, 167; Schmidt, *Architect of Unity*, 108.

51. "Ecumenical Meetings Next Summer," *Federal Council Bulletin*, 19, no. 5 (May 1936), 9.

52. "The Church as World Community," *Federal Council Bulletin*, 19, no. 9 (November 1936), 3–4.

53. "Bringing Oxford to America," *Federal Council Bulletin*, 20, no. 9 (November 1937), 9.

54. "Forward from Oxford and Edinburgh," *Federal Council Bulletin*, 21, no. 2 (February 1938), 6.

55. "Prospects for World Council of Churches," *Federal Council Bulletin*, 20, no. 10 (December 1937), 4; "Forward from Oxford and Edinburgh," 6.

56. "Popular Report on Oxford," *Federal Council Bulletin* 20, no. 10 (December 1937), 6.

57. Tamblyn and Brown, Incorporated, "Report of the Christian Unity Fund (Oxford-Edinburgh Continuation Program) to May 1, 1938," 1–2, WCC-LW.

58. "Preliminary Steps Forwarding the Proposal of Oxford and Edinburgh for a World Council of Churches, Extracts from the Minutes of the Meeting of the Committee of Fourteen, Victoria Hotel, London, August 14, 1937; the Joint Meetings of the American Sections of the Life and Work and Faith and Order Movements, Hotel George Washington, New York, September 30, 1937; and the Special Joint Committee of the above movements at 230 Park Avenue, New York, October 9, 1937" (New York: World Conference on Faith and Order, Universal Christian Council for Life and Work), 5–7, WCC-YDS.

59. "United Program of Life and Work and Faith and Order," *Federal Council Bulletin*, 20, no. 9 (November 1937), 13.

60. "New Evidences of Ecumenical Unity," *Federal Council Bulletin* 21, no. 2 (February 1938), 5; "Forward from Oxford and Edinburgh," 6–7.

61. Henry P. Van Dusen to Samuel McCrea Cavert, 10 March 1938, 1, WCC-HPVD.

62. "Proceedings of the Conference—Proposed World Council of Churches, Utrecht Conference, May, 1938," 1, 4–8; "Statement of Action Taken at Utrecht Conference," 6, WCC-YDS; Visser 't Hooft, "The Genesis of the World Council of Churches," 704.

63. "Proceedings of the Conference—Proposed World Council of Churches, 8; Cavert, *The American Churches in the Ecumenical Movement*, 167–168; "Holland Brings World Council Near," *Federal Council Bulletin* 21, no. 6 (June 1938), 6.

64. Commenting a few months later on this arrangement, Visser 't Hooft saw it the same way: "[I]t should especially be underlined that there is a place within the framework of the Council as a whole for different types of pioneering work which will not commit the Council itself . . . but which will nevertheless . . . exert real influence upon the churches. This is particularly true of the study work . . . which should continue to make the same impact . . . as it made through the preparation of the Oxford and Edinburgh Conferences." Visser 't Hooft, "What Is the World Council of Churches?" *Christendom* 4, no. 1 (winter 1939), 23–24.

65. Visser 't Hooft, *Memoirs*, 81.

66. "Holland Brings World Council Near," 7; Visser 't Hooft, "The Genesis of the World Council of Churches," 705.

67. "Proposed World Council of Churches—Minutes of the Administrative Committee, Meeting at Utrecht on Friday, May 13, 1938," WCC-YDS.

68. Henry P. Van Dusen to Samuel McCrea Cavert, 13 October 1938, "Henry P. Van Dusen Correspondence," Reinhold Niebuhr Papers, the Collection of the Manuscript Division, Library of Congress (hereafter, Niebuhr Papers).

69. Samuel McCrea Cavert to John C. Bennett, 15 June 1938, Bennett Papers.

70. "*Christendom*: An Ecumenical Quarterly," *Federal Council Bulletin*, 21, no. 8 (October, 1938), 8; *The 1939 Meeting of the Continuation Committee held at St. George's School, Clarens, Switzerland, August 21–23, 1939* (Oxford and New York: The [Continuation] Committee, 1939), Pamphlet no. 92, Series I, 9.

71. *Christendom* 4, no. 1 (January 1939), 1. The Theological Discussion Group members were Edwin Aubrey, Bennett, Cavert, Angus Dun, Georgia Harkness, Lynn Harold Hough, John Mackay, Benjamin Mays, and Niebuhr.

72. *The 1938 Meeting of the Continuation Committee held at St. George's School, Clarens, Switzerland, August 29–September 1, 1938* (Oxford and New York: The [Continuation] Committee, 1938), Pamphlet no. 91, Series I, 9, 28, 33–37, 47–48; *The 1939 Meeting of the Continuation Committee*, 6.

73. *The 1939 Meeting of the Continuation Committee*, 6, 9–76.

SIX / MAKING A NEW INTERNATIONAL ORDER IN THE WAR YEARS

1. Donald Meyer, *The Protestant Search for Political Realism, 1919–1941* (Berkeley: University of California Press, 1960, 2d ed., Middletown, Conn.: Wesleyan University Press, 1988), xvi; Wayne H. Cowan, "Introduction," *Witness to a Generation: Significant Writings from Christianity and Crisis (1941–1966)*, ed. Wayne H. Cowan (Indianapolis: Bobbs-Merrill, 1966), xv.

2. Letter from W. A. Visser 't Hooft to Samuel McCrea Cavert, 19 December 1939, Archives of the World Council of Churches, Geneva, Switzerland, cited in William J. Schmidt, *Architect of Unity: A Biography of Samuel McCrea Cavert* (New York: Friendship Press, 1975), 133–134, n. 14.

3. Ibid., 117–141; W. A. Visser 't Hooft, "The Genesis of the World Council of Churches," in A History of the Ecumenical Movement, 1517–1948, ed. Ruth Rouse and Stephen Neill (Philadelphia: Westminster Press, 1968, 709–710; William Adams Brown, "Maintaining the Christian Network," *Christendom*, 5, no. 3 (summer 1940), 460.

4. Henry Smith Leiper, "Plans Completed for World Conference, Oxford, 1937," *Federal Council Bulletin*, 19, no. 8 (October 1936), 6–8.

5. "A Challenge to Christendom," *Federal Council Bulletin*, 17, no. 2 (February 1934), 5; "A Truly Christian Appeal," *Federal Council Bulletin*, 17, no. 6 (June 1934), 5; "German Guest Welcomed," *Federal Council Bulletin*, 18, no. 5 (May 1935), 10; Samuel McCrea Cavert, "How Christians May Show Sympathy for Jews," *Federal Council Bulletin*, 18, no. 8 (October 1935), 4–5; Frank Ritchie, "Refugees a Challenge to Christian People," *Federal Council Bulletin*, 18, nos. 9 and 10 (November–December 1935), 12; "Christians Welcome Jewish Visitors," *Federal Council Bulletin*, 19, no. 3 (March 1936), 7; Samuel McCrea Cavert, "Why Christians Must Oppose Anti-Semitism," *Federal Council Bulletin*, 19, no. 7 (September 1936), 5.

6. Samuel McCrea Cavert, "This Humanity," *Federal Council Bulletin*, 21, no. 10 (December 1938), 3–4; "Christians Unite in Sympathy for Jews," *Federal Council Bulletin*, 21, no. 10 (December 1938), 9; "Thirtieth Anniversary Marks Interest in Unity," *Federal Council Bulletin*, 22, no. 1 (January 1939), 7; "Support for German Refugees," *Federal Council Bulletin*, 22, no. 3 (March 1939), 7; "Friendly Refugee Policy Is Urged," *Federal Council Bulletin*, 22, no. 4 (April 1939), 8–9; "Relief for Chinese and Refugees Continues," *Federal Council Bulletin*, 22, no. 7 (September 1939), 8–9.

7. Francis P. Miller, *Man from the Valley: Memoirs of a Twentieth-Century Virginian* (Chapel Hill: University of North Carolina Press, 1971), 90–92; Mark Lincoln Chadwin, *The Hawks of World War II* (Chapel Hill: University of North Carolina Press, 1968), 32–36, 47–48; Robert D. Schulzinger, *The Wise Men of Foreign Affairs: The History of the Council on Foreign Relations* (New York: Columbia University Press, 1984), 70–71.

8. "American War Vote Demanded; Somme Is Cited as Our 'Frontier'; 30 Notables Ask Public to Join Plea for Step Held to Be Only Way to Full Massing of Our Energies Against Germany," *New York Times*, 10 June 1940; Chadwin, *The Hawks of World War II*, 38–39.

9. Miller, *Man from the Valley*, 93–94; Chadwin, *The Hawks of World War II*, 40–73.

10. Miller, *Man from the Valley*, 96–101; Schulzinger, *The Wise Men of Foreign Affairs*, 71.

11. June Bingham, *Courage to Change: An Introduction to the Life and Thought of Reinhold Niebuhr* (New York: Scribner, 1961; reprint, 1972), 251–252; Rich-

ard Wightman Fox, *Reinhold Niebuhr: A Biography* (New York: Pantheon Books, 1985; reprint, San Francisco: Harper and Row, 1987), 196. For more about the origins of *Christianity and Crisis* in relation to the *Christian Century*, see Mark David Hulsether, "Liberals, Radicals, and the Contested Social Thought of Postwar Protestantism: *Christianity and Crisis* Magazine, 1941–1976" (Ph.D. diss., University of Minnesota, 1992), 91–106.

12. Reinhold Niebuhr to John C. Bennett, 31 May 1940, Niebuhr Papers.

13. "The Crisis," *Christianity and Crisis*, 10 February 1941, 1; "Holy Wars," *Christianity and Crisis*, 10 February 1941, 2–3; Reinhold Niebuhr, "The Christian Faith and the World Crisis," *Christianity and Crisis*, 10 February 1941, 4; "The World After the War," *Christianity and Crisis*, 10 February 1941, 3; "British Churchmen and Peace Aims," *Christianity and Crisis*, 10 February 1941, 3.

14. Henry P. Van Dusen to John C. Bennett, 9 May 1941, WCC-HPVD.

15. Henry P. Van Dusen to John C. Bennett, 17 March 1941, Bennett Papers.

16. John Foster Dulles, "The Church's Contribution to a Warless World," *Religion in Life* (winter, 1940), copyright 1939 by Abingdon Press, in *The Spiritual Legacy of John Foster Dulles: Selections from His Articles and Addresses*, ed. Henry P. Van Dusen (Philadelphia: Westminster Press, 1960), 139–150; Mark G. Toulouse, *The Transformation of John Foster Dulles: From Prophet of Realism to Priest of Nationalism* (Macon, Ga.: Mercer University Press, 1985), 55.

17. "To Study Peace and War Problems," *Federal Council Bulletin*, 23, no. 2 (February 1940), 6; "The Churches and the International Situation," *Federal Council Bulletin*, 23, no. 4 (April 1940), 7–9; Toulouse, *The Transformation of John Foster Dulles*, 55.

18. "Study Guide on International Problems," *Federal Council Bulletin*, 23, no. 5 (May 1940), 13; Toulouse, *The Transformation of John Foster Dulles*, 56.

19. "The American Churches in Time of War," *Federal Council Bulletin*, no. 24, no. 1 (January 1941), 6–7; Robert W. Potter, "Policy Urged on Churches," *New York Times*, 11 December 1940; Walter W. Van Kirk, "Churches to Study Bases of Durable Peace," *Federal Council Bulletin*, 24, no. 2 (February 1941), 13; Toulouse, *The Transformation of John Foster Dulles*, 56–57. Dulles coined the phrase "a just and durable peace."

20. Toulouse, *The Transformation of John Foster Dulles*, 61–62.

21. "Minutes. Committee of Direction of the Commission to Study the Bases of a Just and Durable Peace, New York, March 21, 1941," Niebuhr Papers; Toulouse, *The Transformation of John Foster Dulles*, 63–64.

22. "A World-Wide Communion Sunday," *Federal Council Bulletin*, 23, no. 5 (May 1940), 5; "The Sacrament for a Suffering World," *Federal Council Bulletin*, 23, no. 7 (September 1940), 5; "Unprecedented Communion Celebration," *Federal Council Bulletin*, 24, no. 9 (November 1941), 6.

23. Samuel McCrea Cavert, *The American Churches in the Ecumenical Movement, 1900–1968* (New York: Association Press, 1968), 183; Schmidt, *Architect of Unity*, 136.

24. "European Visit Deferred," *Federal Council Bulletin*, 25, no. 1 (January 1942), 10; Cavert, *The American Churches in the Ecumenical Movement*, 183; Schmidt, *Architect of Unity*, 137.

25. "A Message to Our Fellow Christians, from the Federal Council of the Churches of Christ in America, Adopted December 30, 1941," *Federal Council Bulletin*, 25, no. 1 (January 1942), 3–4. Support for the war was not given unreservedly even by the "realists." John Bennett reminded those involved in the ecumenical movement that the church had the task of upholding the government while maintaining a critical perspective on it. See John C. Bennett, "In Such a Time," *Christendom*, 7, no. 2 (spring 1942), 162.

26. "The Study Conference on the Bases of Peace," *Federal Council Bulletin*, 25, no. 4 (April 1942), 9–10; Cavert, *The American Churches in the Ecumenical Movement*, 179.

27. "The Study Conference on the Bases of Peace," *Federal Council Bulletin*, 25, no. 4 (April 1942), 9–10; "Churches Use 'Delaware,'" *Federal Council Bulletin*, 25, no. 8, pt. 2 (October 1942), 2.

28. Henry P. Van Dusen, "Issues of the Peace," *Christendom*, 7, no. 1 (winter 1942), 2–12.

29. Henry P. Van Dusen, "The Churches Speak," *Christianity and Crisis*, 16 April 1942, 1–2.

30. William Adams Brown, "The Forgotten Factor in Post-War Reconstruction," *Christendom*, 7, no. 4 (autumn 1942), 481.

31. Toulouse, *The Transformation of John Foster Dulles*, 67; "Six Pillars of Peace," *Christianity and Crisis*, 31 May 1943, 5; Bradford S. Abernethy, "Political Propositions for Peace Issued," *Federal Council Bulletin*, 26, no. 4 (April 1943), 11–12.

32. "Six Pillars of Peace," *Christianity and Crisis*, 31 May 1943, 5–6; "Six Pillars of Peace," *Christianity and Crisis*, 28 June 1943, 6–8.

33. "The Moscow Declarations and The 'Six Pillars of Peace,'" *Federal Council Bulletin*, 26, no. 10 (December 1943), 3; "The Christian Mission on World Order," *Federal Council Bulletin*, 26, no. 9 (November 1943), 9; Toulouse, *The Transformation of John Foster Dulles*, 69.

34. Henry P. Van Dusen, "Six Pillars of Peace," *Christianity and Crisis*, 22 March 1943, 1–2; Toulouse, *The Transformation of John Foster Dulles*, 71.

35. Herman Will, *A Will for Peace: Peace Action in the United Methodist Church, A History* (Washington, D.C.: General Board of Church and Society of the United Methodist Church, 1984), 81–83; G. Bromley Oxnam, "The Crusade for a New World Order," *Christianity and Crisis*, 26 July 1943, 12–13; Robert Moats Miller, *Bishop G. Bromley Oxnam: Paladin of Liberal Protestantism* (Nashville, Tenn.: Abingdon Press, 1990), 280–287; Robert A. Divine, *Second Chance: The Triumph of Internationalism in America During World War II* (New York: Atheneum, 1967), 161–162.

36. Dennis L. Tarr, "The Presbyterian Church and the Founding of the UN," *Journal of Presbyterian History*, 53 (spring 1975), 3–32.

37. *Changing World* (May 1944), 5; *Christian Century*, 22 May 1944, 356; *Christian Century*, 19 April 1944, 485–486; *Post War World*, 15 April 1944, 1.

38. "The Christian Mission on World Order," *Federal Council Bulletin*, 26, no. 9 (November 1943), 9; "Christian Mission on World Order," *Christianity and Crisis*, 20 September 1943, 7.

39. "Princeton International Round-Table," *Federal Council Bulletin*, 26, no. 7 (September 1943), 7; "An International Christian Round Table," *Christianity and Crisis*, 26 July 1943, 1–2; "Princeton International Round Table," *Christendom*, 8, no. 4 (autumn 1943), xv; Toulouse, *The Transformation of John Foster Dulles*, 77.

40. "The Moscow Declarations and The 'Six Pillars of Peace,'" 3.

41. Ruth Russell, *A History of the United Nations Charter: The Role of the United States, 1940–1945* (Washington, D.C.: Brookings Institution, 1958), 216–217, 594; "Informal Discussions on Peace Organization," *The Department of State Bulletin*, 22 October 1944, 450–453.

42. John Foster Dulles, "America's Role in the Peace," *Christianity and Crisis*, 22 January 1945, 5; John Foster Dulles, "Collaboration Must Be Practical," *Vital Speeches of the Day*, 9 (February 1945), 246–249; "Professors Horton and Hocking to Head Pre-Cleveland Conference Commissions," *Federal Council Bulletin*, 27, no. 8 (October 1944), 11; "The Churches and a Just and Durable Peace," *Christendom*, 5, no. 2 (spring 1945), xiii.

43. "Cleveland Conference on a Just and Durable Peace," "The Laymen at Cleveland," "The Cleveland Conference and Basic Issues," *Federal Council Bulletin*, 28, no. 2 (February 1945), 3–8; "Commission on a Just and Durable Peace," *Christianity and Crisis*, 19 February 1945, 7–8; "The Churches and a Just and Durable Peace," xiii-xiv; Toulouse, *The Transformation of John Foster Dulles*, 80.

44. "Appendix D, The United Nations Conference on International Organization: List of Delegations, United States Delegation," *Charter of the United Nations: Report to the President on the Results of the San Francisco Conference by the Chairman of the Delegation, the Secretary of State*, Publication 2349, Conference Series 71 (Washington, D.C.: Department of State, 26 June 1945), 255; "Mr. Dulles Given Leave from Commission," *Federal Council Bulletin*, 28, no. 5 (May 1945), 10; Miller, *Bishop G. Bromley Oxnam*, 267.

45. Russell, *A History of the United Nations Charter*, 594–595; "United Nations Conference on International Organization," *Department of State Bulletin*, 15 April 1945, 671–672; "Appendix D," *Report to the President*, 262–266.

46. Arthur H. Vandenberg, Jr., ed., with the collaboration of Joe Alex Morris, *The Private Papers of Senator Vandenberg* (Boston: Houghton Mifflin, 1952), 171.

47. Richard M. Fagley, "The Churches and San Francisco," *Federal Council Bulletin*, 28, no. 6 (June 1945), 7; Edward L. Parsons, "Report from San Francisco," *Christianity and Crisis*, 11 June 1945, 1–3; Russell, *A History of the United Nations Charter*, 635–641.

48. Russell, *A History of the United Nations Charter*, 778–781, 808–842, 910–918; and "Appendix M, Charter of the United Nations," 1035–1053. The Soviets' position changed after Truman bluntly told Stalin at the Potsdam Con-

ference in May that he would accomplish the United Nations whether or not the Soviet Union became a member.

49. *Secretary's Report for the Period August, 1939–October, 1941* (Oxford and Washington, Conn.: The Secretary, 1941), Pamphlet no. 96, Series I, 3, 7; *Report of the American Section of the Commission on Intercommunion* (Washington, Conn.: Office of the Associate Secretary for America, 1942), Pamphlet no. 98, Series I; *Secretary's Report, 1942–1943* (November 1942), Pamphlet no. 97, Series I, 3.

50. *The Nature of the Church: A Report of the American Theological Committee* (Chicago: Willett, Clark and Company, 1945), Pamphlet no. 100, Series I.

51. John C. Bennett to Collaborators for the Study Department in the United States, 6 March 1940, WCC-HPVD. Bennett summarized the genesis of the debate and the substance of Visser 't Hooft's argument in a three-year retrospective report of the project; see John C. Bennett, "Results of an Ecumenical Study," *Christendom*, 9, no. 2 (spring 1944), 142–152.

52. Bennett formed his group in 1939 when he taught at the Pacific School of Religion. See Henry P. Van Dusen to John C. Bennett, 16 November 1939, WCC-HPVD. Members of the Chicago group included Edwin E. Aubrey (chair), James L. Adams (Meadville Theological School), Conrad Bergendoff (Augustana Theological Seminary), W. Barnett Blakemore, Jr. (Disciples Divinity House, University of Chicago), Joseph Haroutunian (Presbyterian Theological Seminary), John Knox (University of Chicago), Georgia Harkness (Garrett Biblical Institute); and Wilhelm Pauck (Chicago Theological Seminary). Noted in "Preaching as an Expression of the Ethical Reality of the Church," A Memorandum by the Chicago Ecumenical Discussion Group (TDG-YDS). See also John C. Bennett to Those who received the Chicago memorandum, n.d., attached to John C. Bennett to Prof. E. S. Brightman, 24 April 1941, WCC-HPVD; John C. Bennett, "The Study Commission at Toronto," *Christendom*, 6, no. 4 (autumn 1941), 633.

53. Henry P. Van Dusen to John C. Bennett, 19 February 1942, Bennett Papers.

54. Paul J. Tillich, Theodore M. Greene, George F. Thomas, Edwin E. Aubrey, and John Knox, *The Christian Answer*, edited with an introduction by Henry P. Van Dusen (New York: Scribner, 1945), viii; Henry P. Van Dusen to the Members of the Theological Discussion Group, 15 April 1941, TDG-YDS. A critical self-evaluation undertaken by the group in the 1941–1942 academic year also may have precipitated their growing cognizance of their consensus and the need to express it explicitly in a joint publication.

55. "Theological Discussion Group, Proposed Program for the year 1942–1943," TDG-YDS.

56. "The Relation of the Church to War," *Federal Council Bulletin*, 26, no. 5 (May 1943), 12.

57. Members of the Theological Discussion Group who belonged to the commission were Edwin E. Aubrey, Roland Bainton, John C. Bennett, Harvie Branscomb, Angus Dun, Theodore M. Greene, Georgia Harkness, Walter M. Horton, John Knox, John A. Mackay, Benjamin E. Mays, H. Richard Niebuhr,

Reinhold Niebuhr, Wilhelm Pauck, Douglas Steere, Henry P. Van Dusen, and Alexander Zabriskie.

58. Samuel McCrea Cavert to John C. Bennett, 11 February 1943; Edwin E. Aubrey to Members of Section 1 of the Commission on "The Relation of the Church to the War in the Light of the Christian Faith," n.d., Bennett Papers.

59. "Theological Discussion Group, Proposed Program for the year 1942–1943," TDG-YDS.

60. Robert L. Calhoun to John C. Bennett, 13 May 1943, Bennett Papers.

61. Henry P. Van Dusen to the Theological Discussion Group, n.d.; Nels F. S. Ferré, "The Relation of the Church to the War in the Light of the Christian Faith"; John Knox, "War as Seen from the Point of View of the Christian Faith"; Henry P. Van Dusen, "The Christian Faith and War," October 1943, TDG-YDS.

62. "The Relation of the Church to the War in Light of the Christian Faith," *Social Action*, 15 December 1944, 3–79.

63. "Historical Review of Church and War," *Federal Council Bulletin*, 28, no. 2 (February 1945), 8.

64. "The Church and the War," *Christianity and Crisis*, 25 December 1944, 5. In the early 1960s it had such a reputation. See *Creeds of the Church: A Reader in Christian Doctrine from the Bible to the Present*, 3d ed., ed. John H. Leith (Chicago: Aldine, 1962; reprint, Atlanta: John Knox Press, 1982), 523.

65. Tillich et al., *The Christian Answer*.

66. Ibid., viii.

67. "Americans Visit England," *Federal Council Bulletin*, 25, no. 5 (May 1942), 12; "Ecumenical Visitation Across the Atlantic," *Christendom*, 8, no. 1 (winter 1943), viii–ix.

68. Henry Smith Leiper to John R. Mott, 5 October 1942, "Appendix E, Report to the Joint Executive Committee on Visitation to Portugal, England, Scotland and Ireland, April 14 to June 3, 1942, by Henry Smith Leiper," 2, Mott Papers.

69. Walter W. Van Kirk, "British and American Post-War Aims," *Federal Council Bulletin*, 25, no. 7, pt. 1 (September 1942), 10.

70. Schmidt, *Architect of Unity*, 138–140; David P. Gaines, *The World Council of Churches: A Study of Its Background and History* (Peterborough, N.H.: Richard R. Smith, 1966), 178.

71. Nils Ehrenström, "Movements for International Friendship and Life and Work, 1925–1948," in *A History of the Ecumenical Movement, 1517–1948*, ed. Ruth Rouse and Stephen Neill (Philadelphia: Westminster Press, 1968), 558; Visser 't Hooft, "The Genesis of the World Council of Churches," 711–712.

72. Visser 't Hooft, *Memoirs*, 175.

73. Schmidt, *Architect of Unity*, 181; Paul G. Macy, "Ecumenical Ambassadors," *Federal Council Bulletin*, 28, no. 6 (June 1945), 10.

74. Visser 't Hooft, *Memoirs*, 186.

75. Schmidt, *Architect of Unity*, 229; William J. Schmidt and Edward Ouellette, *What Kind of a Man? The Life of Henry Smith Leiper* (New York: Friendship Press, 1986), 190; Visser 't Hooft, *Memoirs*, 187.

76. Cavert, *The American Churches in the Ecumenical Movement*, 198; Schmidt, *Architect of Unity*, 182.

77. Cavert, *The American Churches in the Ecumenical Movement*, 198; Visser 't Hooft, "The Genesis of the World Council of Churches," 715; Visser 't Hooft, *Memoirs*, 190–191; Schmidt, *Architect of Unity*, 184.

78. Visser 't Hooft, "The Genesis of the World Council of Churches," 715; Cavert, *The American Churches in the Ecumenical Movement*, 180–181; "Repentance and Humility," *Federal Council Bulletin*, 28, no. 10 (December 1945), 4–5; "German Church Joins World Council," *Christianity and Crisis*, 12 November 1945, 7–8.

SEVEN / FROM THE CENTER TO THE MARGINS

1. W. A. Visser 't Hooft, *Memoirs* (London and Philadelphia: SCM Press/Westminster Press, 1973), 195.

2. David P. Gaines, *The World Council of Churches: A Study of Its Background and History* (Peterborough, N.H.: Richard R. Smith, 1966), 181. *Life* magazine featured an article and several photographs, including a large one of the leadership core standing in front of Geneva's massive Reformation wall monument. See, "Protestants Plan for Peace," *Life*, 10 March 1946, 31–35.

3. Charles P. Taft, "Report on World Council," *Christianity and Crisis*, 13 May 1946, 6–7; "'Wholeness Is the True Nature of the Church,'" *Federal Council Bulletin*, 29, no. 5 (May 1946), 5; and Visser 't Hooft, *Memoirs*, 196.

4. *The World Council of Churches in Its Process of Formation: Minutes and Reports of the Meeting of the Provisional Committee of the World Council of Churches Held at Geneva from February 21st to 23rd, 1946; The Constitutional Documents of the World Council of Churches and an Introduction by W. A. Visser 't Hooft* (Geneva: World Council of Churches, 1946), 14.

5. Ibid., 32–36, 43.

6. Ibid., 55, 78; Visser 't Hooft, *Memoirs*, 197; W. A. Visser 't Hooft, "The Genesis of the World Council of Churches," in *A History of the Ecumenical Movement, 1517–1948*, ed. Ruth Rouse and Stephen Neill (Philadelphia: Westminster Press, 1968), 717.

7. *The World Council of Churches in Its Process of Formation*, 108–109; Douglas Horton, "The Meeting of the Provisional Committee of the World Council of Churches," *Christendom*, 11, no. 3 (summer 1946), 345; and William J. Schmidt, *Architect of Unity: A Biography of Samuel McCrea Cavert* (New York: Friendship Press, 1975), 217.

8. Samuel McCrea Cavert to W. A. Visser 't Hooft, 22 May 1945, Archives of the National Council of the Churches of Christ in the United States of America, Philadelphia, Pennsylvania, cited in Schmidt, *Architect of Unity*, 217 n. 14.

9. *The World Council of Churches in Its Process of Formation*, 109–111.

10. Ibid., 56; Schmidt, *Architect of Unity*, 191–192.

11. *The World Council of Churches in Its Process of Formation*, 57, 196; Samuel McCrea Cavert, *The American Churches in the Ecumenical Movement*, 199; Schmidt, *Architect of Unity*, 213.

12. Douglas Horton, "The Meeting of the Provisional Committee of the World Council of Churches," *Christendom*, 11, no. 3 (summer 1946), 355.

13. *Report of the Study Department [to the Provisional Committee, Buck Hill Falls, Pennsylvania, April 22–24, 1947]*, 3, Henry P. Van Dusen Papers, "Provisional Committee, Buck Hill Falls, 1947," Special Collections, the Burke Library, Union Theological Seminary. See "Recommendations to the Participants in the Ecumenical Studies on 'The Order of God and the Present Disorder of Man,'" n.d., 2–3, WCC-HPVD.

14. See volumes 1–4, *Man's Disorder and God's Design*, The Amsterdam Assembly Series (New York: Harper and Brothers, 1948).

15. James Muilenberg, "An Evaluation of the Methods of the Historical Study of the Bible"; Walter M. Horton, "Neo-Orthodox Conceptions of Biblical Authority"; Amos N. Wilder, "The Status and Content of Biblical Theology," TDG-YDS; "Report of the Discussion of the Theological Discussion Group of Dr. Oldham's Paper on Technics and Civilization, College of Preachers, Washington, D.C., November 7–9, 1947," WCC-HPVD; "U.S. Churchmen Prepare for World Council Assembly," *Christianity and Crisis*, 6 January 1947, 7. By the time the preparatory volumes appeared in print, the study had involved over 160 Americans alone.

16. "The Authority and Significance of the Bible," *Christendom*, 12, no. 2 (spring 1947), 277; "Study Conference on the Bible," *Christianity and Crisis*, 3 March 1947, 7; Visser 't Hooft, *Memoirs*, 205.

17. Carl E. Schneider, "An American's Observations on European Theological Discussion," *Christendom*, 12, no. 3 (summer 1947), 343–344.

18. Henry P. Van Dusen to Nils Ehrenström, 26 June 1939; Henry P. Van Dusen to Nils Ehrenström, 22 July 1939, WCC-HPVD.

19. Henry P. Van Dusen to W. A. Visser 't Hooft, 25 May 1946, WCC-HPVD.

20. Henry P. Van Dusen to W. A. Visser 't Hooft, 18 May 1948, Archives of the World Council of Churches in Formation, "Correspondence of Henry P. Van Dusen," Special Collections, the Burke Library, Union Theological Seminary.

21. J. H. Oldham to John Bennett, 24 February 1948, WCC-HPVD.

22. Schmidt, *Architect of Unity*, 56–57; Melanie A. May, *Bonds of Unity: Women, Theology and the Worldwide Church*, American Academy of Religion Series (Atlanta: Scholars Press, 1989), 17. Virginia Lieson Brereton described the ambiguous position that women leaders held in the ecumenical movement during these years. On one hand, because many of them were wives, daughters, or sisters of the male leaders, they were insiders in the movement and had friends and acquaintances among the wealthy and influential in the dominant denominations. On the other hand, they were outsiders, deriving their identity from women's societies and women's educational institutions. See Virginia Lieson Brereton, "United and Slighted: Women as Subordinated Insiders," in *Between the Times: The Travel of the Protestant Establishment in America, 1900–1960*, ed. William R. Hutchison (Cambridge: Cambridge University Press, 1989), 143–167.

23. Inez M. Cavert, "Extensive Study Being Made of Women in the Church," *Federal Council Bulletin*, 30, no. 5 (May 1947), 10; May, *Bonds of Unity*, 18; Schmidt, *Architect of Unity*, 223–224. For a general survey of women's involvement in the ecumenical movement in the United States, see Gladys Gilkey Calkins, *Follow Those Women: Church Women in the Ecumenical Movement. A History of the Development of United Work Among Women of the Protestant Churches in the United States* (New York: National Council of Churches of Christ in the U.S.A., 1961).

24. William W. Clemes, "Meetings Highlight Role of Women in the Church," *Federal Council Bulletin*, 31, no. 5 (May 1948), 11; May, *Bonds of Unity*, 18.

25. May, *Bonds of Unity*, 18; Gaines, *The World Council of Churches*, 243.

26. May, *Bonds of Unity*, 18; Gaines, *The World Council of Churches*, 243.

27. Henry P. Van Dusen, "The World Council Continues to Take Shape," *Christendom*, 12, no. 1 (winter 1947), 84; Cavert, *The American Churches in the Ecumenical Movement*, 199.

28. "A Call to the Churches for the First Assembly of the World Council," *Federal Council Bulletin*, 31, no. 1 (January 1948), 6; "The World Council in America," *Christendom*, 12, no. 3 (summer 1947), 420–423; Gaines, *The World Council of Churches*, 216.

29. It was a record turnout for the press corps of the city of international conferences. Henry Smith Leiper, "Large Participation Due for Amsterdam Assembly: 127 Denominations Already Present," *Federal Council Bulletin*, 31, no. 1 (January 1948), 7; "Final Planning Session Is Held: Amsterdam Preparations Near Completion," *Federal Council Bulletin*, 31, no. 3 (March 1948), 5–6; Visser 't Hooft, "The Genesis of the World Council of Churches," 719.

30. *Life*, 17 May 1948, 108–110. See also Eleanor Kent Browne to the Delegates, Alternates, etc., 11 May 1948, Niebuhr Papers. Some denominational periodicals ran pre-assembly stories. For example, John C. Bennett, "Guest Editorial: And Now the World Council," *Advance*, 140, no. 5 (May 1948), 4–5. *Advance* was the denominational organ for the Congregational-Christian Church. *The Living Church* of the Protestant Episcopal Church offered a pre-Amsterdam number, 114, no. 26 (June 27, 1948). Articles included Frederick E. Reissing, "Looking Ahead to Amsterdam," 9–10; Samuel McCrea Cavert, "How the Assembly Is Organized," 10–11; Mrs. Samuel McCrea Cavert, "Women at Amsterdam," and Philip T. Zabriskie, "The Youth Program at Amsterdam," 18.

31. "A Prayer for the Assembly," *Federal Council Bulletin*, 31, no. 5 (May 1948), 1; "Prayer for Amsterdam," *Federal Council Bulletin*, 31, no. 5 (May 1948), 4; "Whitsunday—A Day of Prayer," *Federal Council Bulletin*, 31, no. 5 (May 1948), 6.

32. John Oliver Nelson, "The Amsterdam Assembly in Review," *Federal Council Bulletin*, 31, no. 8 (October 1948), 5; Gaines, *The World Council of Churches*, 231.

33. Douglas Horton, "An Overall Appraisal of Amsterdam and Its Results," *Christendom*, 13, no. 4 (autumn 1948), 421; Nelson, "The Amsterdam Assem-

bly in Review," 5; Gaines, *The World Council of Churches*, 224, 233–236; Visser 't Hooft, *Memoirs*, 208–209; James W. Kennedy, *Venture of Faith: The Birth of the World Council of Churches* (New York: Morehouse-Goreham, 1948), 15–16; Ivan Lee Holt, "The Worship Services at Amsterdam," *Christendom*, 13, no. 4 (autumn 1948), 447.

34. Nelson, "The Amsterdam Assembly in Review," 5. Visser 't Hooft, *Memoirs*, 209; Gaines, *The World Council of Churches*, 239–240; *The First Assembly of the World Council of Churches. The Official Report*, Vol. 5, ed. W. A. Visser 't Hooft, Man's Disorder and God's Design, the Amsterdam Assembly Series (New York: Harper and Brothers, 1949), 27–28.

35. Holt, "The Worship Services at Amsterdam," 447–448; Nelson, "The Amsterdam Assembly in Review," 6; Gaines, *The World Council of Churches*, 239–240.

36. Donald Boles quoted in Gaines, *The World Council of Churches*, 241. In the United States alone some sixteen hundred papers ran stories about the assembly.

37. Gaines, *The World Council of Churches*, 242–243.

38. Dulles expressed the ideas in his address in the essay he contributed to the preparatory study, "The Christian Citizen in a Changing World," in *The Church and the International Disorder*, vol. 4, Man's Disorder and God's Design, The Amsterdam Assembly Series (New York: Harper and Brothers, 1948), 73–114. Hromadka expressed the ideas in his address in the essay he contributed to the preparatory study, "Our Responsibilities in the Post-War World," in *The Church and the International Disorder*, 114–142. See also Nelson, "The Amsterdam Assembly in Review," 6; Walter W. Van Kirk, "The Churches and the International Disorder," *Christendom*, 13, no. 4 (autumn 1948), 488–490; John C. Bennett, "East and West in Amsterdam," *Christianity and Crisis*, 8, no. 16 4 October 1948, 122–123; "Report of Section III, The Church and the Disorder of Society," in *The Church and the Disorder of Society*, vol. 3, Man's Disorder and God's Design, the Amsterdam Assembly Series (New York: Harper and Brothers, 1948), 197–205.

39. Henry P. Van Dusen to Benjamin Strong, 22 November 1948, Henry P. Van Dusen Papers, "Post-Amsterdam," Special Collections, the Burke Library, Union Theological Seminary. See also David Bronson to John C. Bennett, 10 September 1943; John C. Bennett to Andrew G. Kuroda, 27 September 1948, Bennett Papers.

40. Henry P. Van Dusen, "The Business of the World Council," *Christianity and Crisis*, 4 October 1948, 125.

41. Robert T. Handy, *A History of Union Theological Seminary in New York* (New York: Columbia University Press, 1987), 211–291.

42. These core members of the Theological Discussion Group also continued to publish monographs on subjects they had begun to address in conjunction with the ecumenical movement. Bennett wrote several books about Christianity and international relations, among them *Nuclear Weapons and the Conflict of Conscience* (1962), *Christian Faith and Political Choice* (1963), and *Foreign Policy*

in Christian Perspective (1966). Niebuhr's enduring preoccupation with a realist approach to theology, political theory, and international relations found expression in such works as *The Irony of American History* (1951), *Christian Realism and Political Problems* (1953), and *The Structure of Nations and Empires* (1959). Less prolific was Van Dusen, who wrote a book dealing indirectly with international relations, a biography of UN General Secretary Dag Hammarskjöld (1967). Attending to ecumenism itself, Cavert wrote a history of the movement, *The American Churches in the Ecumenical Movement, 1900–1968* (1968).

43. Alden Whitman, "Reinhold Niebuhr Is Dead; Protestant Theologian, 78," *New York Times*, 2 June 1971, 1, 45.

Bibliography

MANUSCRIPT COLLECTIONS

Archives of the Student Volunteer Movement for Foreign Missions. Manuscript Group no. 42. Special Collections. Yale Divinity School Library.

Archives of the World Council of Churches. Manuscript Group no. 500. Special Collections. Yale Divinity School Library.

Archives of the World Council of Churches in Formation. Special Collections. The Burke Library. Union Theological Seminary.

Archives of the World's Student Christian Federation. Manuscript Group no. 46. Special Collections. Yale Divinity School Library.

Archives of the YMCA-Student Division. Manuscript Group no. 58. Special Collections. Yale Divinity School Library.

Henry P. Van Dusen Papers. Special Collections. The Burke Library. Union Theological Seminary.

John C. Bennett Papers. Special Collections. The Burke Library. Union Theological Seminary.

John R. Mott Papers. Manuscript Group no. 45. Special Collections. Yale Divinity School Library.

Reinhold Niebuhr Papers. The Collection of the Manuscript Division. Library of Congress.

Theological Discussion Group Papers. Manuscript Group no. 43. Special Collections. Yale Divinity School Library.

William Adams Brown Papers. Special Collections. The Burke Library. Union Theological Seminary.

World Council of Churches. *Commission on Faith and Order: Official Numbered Publications, 1910–1948.* Geneva, 1970. Microfilm.

BOOKS AND ARTICLES

Anonymous works are listed in a separate section following this one.

Abernethy, Bradford S. "Political Propositions for Peace Issued." *Federal Council Bulletin*, 26, no. 4 (April 1943), 11–12.

Abrams, Roy H. *Preachers Present Arms: A Study of War-Time Attitudes and Activities of the Churches and the Clergy in the United States, 1914–1918*. Philadelphia: Round Table Press, 1933.

Ahlstrom, Sydney E. *A Religious History of the American People*. New Haven, Conn.: Yale University Press, 1972.

Anderson, H. George. "Ecumenical Movements." In *Altered Landscapes: Christianity in America, 1935–1985*, edited by David W. Lotz with Donald W. Shriver, Jr., and John F. Wilson. Grand Rapids, Mich.: William B. Eerdmans, 1989, 92–105.

Artman, J. M., and Ruth Shonle. "Biennial Report of Trends in Religious and Character Education." *Religious Education*, 22, no. 6 (June 1927), 661–684, 690–692.

Aubrey, Edwin E. "Church and Community." In *Church and Community*. The Church, Community, and State Series. London: George Allen and Unwin, 1937, 171–190.

Bainton, Roland. *Christian Attitudes Toward War and Peace: A Historical Survey and Critical Re-evaluation*. Nashville, Tenn.: Abingdon Press, 1960.

Baker, James Chamberlain. *The First Wesley Foundation: An Adventure in Christian Higher Education*. Nashville: Parthenon, 1960.

Barth, Karl. "The Inward Man." *Student World*, 21, no. 3 (July 1928), 309–315.

Beisner, Robert L. *From the Old Diplomacy to the New, 1865–1900*. 2d ed. New York: Thomas Y. Crowell, 1975.

Bennett, John C. "After Liberalism—What?" *Christian Century*, 8 November 1933, 1403–1406.

———. "The Causes of Social Evil." In *The Christian Faith and the Common Life*. The Church, Community, and State Series. London: George Allen and Unwin, 1937, 175–196.

———. "East and West in Amsterdam." *Christianity and Crisis*, 4 October 1948, 122–123.

———. "Editorial Notes." *Christianity and Crisis*, 1 October 1945, 2.

———. "Guest Editorial: And Now the World Council." *Advance*, 140, no. 5 (May 1948), 4–5.

———. "In Such a Time." *Christendom*, 7, no. 2 (spring 1942), 162–168.

———. "Results of an Ecumenical Study." *Christendom*, 9, no. 2 (spring 1944), 142–152.

———. "The Study Commission at Toronto." *Christendom*, 6, no. 4 (autumn 1941), 633.

Bethge, Eberhard. *Dietrich Bonhoeffer: Man of Vison, Man of Courage*. Translated by Eric Mosbacher et al. New York: Harper and Row, 1970. Reprint, 1977.

Betts, George Herbert. "What Makes Education Religious?" *Religious Education*, 18, no. 2 (April 1923), 84–87.

Bingham, June. *Courage to Change: An Introduction to the Life and Thought of Reinhold Niebuhr*. New York: Scribner, 1961. Reprint, 1972.

Blackwelder, Oscar F. "An Inside Story." *The Lutheran*, 7 January 1937, 2, 19.

Blanchard, Leslie. "Impressions of the Federation Meeting." *Intercollegian*, 38, no. 1 (October 1920), 4.

Bloodgood, Francis J. "Report of the Edinburgh Conference Prepared." *Living Church*, 4 September 1937, 287–288, 293.

Boegner, Marc. *The Long Road to Unity: Memoirs and Anticipations*. Translated by Rene Hague. London: William Collin Sons and Co., 1970.

Braeman, John, Robert Hamlett Bremner, and David Brody. *Change and Continuity in Twentieth-Century America: The 1920s*. Columbus: Ohio State University Press, 1968.

Bramwell, Anna C., ed. *Refugees in the Age of Total War*. London: Unwin Hyman, 1988.

Brent, Rt. Rev. Charles H. "The Call to Unity." *Federal Council Bulletin*, 10, no. 8 (October 1927), 9–10.

Bridgman, Ralph. "What Is Missionary Education?" *Student Volunteer Movement Bulletin*, 4, no. 3 (May 1923), 116–117.

Brown, William Adams. *The Essence of Christianity*. New York: Scribner, 1906.

———. "The Forgotten Factor in Post-War Reconstruction." *Christendom*, 7, no. 4 (autumn 1942), 481–488.

———. "The Homeless Liberal." *Religious Education*, 22, no. 1 (January 1927), 12–18.

———. "Maintaining the Christian Network." *Christendom*, 5, no. 3 (summer 1940), 460.

———. *Toward a United Church: Three Decades of Ecumenical Christianity*. New York: Scribner, 1946.

Brunner, H. Emil. *The Theology of Crisis*. New York: Scribner, 1930.

Busch, Eberhard. *Karl Barth: His Life from Letters and Autobiographical Texts*. Translated by John Bowden. London: SCM Press, 1976.

Calhoun, Robert L. "The Dilemma of Humanitarian Modernism." In *The Christian Understanding of Man*. The Church, Community, and State Series. London: George Allen and Unwin, 1937, 45–81.

Calkins, Gladys Gilkey. *Follow Those Women: Church Women in the Ecumenical Movement. A History of the Development of United Work Among Women of the Protestant Churches in the United States*. New York: National Council of Churches of Christ in the U.S.A., 1961.

Campbell, E. Fay. "Why I Returned My Pin." *Intercollegian*, 41, no. 7 (April 1924), 9–10.

Carpenter, Joel A. "From Fundamentalism to the New Evangelical Coalition." In *Evangelicalism and Modern America*, edited by George Marsden, 3–16. Grand Rapids, Mich.: William B. Eerdmans, 1984.

Carter, Paul A. *The Decline and Revival of the Social Gospel: Social and Political Liberalism in American Protestant Churches, 1920–1940.* Hamden, Conn.: Archon Books, 1954.

Cauthen, Kenneth. *The Impact of American Religious Liberalism.* New York: Harper and Row, 1962.

Cavert, Inez M. "Extensive Study Being Made of Women in the Church." *Federal Council Bulletin*, 30, no. 5 (May 1947), 10.

Cavert, Samuel McCrea. *The American Churches in the Ecumenical Movement, 1900–1968.* New York: Association Press, 1968.

———. "American vs. European Thinking About the Post-War World." *Christianity and Crisis*, 3, no. 13 (26 July 1943), 7–9.

———. "How Christians May Show Sympathy for Jews." *Federal Council Bulletin*, 18, no. 8 (October 1935), 4–5.

———. "How the Assembly Is Organized." *Living Church*, 27 June 1948, 10–11.

———. "The Issues at Edinburgh." *Federal Council Bulletin*, 20, no. 7 (September 1937), 7–9.

———. "This Humanity." *Federal Council Bulletin*, 21, no. 10 (December 1938), 3–4.

———. "Whither the Church?" *Federal Council Bulletin*, 19, no. 2 (February 1936), 13.

———. "Why Christians Must Oppose Anti-Semitism." *Federal Council Bulletin*, 19, no. 7 (September 1936), 5.

Cavert, Twila Lytton. "'From East and West They Came.'" *The Intercollegian*, 46, no. 1 (October 1928), 17–18.

———. "Women at Amsterdam." *Living Church*, 27 June 1948, 18.

Chadwin, Mark Lincoln. *The Hawks of World War II.* Chapel Hill: University of North Carolina Press, 1968.

Childs, John L. "Should the Policies of the Student Volunteer Movement Be Modified?" *Intercollegian*, 41, no. 3 (December 1923), 4–6.

Clemes, William W. "Meetings Highlight Role of Women in the Church." *Federal Council Bulletin*, 31, no. 5 (May 1948), 11.

Coe, George A. "New Social Horizons." *Intercollegian*, 37, no. 5 (February 1920), 3.

———. *What Ails Our Youth?* New York: Scribner, 1924.

The Commission of Appraisal. William Ernest Hocking, chairman. *Re-thinking Missions: A Laymen's Inquiry After One Hundred Years.* New York: Harper and Brothers Publishers, 1932.

Conners, James L. "Preaching Mission Begins in Albany." *The Living Church*, 26 September 1936, 347.

Cope, Henry F. *Education for Democracy.* New York: Macmillan, 1920.

———. "Responsibility to the Youth in Colleges." *Religious Education*, 16, no. 5 (October 1921), 267–271.

Cowan, Wayne H., ed. *Witness to a Generation: Significant Writings from Christianity and Crisis (1941–1966).* Indianapolis: Bobbs-Merrill, 1966.

Cowley, Malcolm. *Exile's Return: A Literary Odyssey of the 1920s.* New York: Norton, 1934. Reprint, Viking Press, 1956. Penguin, 1986.

Cremin, Lawrence A. *American Education: The Metropolitan Experience, 1876–1980.* New York: Harper and Row, 1988.

Cully, Kendig Brubaker. "A Later Look at Harrison Sacket Elliott." In *Pioneers of Religious Education in the 20th Century: A Festschrift for Herman E. Wornom,* edited by Boardman W. Kathan, 57–66. Special issue, *Religious Education,* 73 (September–October 1978).

Curti, Merle. *American Philanthropy Abroad: A History.* New Brunswick, N.J.: Rutgers University Press, 1963.

———. "Reflections on the Genesis and Growth of Peace History." *Peace and Change,* 11, no. 1 (spring 1985), 1–18.

———. *The Social Ideas of American Educators.* American Historical Association Commission on the Social Sciences. Paterson, N.J.: Pageant Books, 1959.

de Blois, Austen K. "Ecumenical Fellowship: The World Conference at Oxford." *Watchman-Examiner,* 25, no. 38 (September 1937), 1060–1062.

Delloff, Linda-Marie, Martin E. Marty, Dean Peerman, and James M. Wall. *A Century of the Century.* Grand Rapids, Mich.: William B. Eerdmans, 1984.

Divine, Robert A. *Second Chance: The Triumph of Internationalism in America During World War II.* New York: Atheneum Press, 1967.

Douglass, H. Paul. "American Progress in Christian Unity Since Oxford and Edinburgh." *Federal Council Bulletin,* 21, no. 3 (March 1938), 7–10.

———. "Church and Community in the United States." In *Church and Community.* The Church, Community, and States Series. London: George Allen and Unwin, 1937, 193–259.

Dulles, John Foster. "America's Role in the Peace." *Christianity and Crisis,* 22 January 1945, 2–6.

———. "The Christian Citizen in a Changing World." In *The Church and the International Disorder.* Vol. 4. Man's Disorder and God's Design. The Amsterdam Assembly Series. New York: Harper and Brothers, 1948, 73–114.

———. "Collaboration Must Be Practical." *Vital Speeches of the Day,* 9 (February 1945), 246–249.

———. "The Problem of Peace in a Dynamic World." In *The Universal Church and the World of Nations.* The Church, Community, and State Series. London: George Allen and Unwin, 1937, 145–168.

Dykeman, Wilma. *Prophet of Plenty: The First Ninety Years of W. D. Weatherford.* Knoxville: University of Tennessee Press, 1966.

Eagan, Eileen. *Class, Culture, and the Classroom: The Student Peace Movement of the 1930s.* Philadelphia: Temple University Press, 1981.

Eddy, Sherwood. *Eighty Adventurous Years: An Autobiography.* New York: Harper and Brothers, 1955.

———. *A Pilgrimage of Ideas, or The Re-Education of Sherwood Eddy.* New York: Farrar and Rhinehart, 1934.

Edwards, R. H., J. M. Artman, and Galen M. Fisher. *Undergraduates: A Study of Morale in Twenty-Three American Colleges and Universities*. Garden City, N.Y.: Doubleday, Doran, 1928.

Ehrenström, Nils. "Movements for International Friendship and Life and Work, 1925–1948." In *A History of the Ecumenical Movement, 1517–1948*. Ed. Ruth Rouse and Stephen Neill. Philadelphia: Westminster Press, 1968, 545–598.

Elliott, A. J. "Can College Fraternities Survive?" *Intercollegian*, 41, no. 7 (April 1924), 3–4.

Elliott, A. R. "New View on Missions." *Intercollegian*, 50, no. 4 (January 1933), 96.

Elliott, Harrison Sacket. *The Why and How of Group Discussion*. New York: Association Press, 1923.

Ericksen, Robert P. *Theologians Under Hitler: Gerhard Kittell, Paul Althaus, and Emanuel Hirsch*. New Haven, Conn.: Yale University Press, 1985.

Fackré, Gabriel. "Theology: Ephemeral, Conjunctural, and Perennial." In *Altered Landscapes: Christianity in America, 1935–1985*, edited by David W. Lotz with Donald W. Shriver, Jr., and John F. Wilson. Grand Rapids, Mich.: William B. Eerdmans, 1989.

Fagley, Richard M. "The Atomic Bomb and the Crisis of Man." *Christianity and Crisis*, 5, no. 16 (1 October 1945), 5–6.

———. "The Churches and San Francisco." *Federal Council Bulletin*, 28, no. 6 (June 1945), 7.

Fairbank, John King. "Assignment for the '70s." *American Historical Review*, 74, no. 3 (February 1969), 861–879.

———, ed. *The Missionary Enterprise in China and America*. Cambridge, Mass.: Harvard University Press, 1974.

Farmer, H. H. "The Faith by Which the Church Lives." *International Review of Missions*, 28, no. 110 (April 1939), 174–184.

Fass, Paula S. *The Damned and the Beautiful: American Youth in the 1920s*. New York: Oxford University Press, 1977.

Feingold, Henry L. *The Politics of Rescue: The Roosevelt Administration and the Holocaust, 1938–1945*. New Brunswick: N.J.: Rutgers University Press, 1970.

Fisher, Galen M., ed. *Religion in the Colleges*. New York: Association Press, 1928.

Fleming, D. J. "The Convention's Significance to American Education." *Intercollegian*, 41, no. 5 (February 1924), 7–8.

———. "Embodying International Goodwill." *Intercollegian*, 40, no. 9 (June 1923), 9–10.

———. In "Review of Books." *International Review of Missions*, 13, no. 51 (July 1924), 449–456.

Foulkes, William Hiram. "The National Preaching Mission." *Presbyterian Tribune*, 7 January 1937, 7–8.

Fowler, James W. *To See the Kingdom: The Theological Vision of H. Richard Niebuhr*. Nashville, Tenn.: Abingdon Press, 1974.

Fox, John P. "German and European Jewish Refugees, 1933–1945: Reflections on the Jewish Condition Under Hitler and the Western World's Response to Their Expulsion and Flight." In *Refugees in the Age of Total War*, edited by Anna C. Bramwell, 69–85. London: Unwin Hyman, 1988.

Fox, Richard Wightman. "The Niebuhr Brothers and the Liberal Protestant Heritage." In *Religion and Twentieth-Century American Intellectual Life*, edited by Michael J. Lacey. Cambridge: Woodrow Wilson International Center for Scholars and Cambridge University Press, 1989.

———. *Reinhold Niebuhr: A Biography*. San Francisco: Harper and Row, 1987.

Gaines, David P. *The World Council of Churches: A Study of Its Background and History*. Peterborough, N.H.: Richard R. Smith, 1966.

Gauss, Christian. *Life in College*. New York: Scribner, 1930.

Genizi, Heim. *American Apathy: The Plight of Christian Refugees from Nazism*. Ramat-Gan, Israel: Bar-Ilan University, 1983.

Hall, David. "The Victorian Connection." In *Victorian America*, edited by Daniel Walker Howe. Philadelphia: University of Pennsylvania Press, 1976.

Hall, R. O. "The Price of World Federation, Peking, 1922." *Student World*, 15, no. 3 (July 1922), 139–145.

Handy, Robert T. "The American Religious Depression." *Church History*, 29 (March 1960), 3–16.

———. *A History of Union Theological Seminary in New York*. New York: Columbia University Press, 1987.

———, ed. *The Social Gospel in America, 1870–1920: Gladden, Ely, Rauschenbusch*. New York: Oxford University Press, 1966.

———. *Undermined Establishment: Church-State Relations in America, 1880–1920*. Princeton, N.J.: Princeton University Press, 1991.

Harlow, Ralph S. "The Indianapolis Convention." *Intercollegian*, 41, no. 5 (February 1924), 4–7.

Harris, Cyril. *The Religion of Undergraduates*. New York: Scribner, 1924.

Healy, David. *U.S. Expansionism: The Imperialist Urge in the 1890s*. Madison: University of Wisconsin Press, 1970.

Heimann, Eduard. "Problems of European Reconstruction." *Christianity and Crisis*, 18 May 1942, 5–7.

Hemingway, Ernest. *A Moveable Feast*. New York: Scribner's, 1964. Reprint, Macmillan, 1987.

Hesselink, I. John. "Emil Brunner: A Centennial Perspective." *Christian Century*, 13 December 1989, 1171–1174.

High, Stanley. *The Revolt of Youth*. New York: Abingdon Press, 1923.

Hobson, Henry W. "The Birth at Madras." *International Review of Missions*, 28, no. 111 (July 1939), 337–346.

Hodgson, Leonard. "Faith and Order, 1937–1947." *Christendom*, 12, no. 3 (summer 1947), 281–289.

Hogan, Michael J. *The Marshall Plan: America, Britain, and the Reconstruction of Western Europe, 1947–1952*. Cambridge: Cambridge University Press, 1987. Reprint, 1988.

Hogg, William Richey. *Ecumenical Foundations: A History of the International*

Missionary Council and Its Nineteenth-Century Background. New York: Harper and Brothers, 1952.

Holt, Ivan Lee. "The Worship Services at Amsterdam." *Christendom*, 13, no. 4 (autumn 1948), 446–448.

Hoover, Lyman. "Fraternities and a Fraternal World." *Intercollegian*, 42, no. 4 (January 1925), 115–116.

Hopkins, Charles Howard. *History of the Y.M.C.A. in North America.* New York: Association Press, 1951.

———. *John R. Mott, 1865–1955: A Biography.* Grand Rapids, Mich.: William B. Eerdmans, 1979.

———. *The Rise of the Social Gospel in American Protestantism, 1865–1915.* New Haven, Conn.: Yale University Press, 1940.

Hordern, William E. *A Layman's Guide to Protestant Theology.* Rev. ed. New York: Macmillan, 1955. Reprint, 1978.

Horton, Douglas. "The Meeting of the Provisional Committee of the World Council of Churches." *Christendom*, 11, no. 3 (summer 1946), 341–355.

———. "An Overall Appraisal of Amsterdam and Its Results." *Christendom*, 13, no. 4 (autumn 1948), 421.

Horton, Walter. "The Christian Understanding of Man." In *The Christian Understanding of Man.* The Church, Community, and State Series. London: George Allen and Unwin, 1937, 217–241.

Hromadka, Josef. "Our Responsibilities in the Post-War World." In *The Church and the International Disorder.* Vol. 4. Man's Disorder and God's Design. The Amsterdam Assembly Series. New York: Harper and Brothers, 1948, 114–142.

Hudson, Winthrop S., and John Corrigan. *Religion in America: An Historical Account of the Development of American Religious Life.* 5th ed. New York: Macmillan, 1992.

Hume, Robert A. "Missions in the New Day." *Religious Education*, 15, no. 6 (December 1920), 337–339.

Hume, Theodore. "Moral Man and Immoral Society." *Christian Century*, 4 January 1933, 18.

Hutchison, John A. *We Are Not Divided: A Critical and Historical Study of the Federal Council of the Churches of Christ in America.* New York: Round Table Press, 1941.

Hutchison, William R. *Errand to the World: American Protestant Thought and Foreign Missions.* Chicago: University of Chicago Press, 1987.

———. *The Modernist Impulse in American Protestantism.* Cambridge, Mass.: Harvard University Press, 1976.

———, ed. *Between the Times: The Travail of the Protestant Establishment in America, 1900–1960.* Cambridge: Cambridge University Press, 1989.

Iriye, Akira. *From Nationalism to Internationalism: U.S. Foreign Policy to 1914.* London: Routledge and Kegan Paul, 1977.

Karlström, Nils. "Movements for International Friendship and Life and Work, 1910–1925." *In A History of the Ecumenical Movement, 1517–1948.* Ed. Ruth Rouse and Stephen Neill. Philadelphia: Westminster Press, 1968, 509–544.

Katz, Daniel, and Floyd Henry Allport. *Student Activities: A Report of the Syracuse Reaction Study.* Syracuse, N.Y.: Craftsman Press, 1931.

Keller, Floyd. "A New Pan-Protestant Project." *America,* 7 February 1920, 342.

Keller, Rosemary Skinner. *Georgia Harkness: For Such a Time as This.* Nashville, Tenn.: Abingdon Press, 1992.

Kelsey, Earl H. "The Convention in the College Press." *Intercollegian,* 37, no. 7 (April 1920), 10.

Kennedy, James W. *Venture of Faith: The Birth of the World Council of Churches.* New York: Morehouse-Gorham, 1948.

Kershner, Frederick D. "Book Review." *Religious Education,* 17, no. 2 (February 1932), 189.

Kohn, Eugene. "The Jewish Problem and Its Solution." *Christianity and Crisis,* 23 March 1942, 2–5.

Krishnaya, Stephen G. "Student Impressions of Indianapolis." *Student Volunteer Movement Bulletin,* 5, no. 2 (February 1924), 89–90.

Latourette, Kenneth Scott. "Are Our Campuses a Menace to Peace?" *Intercollegian,* 42, no. 1 (October 1924), 4–5.

———. "Community and Church: An Historical Survey and Interpretation." In *Church and Community.* The Church, Community, and States Series. London: George Allen and Unwin, 3–17.

———. A History of the Expansion of Christianity. 7 vols. New York: Harper, 1937–1945.

———. "The Laymen's Foreign Missions Inquiry: The Report of Its Commission on Appraisal." *International Review of Missions,* 22, no. 86 (April 1933), 153–173.

Leiper, Henry Smith. "Christians of the World Face German Situation." *Federal Council Bulletin,* 16, nos. 9 and 10 (November–December 1933), 8.

———. "Christians of the World Plan United Front." *Federal Council Bulletin,* 18, no. 8 (October 1935), 6–7.

———. "Developments in World Council Series." *Federal Council Bulletin,* 27, no. 7 (September 1944), 6.

———. "Geneva Meeting Marks Advance in World Unity." *Federal Council Bulletin,* 15, no. 8 (October 1932), 19–20.

———. "Large Participation Due for Amsterdam Assembly: 127 Denominations Already Present." *Federal Council Bulletin,* 31, no. 1 (January 1948), 7.

———. "Moving Toward the World Council." *Federal Council Bulletin,* 22, no. 3 (March 1939), 6–7.

———. "Plans Completed for World Conference, Oxford, 1937." *Federal Council Bulletin,* 19, no. 8 (October 1936), 6–8.

———. "Universal Life and Work Develops Permanent Organization." *Federal Council Bulletin,* 13, no. 10 (December 1930), 12–13.

———. "World Assembly Activity Increases: Details Cleared as Amsterdam Meeting Nears." *Federal Council Bulletin,* 31, no. 5 (May 1948), 8–9.

———. "World Conference at Oxford Next Month." *Federal Council Bulletin,* 20, no. 5 (June 1937), 6.

Leith, John H., ed. *Creeds of the Church: A Reader in Christian Doctrine from the Bible to the Present.* 3d ed. Atlanta: John Knox Press, 1962. Reprint, 1982.

Leuchtenberg, William E. *The Perils of Prosperity, 1914–1932.* Chicago: University of Chicago Press, 1958. Reprint, 1973.

———. "Progressivism and Imperialism: The Progressive Movement and American Foreign Policy, 1898–1916." *Mississippi Valley Historical Review,* 39 (December 1952), 483–504.

Levine, David O. *The American College and the Culture of Aspiration, 1915–1940.* Ithaca, N.Y.: Cornell University Press, 1986.

Lewis, Guy. "Sport, Youth Culture and Conventionality, 1920–1970." *Journal of Sport History,* 4, no. 2 (summer 1977), 129–150.

Lobingier, John Leslie. "What Shall We Do with the Young People?" *Religious Education,* 15, no. 3 (June 1920), 155–160.

Loucks, Grace. "Whither Bound—Discussion Groups?" *Intercollegian,* 44, no. 7 (April 1927), 199–200.

Macfarland, Charles S. "Among the Best New Books." *Federal Council Bulletin,* 16, no. 4 (April 1933), 13–14.

———. "Among the Best Books." *Federal Council Bulletin,* 17, no. 2 (February 1935), 14.

———. *The Churches of Christ in Time of War.* New York: Missionary Education Movement, 1917.

———. *Pioneers for Peace through Religion.* New York: Fleming H. Revell, 1946.

———. "Three Volumes on Karl Barth." *Federal Council Bulletin,* 14, no. 10 (December 1931), 21–22.

Mackay, John A. "The Ecumenical Road." *Christendom,* 2, no. 4 (autumn 1937), 535–538.

———. "Looking Towards Madras." *Christendom,* 3, no. 4 (autumn 1938), 566–575.

———. "The Theology of the Laymen's Foreign Mission Inquiry." *International Review of Missions,* 22, no. 86 (April 1933), 174–188.

Macy, Paul G. "Ecumenical Ambassadors." *Federal Council Bulletin,* 28, no. 6 (June 1945), 10.

———. "Reports from the Mission on World Order." *Federal Council Bulletin,* 26, no. 10 (December 1943), 10–11.

Mannheim, Karl. *Essays on the Sociology of Knowledge.* Edited by Paul Kecskemeti. New York: Oxford University Press, 1952.

Marchand, Roland. *Advertising the American Dream: Making Way for Modernity, 1920–1940.* Berkeley and Los Angeles: University of California Press, 1985.

———. *The American Peace Movement and Social Reform, 1898–1918.* Princeton, N.J.: Princeton University Press, 1972.

Marsden, George M. *Fundamentalism and American Culture: The Shaping of Twentieth-Century Evangelicalism, 1870–1925.* Oxford: Oxford University Press, 1980.

Marty, Martin E. *The Noise of Conflict, 1919–1941.* Vol. 2 of *Modern American Religion.* Chicago: University of Chicago Press, 1991.

Mathews, Basil. *John R. Mott, World Citizen*. New York: Harper and Brothers, 1934.

Maury, Pierre. "More on Germany." *Student World*, 26, no. 4 (October 1933), 281–284.

May, Henry F. *The End of American Innocence: A Study of the First Years of Our Own Time, 1912–1917*. New York: Knopf, 1959.

May, Melanie A. *Bonds of Unity: Women, Theology and the Worldwide Church*. American Academy of Religion Series. Atlanta: Scholars Press, 1989.

McDowell, John Patrick. *The Social Gospel in the South: The Woman's Home Mission Movement in the Methodist Episcopal Church, South, 1886–1939*. Baton Rouge: Louisiana State University Press, 1982.

McGiffert, Arthur C. "The Church and the World Fellowship." *Religious Education*, 16, no. 3 (June 1921), 131–136.

McLoughlin, William G., Jr. *Modern Revivalism: Charles Grandison Finney to Billy Graham*. New York: Ronald Press, 1959.

Mendenhall, W. O. "Race Discrimination at Detroit." *Intercollegian*, 48, no. 5 (February 1931), 144–146.

Meyer, Donald. *The Protestant Search for Political Realism, 1919–1941*. Berkeley: University of California Press, 1960. 2d ed. Middletown, Conn.: Wesleyan University Press, 1988.

Micou, Paul. *The Church's Inquiry into Student Religious Life*. The National Council, Protestant Episcopal Church, 1923.

———. "The Episcopal Church Mobilizes Its Students." *Intercollegian*, 38, no. 2 (November 1920), 9.

Miller, Francis P. "The Bookshelf." *Intercollegian*, 50, no. 9 (June 1933), 257–260.

———. "A Communication." *Intercollegian*, 41, no. 5 (February 1924), 30.

———. "Edinburgh and the World Council Proposal." *Living Church*, 28 August 1937, 247–248.

———. *Man from the Valley: Memoirs of a Twentieth-Century Virginian*. Chapel Hill: University of North Carolina Press, 1971.

———. "The Task of Federation." *Student World*, 16, no. 1 (January 1923), 24–29.

———, ed. *The Church and the World*. New York: Association Press, 1926.

———, ed. *Religion on the Campus: Report of the Milwaukee National Student Conference*. New York: Association Press, 1927.

Miller, Robert Moats. *Bishop G. Bromley Oxnam: Paladin of Liberal Protestantism*. Nashville, Tenn.: Abingdon Press, 1990.

———. *Harry Emerson Fosdick*. New York: Oxford University Press, 1985.

———. *Protestantism and Social Thought, 1919–1939*. Chapel Hill: University of North Carolina Press, 1958.

Morehouse, Clifford P. "Advance Toward Unity." *Living Church*, 4 September 1937, 273–274.

Moseley, Philip E. "The Small Nations and European Reconstruction." *Christianity and Crisis*, 1 June 1942, 2–5.

Mott, John R. "A Creative International Fellowship." *International Review of Missions*, 17, no. 67 (July 1928), 417–434.

———. "The Ecumenical Movement." *Christendom*, 2, no. 4 (autumn 1937), 529–534.

Munger, Theodore T. *The Freedom of Faith*. Boston: Houghton, Mifflin, 1883.

Nelson, John Oliver. "The Amsterdam Assembly in Review." *Federal Council Bulletin*, 31, no. 8 (October 1948), 5–7.

Nichols, Bruce. "Religion, Refugees, and the U.S. Government." In *Refugees in the Age of Total War*, edited by Anna C. Bramwell, 86–111. London: Unwin Hyman, 1988.

———. *The Uneasy Alliance: Religion, Refugee Work, and U.S. Foreign Policy*. New York: Oxford University Press, 1988.

Niebuhr, H. Richard. *The Kingdom of God in America*. Middletown, Conn.: Wesleyan University Press, 1988.

———. "Man the Sinner." *Journal of Religion*, 15, no. 3 (July 1935), 272–280.

Niebuhr, H. Richard, Wilhelm Pauck, and Francis P. Miller. *The Church Against the World*. Chicago: Willett, Clark and Company, 1935.

Niebuhr, Reinhold. "The Christian Church in a Secular Age." *Student World*, 30, no. 4 (fall 1937), 291–305.

———. "The Christian Faith and the Common Life." In *Christian Faith and the Common Life*. London: George Allen and Unwin, 1937, 69–97.

———. "The Christian Faith and the World Crisis." *Christianity and Crisis*, 10 February 1941, 4–6.

———. "Christianity and Contemporary Politics." *Christian Century*, 17 April 1924, 498–501.

———. *Does Civilization Need Religion?: A Study in the Social Resources of Religion in Modern Life*. New York: Macmillan, 1927. Reprint, 1928.

———. "Editorial Notes." *Christianity and Crisis*, 16 September 1946, 2.

———. "Is Protestantism Self-Deceived?" *Christian Century*, 25 December 1924, 1661–1662.

———. *Leaves from the Notes of a Tamed Cynic*. Chicago: Clark and Colby, 1929. Reprint, San Francisco: Harper and Row, 1980.

———. *Moral Man and Immoral Society: A Study in Ethics and Politics*. New York: Scribner, 1932. Reprint, 1960.

———. "Our World's Denial of God." *Intercollegian*, 44, no. 5 (February 1927), 127–130.

———. "Our World's Denial of God." *Student World*, 20, no. 2 (April 1927), 78–86.

———. "Shall We Proclaim Truth or Search for It?" *Christian Century*, 12 March 1925, 344–346.

———. "What Should Be the Major Emphases of the Churches on the Issues of War and Peace." *Federal Council Bulletin*, 11, no. 1 (January–February 1926), 16.

Olcott, Charles S. *The Life of William McKinley*. 2 vols. Boston: Houghton Mifflin, 1916.

Oldham, J. H. "Introduction." In *The Oxford Conference (Official Report)*. Chicago: Willett, Clark and Company, 1937, 1–44.

———. "Review of Books." *International Review of Missions*, 19, no. 74 (April 1930), 280.

Olmstead, Frank. "The Christian Student and the R.O.T.C." *Intercollegian*, 42, no. 1 (October 1924), 13–14.

Owen, David. "The Indianapolis Convention." *Intercollegian*, 41, no. 1 (October 1923), 14.

Oxnam, G. Bromley. "The Crusade for a New World Order." *Christianity and Crisis*, 26 July 1943, 12–13.

Parsons, Edward L. "Report from San Francisco." *Christianity and Crisis*, 11 June 1945, 12–13.

Paton, William. "The Jerusalem Meeting of the International Missionary Council." *International Review of Missions*, 17, no. 65 (January 1928), 3–10.

———. "The Meeting of the International Missionary Council at Tambaram, Madras." *International Review of Missions*, 28, no. 110 (April 1939), 161–173.

———. "Review of Books." *International Review of Missions*, 19, no. 74 (April 1930), 288–292.

Pauck, Wilhelm, and Marion Pauck. *Paul Tillich, His Life and Thought.* Vol. 1, *Life.* New York: Harper and Row, 1976.

Pells, Richard H. *Radical Visions and American Dreams: Culture and Social Thought in the Depression Years.* New York: Harper and Row, 1973.

Pence, O. E. "Theologs Get Together." *Intercollegian*, 40, no. 8 (May 1923), 21.

Peterson, Patti McGill. "Student Organizations and the Antiwar Movement in America, 1900–1960." *American Studies*, 13, no. 1 (spring 1977), 131–147.

Piper, John F. *The American Churches in World War I.* Athens: Ohio University Press, 1985.

Porter, David R. "The Des Moines Convention." *Student World*, 13, no. 2 (April 1920), 58–69.

———. "A Student League of Nations." *Intercollegian*, 38, no. 1 (October 1920), 3–4.

Potter, Robert W. "Policy Urged on Churches." *New York Times*, 11 December 1940.

Reeves, R. Ambrose "Milwaukee and the Church Universal." *Intercollegian*, 44, no. 5 (February 1927), 119.

Reissing, Frederick E. "Looking Ahead to Amsterdam." *Living Church*, 27 June 1948, 9–10.

Ritchie, Frank. "Refugees a Challenge to Christian People." *Federal Council Bulletin*, 18, nos. 9 and 10 (November–December 1935), 12.

Rodgers, Daniel T. "In Search of Progressivism." *Reviews in American History*, 10, no. 4 (December 1982), 113–132.

Roop, David D. "Collegiate Cavalry at the University of Arizona, 1921–1941." *Arizona and the West*, 27 (1985), 55–72.

Rouse, Ruth. *The World's Student Christian Federation: A History of the First Thirty Years.* London: SCM Press, 1948.

Rouse, Ruth, and Stephen Neill, eds. *A History of the Ecumenical Movement, 1517–1948*. Philadelphia: Westminster Press, 1968.

Roy, Ralph Lord. *Apostles of Discord: A Study of Organized Bigotry and Disruption on the Fringes of Protestantism*. Boston: Beacon Press, 1953.

Russell, Ruth. *A History of the United Nations Charter: The Role of the United States, 1940–1945*. Washington, D.C.: Brookings Institution, 1958.

Rutgers, H. C. "The Meeting of the General Committee." *The Student World*, 15, no. 3 (July 1922), 128–139.

Schaffer, Ronald. "The War Department's Defense of ROTC, 1920–1940." *Wisconsin Magazine of History*, 53, no. 2 (winter 1969–1970), 108–120.

Schmidt, Stephen A. *A History of the Religious Education Association*. Birmingham, Ala.: Religious Education Press, 1983.

Schmidt, William J. *Architect of Unity: A Biography of Samuel McCrea Cavert*. New York: Friendship Press, 1975.

Schmidt, William J., and Edward Ouellette. *What Kind of a Man? The Life of Henry Smith Leiper*. New York: Friendship Press, 1986.

Schneider, Carl E. "An American's Observations on European Theological Discussion." *Christendom*, 12, no. 3 (summer 1947), 341–345.

Schneider, Robert A. "Voice of Many Waters: Church Federation in the Twentieth Century." In *Between the Times: The Travail of the Protestant Establishment in America, 1900–1960*, edited by William R. Hutchison. Cambridge: Cambridge University Press, 1989.

Schulzinger, Robert D. *The Wise Men of Foreign Affairs: The History of the Council on Foreign Relations*. New York: Columbia University Press, 1984.

Scott, Albert T. "A Layman's Inquiry into Foreign Missions." *Far Horizons*, 12, no. 1 (October 1931), 31–32.

Seymour, Jack L., Robert T. O'Gorman, and Charles R. Foster. *The Church in the Education of the Public: Refocusing the Task of Religious Education*. Nashville, Tenn.: Abingdon Press, 1984.

Shedd, Clarence Prouty. *The Church Follows Its Students*. New Haven, Conn.: Yale University Press, 1938.

Silk, Mark. "The Rise of the 'New Evangelicalism.'" In *Between the Times: The Travail of the Protestant Establishment in America, 1900–1960*, edited by William R. Hutchison. Cambridge: Cambridge University Press, 1989.

Smith, H. Shelton. "Conflicting Interchurch Movements in American Protestantism." *Christendom*, 12, no. 2 (spring 1947), 165–176.

Soares, Theodore Gerald. "Is World Fellowship Practicable?" *Religious Education*, 16, no. 3 (spring 1920), 137–140.

Soulen, Richard N. *Handbook of Biblical Criticism*. 2d ed. Atlanta: John Knox Press, 1976. Reprint, 1981.

Southard, Shelby E. "Negro Barred in Preaching Mission." *Living Church*, 17 October 1936, 437.

Speer, Robert E. "The New Offensive." *Intercollegian*, 37, no. 1 (October 1919), 1–3.

———. "The Relation of the Foreign Missionary to the World Situation Today." *Intercollegian*, 41, no. 5 (February 1924), 13–18.

Sperry, Willard L. "American Christianity and the Church Universal." *Christendom*, 3, no. 1 (winter 1938), 55–66.

Stauffer, Milton T. "A Message to Student Volunteers." *Student Volunteer Movement Bulletin*, 3, no. 4 (October 1922), 156–158.

[Stettinius, Edward.] *Charter of the United Nations: Report to the President on the Results of the San Francisco Conference by the Chairman of the Delegation, the Secretary of State*. Publication no. 2349. Conference Series 71. Washington, D.C.: Department of State, 1945.

Taft, Charles P. "Report on World Council." *Christianity and Crisis*, 13 May 1946, 6–7.

Tarr, Dennis L. "The Presbyterian Church and the Founding of the UN." *Journal of Presbyterian History*, 53 (spring 1975), 3–32.

Tatlow, Tissington. "The World Conference on Faith and Order." In *A History of the Ecumenical Movement, 1517–1948*. Ed. Ruth Rouse and Stephen Neill. Philadelphia: Westminster Press, 1968, 405–444.

Thomas, David Edward. "Progress at State Universities, Progress of Religious Education at State University Centers During the Last 20 Years, and Outlook for the Near Future." *Religious Education*, 18, no. 4 (August 1923), 237–240.

Thomas, Ernest. "Through Education to World-Mindedness: The Story of the Toronto Convention." *Religious Education*, 21, no. 2 (April 1926), 131–133.

Thomas, George F. "Corpus Christi and Corpus Christianum." *Christendom*, 7, no. 1 (winter 1942), 24–34.

Thomas, Norman. "Moral Man and Immoral Society." *World Tomorrow*, 14 December 1932, 565, 567.

Tillich, Paul. "The Kingdom of God and History." In *The Kingdom of God and History*. The Church, Community, and State Series. London: George Allen and Unwin, 1937, 105–142.

———. "Natural and Revealed Religion." *Christendom*, 1, no. 1 (autumn 1935), 159–170.

———. "Spiritual Problems of Post-War Reconstruction." *Christianity and Crisis*, 10 August 1942, 2–6.

———. *Systematic Theology*. 3 Vols. Chicago: University of Chicago Press, 1951–1963.

Tillich, Paul J., Theodore M. Greene, George F. Thomas, Edwin E. Aubrey, and John Knox. *The Christian Answer*. Edited with an introduction by Henry P. Van Dusen. New York: Scribner, 1945.

Tippy, Worth M. "'Life and Work' at Eisenach." *Federal Council Bulletin*, 12, no. 9 (November 1929), 17–18.

Tobias, Channing H. "A National Secretary for Africa." *Intercollegian*, 37, no. 6 (March 1920), 12.

Toulouse, Mark G. *The Transformation of John Foster Dulles: From Prophet of Realism to Priest of Nationalism*. Macon, Ga.: Mercer University Press, 1985.

Trachtenberg, Alan. *The Incorporation of America: Culture and Society in the Gilded Age*. New York: Hill and Wang, 1982.

Van Alstyne, Richard W. *The Rising American Empire*. New York: Oxford University Press, 1960.

Vandenberg, Arthur H., Jr., ed. *The Private Papers of Senator Vandendberg*. Boston: Houghton Mifflin, 1952.

Van Dusen, Henry P. "Apprehending Truth Is Conditional." *Intercollegian*, 44, no. 4 (January 1927), 91–92.

————. "The Business of the World Council." *Christianity and Crisis*, 4 October 1948, 123–125.

————. "The Churches Speak." *Christianity and Crisis*, 16 April 1942, 1–2.

————. "Issues of the Peace." *Christendom*, 7, no. 1 (winter 1942), 2–12.

————. "Madras and Christian Thought: A Personal Impression." *Christendom*, 4, no. 2 (spring 1939), 205–217.

————. "Mr. Lippmann's Dilemma." *Intercollegian*, 47, no. 2 (November 1929), 53.

————. *The Plain Man Seeks for God*. New York: Scribner, 1933.

————. "The Plain Man Seeks for God." *Intercollegian*, 50, no. 9 (June 1933), 245.

————. In *Quest of Life's Meaning: Hints Toward a Christian Philosophy of Life for Students*. New York: Association Press, 1926.

————. "Six Pillars of Peace." *Christianity and Crisis*, 22 March 1943, 1–2.

————. "The Spiritual Tone of Indianapolis." *Student Volunteer Movement Bulletin*, 5, no. 2 (February 1924), 104–107.

————. "On the Theology of Crisis." *Intercollegian*, 49, no. 7 (April 1932), 203.

————. "What Are Christian Students Thinking About?" *Intercollegian*, 45, no. 3 (December 1927), 59–60.

————. "The World Council Continues to Take Shape." *Christendom*, 12, no. 1 (winter 1947), 84–92.

————, ed. *The Spiritual Legacy of John Foster Dulles: Selections from His Articles and Addresses*. Philadelphia: Westminster Press, 1960.

Van Kirk, Walter W. "British and American Post-War Aims." *Federal Council Bulletin*, 25, no. 7, pt. 1 (September 1942), 10.

————. "The Churches and the International Disorder." *Christendom*, 13, no. 4 (autumn 1948), 486–497.

————. "Churches to Study Bases of Durable Peace." *Federal Council Bulletin*, 24, no. 2 (February 1941), 13.

————. "Students Face Christian Living in Modern World." *Federal Council Bulletin*, 10, no. 1 (January 1927), 13.

————. "United Action on the Peace Front: Delegates of 15 Nations Charter New Commission." *Federal Council Bulletin*, 29, no. 7 (September 1946), 5–6.

Varg, Paul. *Missionaries, Chinese and Diplomats: The American Protestant Missionary Movement in China, 1890–1952*. Princeton, N.J.: Princeton University Press, 1958.

Visser 't Hooft, W. A. "A Farewell to the Social Gospel." *Student World*, 26, no. 3 (July 1933), 275–276.

———. "German Protestantism at the Crossroads." *Student World*, 26, no. 3 (July 1933), 256–259.

———. "The God of Reason and the God of Faith." *Student World*, 26, no. 4 (October 1933), 371–372.

———. *Memoirs*. London and Philadelphia: SCM Press/Westminster Press, 1973.

———. "Students and the Church." *Student World*, 25, no. 2 (April 1932), 91–92.

———. "What Is the World Council of Churches?" *Christendom*, 4, no. 1 (winter 1939), 21–31.

Visser 't Hooft, Willem Adolf. "The Genesis of the World Council of Churches." In *A History of the Ecumenical Movement, 1517–1948*. Ed. Ruth Rouse and Stephen Neill. Philadelphia: Westminster Press, 1968, 697–724.

Voskuil, Dennis. "Neo-Orthodoxy." *Encyclopedia of the American Religious Experience: Studies of Traditions and Movements*. Vol. 2, edited by Charles H. Lippy and Peter W. Williams, 1147–1157. New York: Scribner, 1988.

Wacker, Grant. "The Holy Spirit and the Spirit of the Age in American Protestantism, 1880–1910." *Journal of American History*, 72, no. 1 (June 1985), 45–62.

Waller, Bolton C. "The Federation and International Brotherhood." *Intercollegian*, 37, no. 7 (April 1920), 7.

Watson, Goodwin B. "How the Discussion Groups Worked Out." *The Student Volunteer Movement Bulletin*, 5, no. 2 (February 1924), 97–101.

Whitman, Alden. "Reinhold Niebuhr Is Dead; Protestant Theologian, 78." *New York Times*, 2 June 1971, 1, 45.

Wiebe, Robert H. *The Search for Order, 1877–1920*. New York: Hill and Wang, 1967.

Will, Herman. *A Will for Peace: Peace Action in the United Methodist Church, A History*. Washington, D.C.: General Board of Church and Society of the United Methodist Church, 1984.

Wilson, Jesse R. "The Boards and the Inquiry." *Far Horizons*, 13, no. 2 (December–January 1933), 31–32.

———. "Reviews." *Far Horizons*, 11, no. 7 (April 1931), 31.

———. "*Re-Thinking Missions*—Dr. Robert E. Speer's Appraisal." *Far Horizons*, 13, no. 3 (February–March 1933), 7–10.

Zabriskie, Alexander C. *Bishop Brent, Crusader for Christian Unity*. Philadelphia: Westminster Press, 1948.

Zabriskie, Philip T. "The Youth Program at Amsterdam." *Living Church*, 27 June 1948, 18.

ANONYMOUS WORKS

"After Milwaukee—What?" *Intercollegian*, 44, no. 4 (January 1927), 98.

"The American Churches in Time of War." *Federal Council Bulletin*, 24, no. 1 (January 1941), 6–7.

"The American Committee for the World Council of Churches." *Christendom*, 10, no. 1 (winter 1945), xiii.

"American War Vote Demanded; Somme Is Cited as Our 'Frontier'; 30 Notables Ask Public to Join Plea for Step Held to Be Only Way to Full Massing of Our Energies Against Germany." *New York Times*, 10 June 1940.

"Americans Visit England." *Federal Council Bulletin*, 25, no. 5 (May 1942), 12.

"Among the Best New Books." *Federal Council Bulletin*, 11, no. 10 (December 1928), 45–46.

"Among the Best New Books." *Federal Council Bulletin*, 12, no. 10 (December 1929), 17–35, 40–48.

"Among the Best New Books." *Federal Council Bulletin*, 15, no. 6 (June 1932), 13.

"Among the New Books." *Federal Council Bulletin*, 10, no. 4 (April 1927), 32–33.

"Appendix—The Relation of the Church to the War in Light of the Christian Faith, Part II, Sections B, C, and D of the Calhoun Report to the Federal Council of Churches, November 1944." *Christendom*, 10, no. 2 (spring 1945), 263–284.

"Archbishop Strengthens Ecumenical Outlook." *Federal Council Bulletin*, 19, no. 1 (January 1936), 9.

"The Authority and Significance of the Bible." *Christendom*, 12, no. 2 (spring 1947), 277.

"Bishop Bell Condemns Use of Atomic Bomb." *Christianity and Crisis*, 17 September 1945, 7.

"Book Notes." *Religious Education*, 18, no. 3 (June 1923), 215–217.

"The Bookshelf." *The Intercollegian*, 47, no. 1 (October 1929), 23–24.

"In Brief." *Intercollegian*, 37, no. 5 (February 1920), 4.

"Bringing Oxford to America." *Federal Council Bulletin*, 20, no. 9 (November 1937), 9.

"British Churchmen and Peace Aims." *Christianity and Crisis*, 10 February 1941, 3.

"A Call to the Churches for the First Assembly of the World Council." *Federal Council Bulletin*, 31, no. 1 (January 1948), 6.

"A Challenge to Christendom." *Federal Council Bulletin*, 17, no. 2 (February 1934), 5.

"A Chance for the Black Race: An Address by F. Eugene Corbre." *Intercollegian*, 41, no. 5 (February 1924), 19–20.

"The Crisis." *Christianity and Crisis*, 10 February 1941, 1–2.

"Christendom: An Ecumenical Quarterly." *Federal Council Bulletin*, 21, no. 8 (October 1938), 8.

"The Christian Mission on World Order." *Federal Council Bulletin*, 26, no. 9 (November 1943), 9.

"Christians Unite in Sympathy for Jews." *Federal Council Bulletin*, 21, no. 10 (December 1938), 9.

"Christians Welcome Jewish Visitors." *Federal Council Bulletin*, 19, no. 3 (March 1936), 7.

The Church and the Disorder of Society. Vol. 3. Man's Disorder and God's Design. The Amsterdam Assembly Series. New York: Harper and Brothers, 1948.

The Church and the International Disorder. Vol. 4. Man's Disorder and God's Design. The Amsterdam Assembly Series. New York: Harper and Brothers, 1948.

"The Church and the War." *Christianity and Crisis*, 25 December 1944, 5–7.

"The Church as World Community." *Federal Council Bulletin*, 19, no. 9 (November 1936), 3–4.

"The Church—If War Should Come." *Federal Council Bulletin*, 22, no. 6 (June 1939), 3–4.

"Church Leaders of Many Nations Assemble at Prague." *Federal Council Bulletin*, 11, no. 8 (October 1928), 19–21.

"The Churches and a Just and Durable Peace." *Christendom*, 5, no. 2 (spring 1945), xiii–xiv.

"The Churches and the International Situation." *Federal Council Bulletin*, 23, no. 4 (April 1940), 7–9.

"Churches Undertake Constructive Policy on Race Relations." *Federal Council Bulletin*, 5, no. 2 (February–March 1922), 1–3.

"Churches Use 'Delaware.'" *Federal Council Bulletin*, 25, no. 8, pt. 2 (October 1942), 2–3.

"Churchmen Speak on Atomic Bomb." *Federal Council Bulletin*, 28, no. 7 (September 1945), 6.

"The Cleveland Conference and Basic Issues." *Federal Council Bulletin*, 28, no. 2 (February 1945), 3–4.

"Cleveland Conference on a Just and Durable Peace." *Federal Council Bulletin*, 28, no. 2 (February 1945), 6–8.

"The Colored Associations." *Intercollegian*, 40, no. 7 (April 1923), 24.

"Coming to Grips with the Racial Problem." *Federal Council Bulletin*, 4, no. 5 (August–September 1921), 100.

"Commission on a Just and Durable Peace." *Christianity and Crisis*, 19 February 1945, 7–8.

"Commission on Unity Begins Work." *Federal Council Bulletin*, 20, no. 8 (October 1937), 13.

"Conference on International Crisis." *Federal Council Bulletin*, 22, no. 5 (May 1939), 11.

"Conference Statistics." *Intercollegian*, 44, no. 5 (February 1927), 131.

"Contemplating the Atomic Bomb." *Federal Council Bulletin*, 28, no. 7 (September 1945), 4.

"Delegates Begin Intensive Preparations for Amsterdam." *Christianity and Crisis*, 5 July 1948, 95.

"Department Reorganization Is Announced." *Federal Council Bulletin*, 31, no. 2 (February 1948), 19.

"Dr. Oldham's Appeal to the Churches." *Federal Council Bulletin*, 18, nos. 9 and 10 (November–December 1935), 4.

"Ecumenical Church Leaders to Meet." *Christianity and Crisis*, 13 November 1944, 7.

"Ecumenical Meetings Next Summer." *Federal Council Bulletin*, 19, no. 5 (May 1936), 9.

"Ecumenical Notes." *Federal Council Bulletin*, 23, no. 2 (February 1940), 8.

"Ecumenical Visitation Across the Atlantic." *Christendom*, 8, no. 1 (winter 1943), viii–ix.

"'Eddy & Co.' in the East." *Intercollegian*, 42, no. 5 (February 1925), 171.

"Edinburgh Approves World Council Plan." *Living Church*, 28 August 1937, 257–258.

"Editorial." *Religious Education*, 17, no. 4 (August 1922), 308.

"Editorial." *Student Volunteer Movement Bulletin*, 5, no. 2 (February 1924), 117–118.

"Editorial." *Student World*, 15, no. 3 (July 1922), 85–86.

"Editorial Board." *Christianity and Crisis*, 10 February 1941, 8.

"Editorials." *Intercollegian*, 44, no. 5 (February 1927), 137.

"European Visit Deferred." *Federal Council Bulletin*, 25, no. 1 (January 1942), 10.

"Evanston (Interdenominational Conference, December 29–January 1)." *Intercollegian*, 43, no. 5 (February 1926), 148–152.

"Federal Council Adopts Unity Commission." *Living Church*, 17 April 1937, 498.

"Final Planning Session Is Held: Amsterdam Preparations Near Completion." *Federal Council Bulletin*, 31, no. 3 (March 1948), 5–7.

The First Assembly of the World Council of Churches: The Official Report. Vol. 5. Ed. W. A. Visser 't Hooft. Man's Disorder and God's Design. The Amsterdam Assembly Series. New York: Harper and Brothers, 1949.

"5,000 Take Part in Interfaith Service." *Living Church*, 21 August 1937, 239.

"Forward from Oxford and Edinburgh." *Federal Council Bulletin*, 21, no. 2 (February 1938), 6–7.

"Friendly Refugee Policy Is Urged." *Federal Council Bulletin*, 22, no. 4 (April 1939), 8–9.

"Furthering the Ecumenical Movement." *Federal Council Bulletin*, 21, no. 4 (April 1938), 8.

"German Church Joins World Council." *Christianity and Crisis*, 12 November 1945, 7–8.

"German Guest Welcomed." *Federal Council Bulletin*, 18, no. 5 (May 1935), 10.

"The Good and Bad of Fraternities." *Intercollegian*, 43, no. 7 (April 1926), 200–205.

"A Growing Fellowship, Excerpts from Dr. Visser 't Hooft's Annual Report." *Christendom*, 11, no. 1 (winter 1946), 114–116.

"High Peaks in Convention Discussion." *Intercollegian*, 41, no. 5 (February 1924), 19–20.

"High Peaks in Convention Discussion: Proposals on Race and a Chance for the Black Race: An Address by F. Eugene Corbie." *Intercollegian*, 41, no. 5 (February 1924), 19.

"High Peaks in Convention Discussion: Proposals on War and They Discussed War." *Intercollegian*, 41, no. 5 (February 1924), 20.

"Historical Review of Church and War." *Federal Council Bulletin*, 28, no. 2 (February 1945), 8.

"Holland Brings World Council Near." *Federal Council Bulletin*, 21, no. 6 (June 1938), 6–7.

"Holy Wars." *Christianity and Crisis*, 10 February 1941, 2–3.

"Informal Discussions on Peace Organization." *Department of State Bulletin*, 22 October 1944, 450–453.

"An International Christian Round Table." *Christianity and Crisis*, 26 July 1943, 8.

"The Jerusalem Conference." *Federal Council Bulletin*, 11, no. 4 (April 1928), 3–4.

"The Laymen at Cleveland." *Federal Council Bulletin*, 28, no. 2 (February 1945), 4.

"Lectures for Study Conference." *Federal Council Bulletin*, 25, no. 3 (March 1945), 13–14.

"The 'Life and Work' Study Program." *Christendom*, 5, no. 2 (spring 1940), 310–311.

"Madras." *Federal Council Bulletin*, 21, no. 1 (January 1938), 9.

"The Meaning of Lausanne, A Symposium." *Federal Council Bulletin*, 10, no. 8 (October 1927), 25–26.

"Meeting the Crisis in Our Relations with German Protestantism." *Federal Council Bulletin*, 16, nos. 9 and 10 (November–December 1933), 5–6.

"A Message to Our Fellow Christians, from the Federal Council of the Churches of Christ in America, Adopted December 30, 1941." *Federal Council Bulletin*, 25, no. 1 (January 1942), 3–5.

"Militarism in the Colleges." *Intercollegian*, 44, no. 3 (December 1926), 77.

"Military Training." *Intercollegian*, 46, no. 6 (March 1929), 189.

"The Moscow Declarations and the 'Six Pillars of Peace.'" *Federal Council Bulletin*, 26, no. 10 (December 1943), 3–4.

"Mr. Dulles Given Leave from Commission." *Federal Council Bulletin*, 28, no. 5 (May 1945), 10.

"The National Preaching Mission." *Federal Council Bulletin*, 19, no. 8 (October 1936), 8–9.

"New Commission for the Study of Christian Unity." *Federal Council Bulletin*, 20, no. 5 (May 1937), 6.

"New Evidences of Ecumenical Unity." *Federal Council Bulletin*, 21, no. 2 (February 1938), 5.

"New Interest in Racial Problems." *Federal Council Bulletin*, 4, no. 3 (April–May 1921), 60.

"New Lessons in Democracy." *Intercollegian*, 37, no. 7 (April 1920), 2.

"New Secretary for International Church Relations." *Federal Council Bulletin*, 13, no. 6 (June 1930), 22.

"New Spirit Seen in Session at Oxford." *Living Church*, 14 August 1937, 202–203.

"News from the Field." *Intercollegian*, 42, no. 4 (January 1925), 141.

"News from the Field." *Intercollegian*, 43, no. 8 (May 1926), 255–256.

"News from the Madras Conference." *Federal Council Bulletin*, 22, no. 2 (February 1939), 8.

"Next Step in War Discussions." *Intercollegian*, 42, no. 1 (October 1924), 1–2.

"The Note of Personal Decision Comes Back." *Federal Council Bulletin*, 19, no. 9 (November 1936), 4–5.

"Notes on Contributors." *Student World*, 15, no. 2 (April 1922), 84.

"The Original Greek Letter Fraternity." *Intercollegian*, 41, no. 7 (April 1924), 2.

"Oxford and Edinburgh in Washington." *Federal Council Bulletin*, 21, no. 1 (January 1938), 10–11.

"Oxford and Edinburgh Mark New World Unity." *Federal Council Bulletin*, 20, no. 7 (September 1937), 6–7.

The Oxford Conference (Official Report). Chicago: Willett, Clark and Company, 1937.

"The Perilous Consequences of Apathy." *Federal Council Bulletin*, 23, no. 6 (June 1940), 3–4.

"Popular Report on Oxford." *Federal Council Bulletin*, 20, no. 10 (December 1937), 6.

"Post-War Reconstruction." *Christianity and Crisis*, 9 February 1942, 1–2.

"Practicing Unity on a Statewide Basis." *Federal Council Bulletin*, 20, no. 9 (November 1937), 6.

"Prayer for Amsterdam." *Federal Council Bulletin*, 31, no. 5 (May 1948), 4.

"A Prayer for the Assembly." *Federal Council Bulletin*, 31, no. 5 (May 1948), 1.

"Preaching Mission Advances Across the Country." *Federal Council Bulletin*, 19, no. 9 (November 1936), 6–7.

"The Preaching Mission and the Unity of the Church." *Federal Council Bulletin*, 20, no. 1 (January 1937), 3–4.

"Preaching Mission—Begun or Over?" *Christian Advocate*, 17 December 1936, 1228.

"Preparing for Ecumenical Conference, 1937." *Federal Council Bulletin*, 18, nos. 9 and 10 (November–December 1935), 15.

"The Present Strategy of Christian Advance." *Federal Council Bulletin*, 18, no. 8 (October 1935), 3.

"Princeton International Round Table." *Christendom*, 8, no. 4 (autumn 1943), xv.

"Princeton International Round-Table." *Federal Council Bulletin*, 26, no. 7 (September 1943), 7.

"Professors Horton and Hocking to Head Pre-Cleveland Conference Commissions." *Federal Council Bulletin*, 27, no. 8 (October 1944), 11.

"Progress Report for World Council: Provisional Committee Holds First Meeting in United States." *Federal Council Bulletin*, 30, no. 5 (May 1947), 6.

"Proposals on Race Problems." *Intercollegian*, 41, no. 5 (February 1924), 19–20.

"Proposals on War." *Intercollegian*, 41, no. 5 (February 1924), 20.

"Proposed Bases for Lasting Peace." *Christian Century*, 18 March 1942, 360–362.

"Prospects for World Council of Churches." *Federal Council Bulletin*, 20, no. 10 (December 1937), 4.

"Protestants Plan for Peace," *Life*, 10 March 1946, 31–35.

"Provisional No Longer." *Intercollegian*, 46, no. 3 (December 1928), 68.

"To Public Leaders and Our People." *Federal Council Bulletin*, 27, no. 2 (February 1944), 6.

"Race Questions and Indianapolis." *Intercollegian*, 41, no. 2 (November 1923), 2.

"The Relation of the Church to the War in the Light of the Christian Faith." *Social Action*, 15 December 1944, 3–79.

"The Relation of the Church to War." *Federal Council Bulletin*, 26, no. 5 (May 1943), 12.

"Relief for Chinese and Refugees Continues." *Federal Council Bulletin*, 22, no. 7 (September 1939), 8–9.

"Reorganization of the Joint Executive Committee." *Christendom*, 9, no. 4 (Autumn, 1944), xiv–xv.

"Repentance and Humility." *Federal Council Bulletin*, 28, no. 10 (December 1945), 4–5.

"Review of Books." *International Review of Missions*, 14, no. 53 (January 1925), 140–141.

"The Sacrament for a Suffering World." *Federal* Council Bulletin, 23, no. 7 (September 1940), 5.

"Six Pillars of Peace." *Christianity and Crisis*, 31 May 1943, 5–6.

"Six Pillars of Peace." *Christianity and Crisis*, 28 June 1943, 6–8.

"Some of the Best New Religious Books." *Federal Council Bulletin*, 11, no. 1 (January 1928), 32.

"Southern Women Against Lynching." *Federal Council Bulletin*, 6, no. 3 (April–May 1923), 7.

"Spring Meeting of the Joint Executive Committee." *Christendom*, 8, no. 3 (summer 1943), 437–438.

"Statement on Control of the Atomic Bomb." *Federal Council Bulletin*, 28, no. 7 (October 1945), 6.

"The Study Commission at Toronto." *Christendom*, 6, no. 4 (autumn 1941), 633.

"Study Conference on the Bible." *Christianity and Crisis*, 3 March 1947, 7.

"Student Volunteer Council Meets." *Intercollegian*, 37, no. 8 (May 1920), 9.

"The Study Conference on the Bases of Peace." *Federal Council Bulletin*, 25, no. 4 (April 1942), 9–10.

"Study Guide on International Problems." *Federal Council Bulletin*, 23, no. 5 (May 1940), 13.

"To Study Peace and War Problems." *Federal Council Bulletin*, 23, no. 2 (February 1940), 6.

"Support for German Refugees." *Federal Council Bulletin*, 22, no. 3 (March 1939), 7.

"They Discussed War." *Intercollegian*, 41, no. 5 (February 1924), 20.

"Thirtieth Anniversary Marks Interest in Unity." *Federal Council Bulletin*, 22, no. 1 (January 1939), 6–8.

"Toward a World Council of Churches." *Federal Council Bulletin*, 20, no. 7 (September 1937), 9–10.

"A Truly Christian Appeal." *Federal Council Bulletin*, 17, no. 6 (June 1934), 5.

"United Nations Conference on International Organization." *Department of State Bulletin*, 15 April 1945, 671–672.

"United Program of Life and Work and Faith and Order." *Federal Council Bulletin*, 20, no. 9 (November 1937), 13.

The Universal Church in God's Design. Vol. 1. Man's Disorder and God's Design. The Amsterdam Assembly Series. New York: Harper and Brothers, 1948.

"Unprecedented Communion Celebration." *Federal Council Bulletin*, 24, no. 9 (November 1941), 6.

"U.S. Churchmen Prepare for World Council Assembly." *Christianity and Crisis*, 6 January 1947, 7.

"War Relief and Reconstruction." *Christendom*, 10, no. 2 (spring 1945), 285–287.

"What Answer Will Christians Make?" *Federal Council Bulletin*, 21, no. 7 (September 1938), 3–4.

"What Part Will We Play in the Peace?" *Federal Council Bulletin*, 23, no. 1 (January 1940), 3–4.

"What Should the Church Do About Anti-Semitism?" *Federal Council Bulletin*, 6, no.3 (April–May 1923), 18.

"What Some Delegates Thought." *Intercollegian*, 43, no. 5 (February 1926), 150–151.

"Whitsunday—A Day of Prayer." *Federal Council Bulletin*, 31, no. 5 (May 1948), 6.

"'Wholeness Is the True Nature of the Church.'" *Federal Council Bulletin*, 29, no. 5 (May 1946), 5.

"The World After the War." *Christianity and Crisis*, 10 February 1941, 3.

"World Conference Announced for 1937." *Federal Council Bulletin*, 18, no. 4 (April 1935), 10–11.

"World Conference of Churches in 1935." *Federal Council Bulletin*, 15, no. 1 (January 1932), 19.

"The World Council in America." *Christendom*, 12, no. 3 (summer 1947), 420–423.

The World Council of Churches in Its Process of Formation: Minutes and Reports of the Meeting of the Provisional Committee of the World Council of Churches Held at Geneva from February 21st to 23rd, 1946; The Constitutional Documents of the World Council of Churches and an Introduction by W. A. Visser 't Hooft. Geneva: World Council of Churches, 1946.

"World's Student Christian Federation Annual Report for the Year 1924–1925." *Student World*, 19, no. 1 (January 1926), 3–47.

"A World-Wide Communion Sunday." *Federal Council Bulletin*, 23, no. 5 (May 1940), 5.

"Why Race Relations Sunday." *Federal Council Bulletin*, 6, no. 6 (November–December 1923), 12–13.

"Young Theologians." *Federal Council Bulletin*, 13, no. 3 (March 1930), 28.

Youth and Renaissance Movements. New York: Council of Christian Churches, 1923.

UNPUBLISHED WORKS

Bennett, John C. Interview with Teresa Thompson, 20 June 1990.

Coston, Herbert Reece, Jr. "The World's Student Christian Federation as an Ecumenical Training Ground." Ph.D. diss., Northwestern University, 1963.

Hulsether, Mark David. "Liberals, Radicals, and the Contested Social Thought of Postwar Protestantism: *Christianity and Crisis* Magazine, 1941–1976." Ph.D. diss., University of Minnesota, 1992.

Showalter, Nathan D. "The End of a Crusade: The Student Volunteer Movement for Foreign Missions and the Great War." Th.D. diss., Harvard University, 1990.

Smalley, Martha Lund. "Historical Sketch of the Student Volunteer Movement for Foreign Missions." In "Archives and Manuscript Register, Manuscript Group Number 42, Archives of the Student Volunteer Movement for Foreign Missions." New Haven, Conn.: Yale Divinity School, 1980.

Smith, Timothy L. "The World Council of Churches and the Refugee Crisis in Western Europe, 1945–1948: An Essay on Disorder and Design." February 28, 1974. Johns Hopkins University, Baltimore, Maryland.

Thompson, Dean Keith. "Henry Pitney Van Dusen: Ecumenical Statesman." Ph.D. diss., Union Theological Seminary, Richmond, Virginia, 1974.

Index